A Dictionary of British America,
1584–1783

A Dictionary of British America, 1584–1783

Mary K. Geiter and W. A. Speck

First published 2007 by
PALGRAVE MACMILLAN
Houndmills, Basingstoke, Hampshire RG21 6XS and
175 Fifth Avenue, New York, N.Y. 10010
Companies and representatives throughout the world

PALGRAVE MACMILLAN is the global academic imprint of the Palgrave Macmillan division of St. Martin's Press, LLC and of Palgrave Macmillan Ltd. Macmillan® is a registered trademark in the United States, United Kingdom and other countries. Palgrave is a registered trademark in the European Union and other countries.

ISBN-13: 978–0–230–00228–9   hardback
ISBN-10: 0–230–00228–5   hardback
ISBN-13: 978–0–230–00229–6   paperback
ISBN-10: 0–23–0–00229–3   paperback

This book is printed on paper suitable for recycling and made from fully managed and sustained forest sources. Logging, pulping and manufacturing processes are expected to conform to the environmental regulations of the country of origin.

A catalogue record for this book is available from the British Library.

A catalogue record for this book is available from the Library of Congress.

10   9   8   7   6   5   4   3   2   1
16   15   14   13   12   11   10   09   08   07

Printed and bound in China

To the grandchildren:

Max
Jacob
Freddie
Megan
Brittany
Annie
Ellie
Annemie
Jilly
Kai
Paige

Contents

Chronology

1584   Sir Walter Raleigh discovers Roanoke Island inside the outer banks of what later became North Carolina. Calls it Virginia in honor of Queen Elizabeth, the Virgin Queen.

1585   First settlement on Roanoke Island.

1586   The settlement abandoned.

1587   Second settlement established by John White.

1590   White returns to Roanoke Island but fails to find any settlers.

1603   Queen Elizabeth dies. King James VI of Scotland becomes James I of England.

1606   The Virginia and Plymouth Companies incorporated.

1607   May   144 settlers sent by Virginia Company settle at Jamestown.

       Aug   Plymouth Company establishes a fort at Sagadahoc in Maine. Soon abandoned.

       Dec   John Smith captured by Powhatan, saved by his daughter Pocahontas.

1609   May   William Bradford and the Pilgrims migrate from England to Holland.

       May   Second charter to Virginia Company.

       Sept   Henry Hudson explores river which is given his name.

1609–1610   Starving time in Virginia.

1610   June   Governor Lord de la Warr arrives in Virginia in time to stop abandonment of Jamestown.

1611   May   Sir Thomas Dale succeeds de la Warr as Governor of Virginia. He introduces military law, published as *Laws Divine Moral and Martial*.

1612   Settlement in Bermuda. Tobacco planted in Virginia.

1614   April   Marriage of Pocahontas and John Rolfe.

1618   Nov   Virginia Company issues charter of privileges, ending martial law and providing for an elected assembly.

1619   July   Assembly convened in Jamestown – first in North America.

       Aug   Twenty Africans sold by Dutch into servitude in Virginia – first slaves.

1620   Nov   Plymouth settled by the Pilgrims. Mayflower Compact.

1622   St Christopher (St Kitts) settled in Leeward Islands.

       March   Massacre of 350 colonists by Indians led by Openchancanough in Virginia.

1624   May   Virginia Company dissolved. Dutch establish New Netherland.

1625   Death of James I. Charles I succeeds.

       Virginia becomes a Crown colony.

       Barbados settled.

1626   May   Dutch West India Company director Peter Minuit buys Manhattan Island from Indians for goods worth 60 guilders. Establishes New Amsterdam there.

       Settlement at site of Salem.

1628   Nevis settled.

1629   Massachusetts Bay Company incorporated.

       Oct   John Winthrop elected governor.

1630   Sept   Boston settled by the Puritans.

       Providence Island settled.

1632   Antigua and Montserrat settled.

       June   Charter for Maryland granted to George Calvert, 1st Lord Baltimore.

1633   Dutch establish fort on Connecticut river on site of Hartford.

1634   St Mary's, first settlement in Maryland, established by Cecili Calvert, 2nd Lord Baltimore.

1636 May   Sir Henry Vane elected governor of Massachusetts. Thomas Hooker settles Hartford in Connecticut.
      June   Roger Williams settles Providence in Rhode Island.
      Oct   Harvard College founded.
1636–1637 Pequot War.
1637 May   John Winthrop defeats Sir Henry Vane in election for governor of Massachusetts.
      Nov   Trial of Anne Hutchinson accused of antinomianism in Boston.
      New Haven settled.
1638 New Sweden Company establishes a settlement on the Delaware of Swedes and Dutch.
      March   Anne Hutchinson excommunicated and banished from Massachusetts.
1639 Jan   Fundamental Orders of Connecticut.
1642–1648 Civil Wars in Britain.
1643 May   Connecticut, Massachusetts, New Hampshire and Plymouth form United Colonies of New England, also know as the New England Confederation.
1644 March   Indian attack on settlers in Virginia. Roger Williams obtains charter for Rhode Island.
1648 The Cambridge Platform defines Calvinist orthodoxy in Massachusetts.
      Dec   Purge of parliament to prepare for trial of Charles I. Purged parliament known as the Rump.
1649 Jan   Execution of Charles I. England becomes a Republic.
      April   Maryland Toleration Act passed.
1650 April   Assembly convenes in Maryland.
      Oct   Rump Parliament orders naval blockade of Virginia in response to the colony's declaration of loyalty to the Crown.
1651 Oct   Rump Parliament passes Navigation Ordinance.
1652 March   Sir William Berkeley, governor of Virginia, yields power to commissioners sent by the Rump to replace him with Richard Bennett. Commissioners also take over government of Maryland. May. Rhode Island declares slavery illegal. Massachusetts claims Maine against claim of Sir Ferdinando Gorges.
      Oct   Massachusetts claims to be an independent commonwealth.
1652–1654 First Anglo–Dutch War provoked largely by Navigation Ordinance.
1653 April   Oliver Cromwell forcibly dissolves the Rump.
      English settlers in Connecticut River valley seize Hartford from Dutch.
      Dec   Instrument of Government makes Cromwell Lord Protector.
1654 Oct   Maryland Governor William Fuller, appointed by Rump parliament, removes toleration from Catholics.
1655 Oliver Cromwell's Western Design takes Jamaica from Spain. Dutch acquire New Sweden.
1656 Jan   Lord Baltimore allowed to regain proprietorship of Maryland by English Protectorate.
1658 Sept   Oliver Cromwell dies.
1660 May   Restoration of Charles II.
      Oct   Navigation Act.
1662 Halfway Covenant in Massachusetts.
      May   Charter granted to Connecticut, including New Haven in the colony.
1663 March   Charles II grants Carolina to eight proprietors.
      July   Royal charter for Rhode Island.
      Staple Act requires Scottish goods to be shipped to colonies via England. i.e. the Empire is English, not British.
1664–1667 Second Anglo–Dutch War.
1664 Sept   New Netherland acquired for Charles II's brother James duke of York [future James II]. Renamed New York and New Jersey.

1665 Feb New Jersey Concessions and Agreements issued by proprietors provide for assembly.
      March Duke's Laws issued by James duke of York in New York.
1667 July Peace of Breda ends Anglo–Dutch War.
1669 Fundamental Constitutions for Carolina.
1670 First settlement in Carolina.
1672–1674 Third Anglo–Dutch War.
1673 New York retaken by the Dutch.
      Plantation Duties Act passed.
1674 Treaty of Westminster. Dutch recognize English claim to New York. John Lord Berkeley
      sells his proprietary rights in New Jersey to John Fenwick and Edward Byllinge.
1675–1676 Metacom's [King Philip's] War.
1676 July New Jersey divided into East and West Jersey.
      Sept Bacon's Rebellion in Virginia.
1677 March Laws, Concessions and Agreements promulgated in West Jersey.
      Covenant Chain negotiated between the Iroquois and the Governor of New York,
      Sir Edmund Andros.
      Culpeper's rebellion in North Carolina.
1679–1681 The Exclusion Crisis erupts when the duke of York's claim as heir to the throne is
      challenged.
1680 Sept New Hampshire becomes a Crown colony.
1681 March Charles II grants Pennsylvania to William Penn.
1682 May Frame of Government in Pennsylvania.
      Aug James duke of York cedes three lower counties along Delaware Bay to Penn.
1683 June Penn's treaty with Indians at Shackamaxon.
      First Assembly convenes in New York, passes Charter of Liberties.
1684 June Charter of Massachusetts revoked.
1685 Feb James II succeeds Charles II.
1686 May Dominion and Territory of New England incorporates Massachusetts, Rhode
      Island, Connecticut and New Hampshire under Sir Edmund Andros.
1688 March New York and New Jersey added to the Dominion.
      June Birth of a son to James II and his wife, Mary of Modena.
      Nov Glorious Revolution in England.
      Dec James II flees to France.
1689 Feb William and Mary declared King and Queen of England and Scotland.
      March News reaches the colonies that James II had fled to France.
      April Andros seized in Boston.
      May Connecticut and Rhode Island resume their charters.
      Leisler's rebellion in New York.
      1 Aug Protestant Association deposes the deputy governor in Maryland, which
      becomes a Crown colony.
      Dec Jacob Leisler assumes title of Governor of New York.
      Outbreak of King William's War.
      St Kitts seized by the French.
1690 Jan William III appoints Henry Sloughter as Governor of New York.
      May Port Royal in Nova Scotia sacked by forces led by Sir William Phips.
      St Kitts retaken.
1691 March Sloughter arrives in New York City.
      May Leisler executed.
      Oct New Charter granted to Massachusetts.
1692 Feb–Sept Witchcraft trials in Salem.
      William Penn deprived of the government of Pennsylvania, which is annexed to New
      York.

1693   Feb   College of William and Mary established in Williamsburg Virginia.
1694   Dec   Death of Queen Mary. William III rules alone.
       Aug   Penn regains Pennsylvania.
1696   Board of Trade and Plantations established. Navigation Act establishes Vice-Admiralty Courts in the colonies.
1697   French take Port York in Hudson's Bay.
       Treaty of Ryswick ends King William's War.
1701   Aug   Iroquois negotiate separate treaty with New France.
       Nov   Penn's Charter of Privileges establishes unicameral legislature in Pennsylvania and allows for secession of Delaware from Pennsylvania.
       Yale College founded.
1702   March   Death of William III. Accession of Queen Anne and start of Queen Anne's War.
       April   New Jersey becomes a Crown colony.
       Sept   St Augustine raided from Charles Town.
1704   Feb   French massacre colonists at Deerfield Massachusetts.
       April   First issue of the *Boston News Letter*, a weekly newspaper.
       Nov   First assembly in Delaware.
       Aug   Charles Town attacked by French and Spanish troops.
1707   Anglo–Scottish Union. Scots admitted to English Empire, making it British.
1708   Connecticut churches adopt Saybrook Platform.
1710   Oct   Port Royal taken, renamed Annapolis. Nearly 4,000 refugees from the Palatinate settle in the Mohawk River valley in New York and in New Bern North Carolina.
1711   July   Abortive expedition from Boston to take Quebec.
1711–1713   Tuscarora War in the Carolinas.
1712   Division of Carolinas into North and South Carolina.
1713   Treaty of Utrecht. French recognize British claims to Newfoundland, Nova Scotia, Hudson Bay, Nevis and St Kitts.
1714   Aug   Death of Queen Anne. Accession of George I.
1715   May   Lord Baltimore, a convert to Anglicanism from Catholicism, regains proprietorship of Maryland.
1719   Nov   South Carolina becomes a Crown colony.
       Dec   *Boston Gazette* launched.
1720   South Sea Bubble.
1721   Sir Robert Walpole becomes Britain's first prime minister.
1725   William Bradford begins publication of *The New York Gazette*.
1726   William Tennent establishes Log College in Pennsylvania to train Presbyterian ministers.
1727   June   Death of George I. Accession of George II.
       Sept   *Maryland Gazette* launched.
1729   North Carolina becomes a Crown colony.
       Base for Royal navy established in Antigua.
       Benjamin Franklin launches the *Pennsylvania Gazette*.
1731   Library Company of Philadelphia established.
1732   June   Charter granted to Georgia. Hat Act passed.
1733   Jan   Georgia settled by James Oglethorpe and 114 colonists.
       May   Molasses Act passed.
       Nov   *New York Journal* launched, edited by John Peter Zenger.
       Dec   Benjamin Franklin begins publication of *Poor Richard's Almanac*.
1735   Trial of Zenger for seditious libel.
1736   Aug   *Virginia Gazette* launched.
1737   Walking Purchase of Indian territory by Penn family in Pennsylvania.

1738   May   George Whitefield arrives in Georgia. His visit sparks off the Great Awakening. New Jersey granted separate governor from New York for first time since it became a crown colony in 1702.

1739   Outbreak of War of Jenkins's Ear.
        Admiral Vernon takes Porto Bello.
        Sept   Stono rebellion in South Carolina.

1740   Abortive attack on Cartagena.
        Oglethorpe besieges St Augustine but forced to retreat.

1741   June   Presbyterian Synod in Philadelphia results in division into Old and New Sides, a schism which lasts until 1758.

1742   Walpole resigns. Lords Carteret and Wilmington form government.

1743   Henry Pelham and the duke of Newcastle head the government.
        George II commands British army at battle of Dettingen.
        American Philosophical Society established.

1744   French declare war on Britain.
        Treaty of Lancaster Pennsylvania between commissioners from Maryland, Pennsylvania and Virginia and the Iroquois, who grant their Ohio lands to the colonies.

1745   June   Colonists take Louisbourg on Cape Breton Island from French.
        Nov   French attack Saratoga and Albany.

1746   College of New Jersey established at Elizabethtown, New Jersey in 1746. It moved to Princeton in 1756 and was later renamed Princeton.

1747   Ohio Company set up to settle western lands claimed by Virginia.

1748   Oct   Treaty of Aix-la-Chapelle restores Louisbourg to France.
        Nov   Lord Halifax becomes President of the Board of Trade.

1749   May   Ohio Company gets a charter.
        June   Base for Royal Navy established at Halifax, Nova Scotia.

1750   June   Iron Act.

1752   June   Georgia becomes a Crown colony.

1753   French plan erection of three forts to strengthen their claim to the Ohio region.
        Oct   George Washington sent by governor of Virginia to object to the plan.

1754   Feb   Virginia plans to build fort on site of modern Pittsburgh. Foiled by the French who start to build Fort Duquesne there.
        Outbreak of French and Indian War.
        March   Death of Henry Pelham. Duke of Newcastle becomes prime minister.
        May   Virginia Militia led by George Washington inflicts defeat on French and Indians in the Great Meadows and builds Fort Necessity there.
        June–July   The Albany Congress. Benjamin Franklin's Plan of Union.
        July   Washington surrenders Fort Necessity to French.
        Oct   King's College founded (later renamed Columbia University).

1755   Feb   General Edward Braddock arrives in America and advances to the Monongahela River where he is defeated and killed in July.
        Sept   6,000 French Acadians expelled from Nova Scotia. Fort William Henry built on Lake George.

1756   French declare war on British in Europe.
        May   French seize Oswego from British.
        Sept–Oct   French expelled from Nova Scotia.
        Dec   William Pitt becomes prime minister.

1757   April   Pitt dismissed.
        June   Formation of the ministry of William Pitt and the duke of Newcastle.
        Aug   French capture Fort William Henry.

1758   July   British defeated at Ticonderoga.
        Nov   British take Louisbourg. British take Fort Duquesne (renamed Pittsburgh).

1759 Feb–April Guadeloupe taken by British.
      July British take Fort Niagara and Ticonderoga.
      Sept Wolfe captures Quebec.
1760 Sept Amherst takes Montreal.
      Oct Death of George II. Accession of George III.
1761 Feb Writs of Assistance case in Massachusetts.
      Oct William Pitt resigns as secretary of state.
1762 Jan Britain declares war on Spain.
      Aug British take Cuba.
      Duke of Newcastle replaced as prime minister by earl of Bute.
1763 Feb Peace of Paris. Guadeloupe and Martinique restored to France in exchange for
      Canada. Cuba restored to Spain in exchange for Florida.
      April Bute replaced by George Grenville.
      May Outbreak of Pontiac's war.
      Oct Proclamation issued by George III establishes Appalachian mountains as western
      boundary of the colonies.
      Nov Pontiac raises siege of Detroit.
      Dec Paxton Boys assassinate Conestoga Indians in jail at Lancaster, Pennsylvania.
1764 April Sugar Act.
      Aug Non-importation agreement in Boston.
1765 March Stamp Act.
      May Quartering Act.
      July Marquis of Rockingham becomes prime minister.
      Aug Thomas Hutchinson's house destroyed.
      Oct Stamp Act Congress in New York City.
1766 March Repeal of Stamp Act. Declaratory Act.
      July Earl of Chatham (William Pitt) replaces Rockingham as prime minister.
      Charles Townshend made Chancellor of the Exchequer.
1767 June American Duties (Townshend) Act.
      Sept Townshend dies. Lord North becomes Chancellor of the Exchequer.
      Dec Non-importation agreements in colonies.
1768 Jan (Colonial) secretariat created. Earl of Hillsborough appointed.
      June Riots in Boston after seizure of John Hancock's sloop.
      Oct Troops commanded by Thomas Gage arrive in Boston.
      Pitt resigns. Duke of Grafton becomes prime minister.
1769 May Virginia Resolves.
      Dec Grafton agrees to repeal all Townshend duties other than those on tea.
1770 Jan Lord North becomes prime minister on Grafton's resignation.
      March Boston Massacre.
      April Townshend duties, except on tea, repealed.
1771 May North Carolina Regulators defeated at Alamance Creek.
1772 June Royal Navy schooner Gaspee burned in Rhode Island.
      Aug The earl of Dartmouth replaces Hillsborough as colonial secretary.
1773 May Tea Act.
      Dec Boston Tea Party.
1774 March–June Coercive Acts.
      May General Gage appointed Governor of Massachusetts.
      Sept First Continental Congress meets in Philadelphia.
      Oct Congress forms Continental Association.
1775 April Battles of Lexington and Concord.
      May Second Continental Congress meets.
      June George Washington given command of continental army.
      Battle of Bunker Hill.

July   Olive Branch Petition.

Aug   George III rejects Olive Branch Petition, declares colonies in rebellion.

Sept–Dec   Abortive American invasion of Canada.

Oct   General William Howe replaces Gage as commander in chief.

Nov   Lord George Germain replaces Dartmouth as colonial secretary.

1776   Feb   Thomas Paine's *Common Sense* published.

March   British troops leave Boston.

May   Congress calls on colonies to adopt their own constitutions.

July   British base established at Staten Island.

Declaration of Independence.

Admiral Richard Howe arrives with British fleet in New York.

Sept   British take New York City.

Dec   Washington retreats across the Delaware.

Washington advances across the Delaware and wins battle of Trenton.

1777   Jan   Washington defeats the British at Princeton.

Sept   British defeat Washington at Brandywine and take Philadelphia, forcing Congress to move to Lancaster and then York, Pennsylvania.

Oct   General John Burgoyne defeated at Saratoga.

Nov   Congress adopts Articles of Confederation subject to ratification by states.

Dec   Washington's forces spend winter at Valley Forge.

1778   Feb   Treaty of alliance between France and the USA.

April   French fleet arrives off New York.

John Paul Jones attacks Whitehaven.

May   Howe replaced as commander in chief by Sir Henry Clinton.

Dec   British take Savannah.

1779   Jan   British take Augusta, Georgia.

Feb   British defeated at Port Royal, South Carolina.

June   Spain declares war on Britain.

Sept   John Paul Jones defeats British ships off Filey.

1780   May   British under Clinton take Charles Town. Lord Cornwallis takes command of British in the southern states.

Aug   British win battle of Camden.

Sept   Benedict Arnold defects to British.

1781   Jan   British defeated at Cowpens.

Feb   Maryland last state to ratify Articles of Confederation.

March   Articles of Confederation implemented.

British defeated at Guilford Court House, North Carolina.

Cornwallis retreats to Yorktown, Virginia.

Oct   battle of Yorktown.

1782   Feb   Lord North replaced as prime minister by the Marquis of Rockingham.

March   Peace talks open in Paris.

April   British navy defeats French at battle of the Saintes.

July   Earl of Shelburne becomes prime minister on Rockingham's death.

1783   Feb   Lord North and Charles James Fox ally to defeat Shelburne, form Coalition under duke of Portland.

Sept   Treaty of Paris.

Introduction

The Colonial era traditionally extends from the founding of Jamestown, England's first success-ful colony, in 1607, to the end of the Seven Years' War, or French and Indian War as it is known in the United States, in 1763. However, this chronology is open to challenge. The unsuccessful settlement at Roanoke Island in the 1580s can be considered as the first serious attempt at founding an English plantation in North America, and indeed is given an entry here. But before that there were voyages of exploration and discovery, and even temporary settlements, by fishermen on Newfoundland for example. One need not subscribe to the myth that the Welsh prince Madoc had colonized Florida in the 12th century to argue that British colonization of America had a long pre-history. Richard Hakluyt's *Principall Navigations, Voyages and Discoveries of the English Nation*, published as early as 1589, documented activities of seamen in the Americas long before the foothold established on the continent at Jamestown. After all Spaniards had been busy creating colonies for over a century before that. As Howard Mumford Jones graphically put it 'When in 1585 a forlorn little band of Englishmen were trying to stick it out on Roanoke Island, 300 poets were competing for a prize in Mexico city' (*O Strange New World: American Culture, the formative years* 1965, p. 85). The fabulous success of the Spaniards in tapping the mineral wealth of South and Central America tempted Englishmen to follow their example and search for the legendary El Dorado.

There were other motives too for colonization, which enthusiasts for overseas expansion such as Hakluyt, in his *Discourse of Western Planting* (1584) and Samuel Purchas in his *Hakluyt Posthumus or Purchas his Pilgrimes* (1625), promoted. The conversion of the natives to the true Protestant faith rather than to Spanish Catholicism or Popery was one, though that did not loom as large as profit in the promotional literature. Another was to relieve Elizabethan and Jacobean England of its alleged surplus population. The ideological justification for imperial expansion preceded rather than followed the successful establishment of colonies. It sprang partly from the refutation of papal allocations of the new world to Portugal and Spain, and partly from the English claims to an imperial jurisdiction over the British Isles under the Tudors.

If the history of the American colonies can be extended back in time before the foundation of Virginia, so its conclusion can be brought forward beyond the traditional date of 1763. Placed in the context of the British Empire rather than of the United States of America it can obviously be taken much further. Even as a prelude to the history of the United States, which this volume is intended to be, it is still somewhat ahistorical to overlook Canada and the West Indies, which are therefore given entries here. It is also to subscribe to a teleological view that the creation of the new republic was inevitable from the end of the Seven Years' War, if not before. Yet, although the eventual separation of the colonies from the mother country was predicted before 1776, it was not anticipated that early. Most predictions in the middle of the 18th century placed it at least 50 years in the future. What precipitated it were the policies of the ministers in London and the reactions to them in the colonies. Arguably ministerial policies did not alienate Americans to the extent of independence being a serious option until Lord North's overreaction to the Boston Tea party in 1773. Until the Coercive Acts of 1774 polarized the situation the issues between the colonists and the British government could have been contained. After that, although there were attempts by both sides to repair the damage, there was no way of going back to the *status quo* before 1763. The colonies declared themselves independent states in 1776. Great Britain did not recognize the independence of the United States of America until the peace of Paris in 1783, which is where this companion to Colonial American history ends.

Not that dates delimited by political events matter as much in colonial history today as they used to do. The times have long gone when it was marked, as Woodrow Wilson complained of the syllabus at Princeton, by details of quarrels between the governors of colonies and their assemblies over obscure issues, which he was thankful he would soon forget. Since the 1960s, when the 'new' social history began to make an impact, historical investigations into the colonial era have moved away from politics to embrace a whole range of phenomena which were relatively neglected previously or even entirely overlooked. Historians became concerned more with economic and social issues such as population and demography, Indians and slaves, and that all-embracing concept 'culture'. The pace of change quickened in the 1980s, under the impact of feminist history, which stressed the roles of women, and of postmodernism, which transformed the very perception of history, particularly in colonial times. Controlling narratives, such as 'the rise of the assemblies' and the victory of liberty over tyranny, almost completely disappeared. So great was the concern that, with the fragmentation of the past, all coherence would be gone from it that the Historical Society was launched in the United States to combat the tendency.

Insofar as a conceptual framework has emerged to replace the grand narratives it is that of Atlantic history. To be sure imperial history, placing the colonial experience within that of Britain, is not new. In the opening decades of the 20th century historians such as Herbert L. Osgood, George Louis Beer and Charles Andrews stressed the importance of looking at the colonies as part of the British Empire. But they wrote at a time when political, constitutional and administrative history were still the central topics of historical inquiry. The 'new' imperial history examines the comparative cultures of Britain and America during the colonial era. Thus investigations have looked at how far the social structures and economies of the mother country and the colonies replicated each other. Contrary to conclusions reached by some historians, who emphasized American exceptionalism, these studies demonstrated that there was considerable replication of British culture in North America.

The older imperial history tended to group the colonies together in terms of their relationship to the British government, distinguishing between Crown, proprietary and corporate colonies. This made sense when historians prioritized administrative and political history, but serves little purpose when investigating cultural phenomena. Thus the fact that Maryland was a proprietary colony while Virginia became a Crown colony was scarcely relevant to the development of a tobacco culture in the Chesapeake Bay. 'Atlantic' historians tend to group the colonies together geographically, though they differ in the ways they carve colonial America up into regions, some preferring two, others three, and yet others four or five. However, there seems to be general agreement on four distinct areas: New England; the middle colonies; the Chesapeake; and the lower south. To these a fifth, the back country, needs to be added as the colonial era progresses from settlements to society.

Although New England was the second area to be settled by English colonists, after Virginia, it traditionally received most attention from historians. This was perhaps because Puritanism was regarded as a seminal influence on the development of American society. It could also have been because the Puritans were more devoted to words, as well as the Word, than their contemporaries, and left behind them an extensive archive of sermons, tracts, diaries and other relatively easily accessible documents, many in print, which made research into their history more amenable than that of most other colonists. The result was the publication of a vast library of studies on the Puritans and Puritanism. When the 'new' social history first began to have an impact in the 1960s it was led by studies of that archetypal phenomenon, the New England town. These studies also pioneered the concept of Atlantic history by comparing the development of towns in New England with those in Old England from which their settlers came.

Following these investigations attention shifted from New England to the Chesapeake Bay. Comparisons between the two regions drew startling contrasts. Where New England was settled largely by 'middle class' families from England, who enjoyed a longer life – expectancy than those they left behind, the Chesapeake attracted in the main young adult males who died like flies in the early years in the disease-ridden environment of the Bay. But where Puritanism allegedly characterized New England so profit motivated Virginians, and those who survived the ordeal created a society dominated by gentry who cultivated tobacco on their plantations. It was even suggested that the Chesapeake was more typical of the societies which emerged after American Independence.

Other historians seeking the origins of modern America in the colonial era claim to have found more typical characteristics in the middle colonies than in those to the north and south of them. Ethnic diversity, for example, which is a crucial ingredient in the United States, was evident in the region between the Hudson River and the Delaware Bay from the outset of colonization. Swedes, Finns and Dutch migrated to it before the English. They were followed by Germans, Scotch Irish and other European settlers, making New York and Pennsylvania polyglot colonies, unlike the English speaking colonists of New England and the Chesapeake. The middle colonies were thus a melting pot long before the 19th century.

Yet if one is looking for a peculiarly American society, different from its European seedbed, the most obvious example is to be found in the lower south, and especially in South Carolina. Here after 1680 a uniquely slave-based rice economy developed, with a majority of the population of African descent, making it much more like the sugar colonies of the West Indies than even the tobacco plantations of the Chesapeake. South Carolina had a black majority of over 60 per cent, compared with a minority of 40 per cent in Virginia. African influences on the culture of the colony have even been detected in some of the techniques of rice production, which some historians insist were imported from Africa.

These regional differences were most marked at the end of the 17th century. By the middle of the 18th century the settlements of the eastern seaboard had grown into societies which were acquiring similar social characteristics. These trends were most discernible in the ports of Boston, Newport, New York City, Philadelphia, Baltimore, Charles Town and Savannah. Although their populations added together comprised at most 10 per cent of the total, which remained overwhelmingly rural, cities have been seen as 'the cutting edge of change' in the late colonial era. Paradoxically on the eve of separation from Britain they were coming to resemble British ports such as Bristol, Liverpool and Glasgow. This 'Anglicanization' of America was facilitated by the import of goods, 'baubles from Britain', from the mother country. As the inhabitants of the eastern seaboard grew in numbers and increased in wealth they created a demand for consumer goods of all kinds which the colonial economies could not satisfy. Consequently the contents of colonial houses of the middle classes as well as the gentry were supplied from Britain, from furniture and fittings to books, paintings and prints.

The growth of a relatively affluent society along the Atlantic coast meant that the greatest regional distinction came to be not that between different coastal areas but between them and the frontier. The differences between the long settled areas and the back country, which only began to be filled up in the central decades of the 18th century, caused friction between them. This exploded into violence in the 1760s with the protests of the 'Paxton boys' in the Susquehanna valley in Pennsylvania, and of the 'regulators' in the piedmont districts of the Carolinas. On the eve of the breach with Britain it seemed as though the colonies were being torn apart by internal tensions.

Among the disruptive forces of those years the Great Awakening was perhaps the most divisive. The revival of Calvinism, with its insistence on a new birth, split communities asunder between 'old' and 'new' lights among the Congregationalists of New England and 'old' and 'new' sides among the Presbyterians of the middle colonies, while Baptists began to make inroads into Anglicanism in the south. Yet paradoxically the Awakening is generally viewed as the first 'American' phenomenon, since it swept across colonial boundaries in a way which no previous movement had done. It united the colonists in Protestant zeal against the 'Popish' French in the Seven Years' War, and when that ended it served as a unifying force against the 'Arminian' tendencies detected behind the policies of George III's ministers and their Anglican allies in the colonies.

This dictionary tries to keep the British as well as the colonists in view. It starts out with a Scottish general, James Abercromby, and ends with a colonial printer, John Peter Zenger. It lists kings and queens and some leading politicians in Britain as well as men and women active in the colonies. There are Acts of parliament as well as of assemblies. When wars are dealt with, although they are given their American rather than their British titles, campaigns on both sides of the ocean are included. The aim is to provide enough information to make the compendium useful as a work of reference for Atlantic as well as for colonial American history.

Note on Entries
Cross references are indicated by bold type. Some events are subsumed under larger headings. Thus readers seeking details of the battle of Saratoga will find them under **The War of American Independence** and the cross reference to **Burgoyne**.

A

ABERCROMBY, JAMES (1706–1781) was born in Scotland, where he represented Banff as MP from 1734 to 1754. Abercromby became the King's painter. He also pursued a military career, becoming deputy governor of Stirling Castle, and rising to be appointed in 1756 second in command in North America to **Lord Loudoun**. When Loudoun was recalled in 1758 he was given the supreme command, and was made colonel in chief of the Royal American Regiment. The campaigns of that year in the **French and Indian War**, however, were unsuccessful, culminating in Abercromby's withdrawal from Ticonderoga. In consequence he too was recalled, to be replaced by **Jeffrey Amherst**.

ACADIA was a term used by the British for the region of **Canada** which the French called Acadie. It referred to the maritime settlements along the Atlantic coast from Maine to modern New Brunswick, which was included in **Nova Scotia** during the colonial period.

ADAMS, ABIGAIL (1744–1818). Born in Weymouth, Massachusetts, she was the daughter of a congregational minister. Her education followed the pattern for girls of the period as she was educated at home. She is famous for her marriage to **John Adams**, second president of the United States, and her advocacy of women's rights in the domestic sphere. Her remark to her husband in 1776 to 'remember the ladies,' expressed her concern that women be recognized as equal partners in the home and that they receive a formal education similar to males. This, she argued, was important preparation for their duties and responsibilities as future republican women.

ADAMS, JOHN (1735–1826) was born at Braintree in Massachusetts. His heritage goes back to the Puritan migration to the colony in 1638. He became a representative to the first and second Continental Congresses; delegate to the Massachusetts state constitutional convention; signer of the **Declaration of Independence**, American Commissioner in Europe; first U.S. ambassador to Holland; a principal negotiator in the 1783 Paris Peace negotiations; and second President of the United States. An avid book collector, Adams' love of books was so great that it was only surpassed by his love of his family and home. His interest in gathering everything in print extended to his having a standing order with a London bookseller to send, 'every book and pamphlet' on the subject of law and government.

Adams was admitted to the bar in 1759, but rose to international prominence by a series of crises that ultimately resulted in America's independence. His rise to local importance coincided with international notice with the death of Boston's prominent attorney, James Gridley and the mental breakdown of **James Otis** which left Adams as Boston's busiest attorney. The 1765 **Stamp Act** sealed Adams' international renown when he responded to the crises with 'A Dissertation on the Canon and the Feudal Law.' First published in the local gazette, the work reached England in a volume entitled, *The True Sentiments of America.* Although the work did not specifically mention the Stamp Act, it implied the Act's significance by emphasizing Americans' long established rights based on English law. The 'Dissertation' was followed by Adams' 'Braintree Instruction' in which the centerpiece was, 'No taxation without representation.'

Ironically, Adams' dictum on liberty and his animosity toward the soldiers who killed five civilians in the 1770 Boston Massacre was tested when he accepted the position of lawyer for the soldiers who were accused of the killings. His dislike of tyranny was balanced on both sides; toward the rabble on the one hand, whom he described as rioters who were at fault, and towards the soldiers on the other, even though they acted in self defense. His successful defense of the case increased his public standing as a man of integrity.

His reputation for integrity resulted in him being chosen as one of five Massachusetts delegates to the first and second Continental Congress. 'The die was cast,' as Adams put it to Jonathan Sewall. From this point, Adams' fame would extend to Europe.

As one of the signers of the Declaration of Independence, Adams, along with **Benjamin Franklin** and Edward Rutledge, was appointed to meet with Admiral Lord Richard **Howe** at the outset of hostilities in hopes of a peaceful settlement toward independence. Howe described Adams as a 'decided character' and put him on the list to be hanged as traitor.

Adams was given more responsibilities which involved him in European diplomacy. His first appointment was as one of three commissioners including **Franklin** and Arthur Lee to France in November 1777 in order to negotiate an alliance. Although he knew no French, he virtually taught himself while on board ship and became proficient enough to communicate effectively when he arrived in Paris.

The American victory over the British at Saratoga in the fall of 1777 convinced the French to lend their support to the Americans, but not as quickly as Adams would have liked. The French foreign minister initially ignored the commissioners' request because of French invasion plans for England. Finally, in February, a formal alliance was made in which the French agreed to fight until Britain recognized the independence of America.

Adams' next trip to Europe occurred in October 1779 as minister plenipotentiary to France. His main business was to conduct peace and commercial negotiations with Britain. Adam's strong aversion to follow French policy in this regard ultimately lost for him any influence with the French. Subsequently, he spent the remainder of the war in Holland trying to secure financial support for America. After the surrender of the British at Yorktown in October 1781, the following year, Adams was recognized as the first U.S. ambassador to the Hague. Furthermore, he was able to secure a loan from the Dutch of 5 million guilders, or 2 million dollars.

Adams returned to Paris to act as one of the principal negotiators in the Peace treaty between the Americans and the British. The treaty not only confirmed first and foremost America's independence from Britain, it marked America's independence from French influence. When he returned to London to the court of **George III**, the king greeted him by saying that although he was the last to consent to colonial separation from Britain, nevertheless with the break made, he would be the first to meet the friendship of the United States as an independent power.

ADAMS, SAMUEL (1722–1803). Born in Boston, Massachusetts, Adams became a primary force in resistance against British measures toward the colonies. As tax collector from the period 1756 to 1765, he was so lenient toward the taxpayers that he fell into arrears for the sum of 10,000 pounds.

While this did not endear him to the British government, he became so popular among the Bostonians that he was elected to Massachusetts assembly in 1765. As tensions between the colonies and the British government increased, Adams was a key player in the organization of resistance. He belonged to the Loyal Nine, North End Caucus, and the Sons of Liberty. He helped to draft the Circular Letter of 1768 protesting against British troop arrivals in Massachusetts. Adams organized the first Committee of Correspondence in 1772 and continued to foment resistance and, ultimately revolt through his own publications and publishing of letters written by governors **Francis Bernard** and **Thomas Hutchinson** that argued for the reduction of colonial liberty. Adams chaired the Town Meeting which adjourned to hold the **Boston Tea Party**.

Adams was chosen as a representative to the Continental Congress from 1774 to 1780 where he was in favor of a loose confederation and sided with the Arthur Lee faction in the dispute over handling French support. In 1780, Adams served on the committee to write his state's constitution in which he supported increased property qualifications for voting rights and a State Senate which represented the property class.

AFFIRMATION ACT 1696 extended to those, principally **Quakers**, who eschewed swearing oaths, the right to affirm instead. This allowed them to be involved in political activities such as parliamentary elections. It had an impact upon the colonies, particularly **Pennsylvania**, where those who attended the **Anglican Church** claimed that, since affirmation had been conceded to Quakers in England, they should reciprocally be given the right to swear oaths.

ALBANY CONGRESS was held in 1754 in Albany, **New York**, with delegates from all the **New England** colonies present together with those from New York, **Pennsylvania** and **Maryland**. The main business of the Congress was to persuade the Iroquois to resume the **Covenant Chain** on the eve of the **French and Indian War**. The occasion was taken to discuss the **Albany Plan** for a permanent union of the colonies.

ALBANY PLAN OF UNION was proposed by **Benjamin Franklin** to unite the North American colonies in order to defend them from French encroachment. Its significance is twofold: from the imperial perspective, the plan threatened to create a separate identity for the colonists from that of the motherland; secondly, it was a visionary document whose ideas were picked up during the **War for American Independence** in the **Articles of Confederation** and the United States Constitution.

The plan was precipitated by the competition for American land and resources between Britain, Spain, and ultimately, France. Between the Treaty of Aix-le-Chapelle in 1748, which was nothing more than recognition of the stalemate between Britain and France in Europe, and the onset of the **French and Indian War** from 1754 to 1763, the British North American colonies felt the squeeze between the French controlled territories and the Atlantic Ocean. During the interval between the Treaty and the resumption of full scale hostilities, conflict increased between British colonials and the French. The French attempted to ring in the British colonies by establishing forts from the Great Lakes to the Mississippi River. The threat was enough to cause London to make secure its own colonial borders and encourage the colonials to establish alliances with the Iroquois and create a common war chest.

A congress met at Albany, New York in 1754 to discuss colonial defense. The initial items on the agenda were negotiations with the Five Nations and the creation of a common war fund. The issue of financing a war provoked further consideration on how the colonies in general would cooperate. Franklin put forward his scheme whereby a grand council, headed by a president general would be responsible for defense, Indian relations, and any new lands acquired by the Crown. While the president general would be appointed by the Crown, representation of the colonies, in a grand council, was to be based upon election to office by the colonial assemblies. Since neither **Nova Scotia** nor **Georgia** had assemblies they were excluded. The number of representatives for each colony in the council was to reflect its population. They were to be elected every three years and to convene annually in Philadelphia. The council would act only in an advisory capacity leaving the president with the crucial veto power. Thus the real control stayed in London. Nevertheless, the idea of proportional representation, as set out by the plan of union, was adopted in the creation of the U.S. constitution, although no claim can be made that the plan directly informed the constitution. The rest of the document concentrated on the need for central control, something that the Americans had come to realize in 1787 with the creation of a federal government and one which attempts certain checks and balances. Military appointments, though nominated by the president, needed the confirmation of the council. Likewise, civil appointments, though nominated by the council, required approbation of the president.

The primary functions of the president and council were to negotiate with the Indians and supervise the settlement of new territories. They were also to be responsible for colonial defense, for which purpose they should be empowered to enlist an army and navy and to raise taxes. The scheme was agreed by the Congress, but was not acceptable to either the colonies or the Crown.

The weakness, and ultimate failure of the plan, was ironically its strength. The idea of central control, particularly when it came to decisions over newly acquired lands, conflicted with individual colonial aspirations and ambitions for expansion. There had been rival land claims between the various colonies such as **Virginia** and **Pennsylvania**, and Pennsylvania and **Connecticut**. The scheme while putting a stop to such problems, also impinged upon local interests. So while the colonials were proudly British, and did not see the plan as a way to independence, they were also jealously defensive of individual local interests. For that reason and from Whitehall's perception that its common purpose raised the specter of a separate identity between the colonies, the plan failed to pass scrutiny.

That the plan was put forward at all and that it passed the first hurdle of the Congress should be considered a watershed of thinking on the colonial side about its attitude toward the future of colonial identity. Though its failure can be put down to competing interests, its introduction can be seen as the beginnings of the recognition of a common purpose.

AMERICAN PHILOSOPHICAL SOCIETY was founded in 1743 in Philadelphia. The Society's principal protagonist was **Benjamin Franklin**, himself a member of the Royal Society for the Promotion of Useful Knowledge in London, which he used as a model for the American society. Its seal depicted an American Indian and a colonist reaching out across the globe to Britannia. Franklin had been instrumental in promoting the advance of science in Philadelphia earlier, helping to establish the Junto Club there in 1728. The Society did not enjoy a continuous existence until after its relaunch in 1768.

AMHERST, JEFFREY (1717–1797) rose to the rank of general in the British army, which he joined in 1735. After military experience in Europe during the War of the Austrian Succession or **King George's War**, and in the opening stages of the Seven Years' War or **French and Indian War**, he was appointed as 'Major General in America' in 1757. As commander of the expedition to take Cape Breton Island from the French in 1758 he launched a successful attack against Louisbourg. The following year Amherst took Ticonderoga and Crown Point from the French, while General **James Wolfe** captured Quebec. Wolfe's death left Amherst to complete the conquest of Canada which he accomplished in 1760 by taking Montreal. He then established his headquarters at New York City, from which he presided over the British campaign in the Caribbean. He also dealt with **Pontiac's War**. His resort to 'germ warfare', by supplying blankets infected with small pox to the Indians, has tarnished his reputation in recent years. At the time he was much feted as a successful commander in chief in North America, a position which **George III** invited him to accept again during the War of American Independence, but which he declined.

ANDROS, SIR EDMUND (1637–1714) was born in Guernsey, where he became bailiff in 1674, and lieutenant governor in 1704, Andros pursued a military career. He took part in an expedition to the West Indies in 1666, where he served as major of the Barbados regiment of foot. He was appointed governor of New York in 1674, a post he held until 1682. Andros implemented the so-called **Duke's Laws** promulgated by the proprietor, James duke of York, and resisted calls for a representative assembly. In 1681 he returned to England and persuaded James that the only way to make the colony profitable was to give in to the demands. James replaced him with **Thomas Dongan**. In 1685, as lieutenant general of Princess Anne's regiment of foot, Andros took part in the repression of the rebellion of the duke of Monmouth. The duke of York, now **James II**, appointed him as governor of the **Dominion of New England**. He arrived in December 1686 and ruled arbitrarily, provoking the **Glorious Revolution in America**. He was seized in Boston and sent to England, but charges laid against him by **Massachusetts** were dropped. From 1692 to 1697 he was governor of **Virginia**, where he quarrelled with **James Blair**. Blair took the quarrel to England and succeeded in having Andros recalled.

ANGLICAN CHURCH. Anglicanism was the creed of the Church of England as by law established. It was enshrined in the Act of Supremacy of 1559 which made the monarch supreme governor of the church 'insofar as the law of Christ allows' and in the thirty-nine articles of 1563, which inclined towards Calvinism. In its liturgy and episcopal form of government, however, it leaned more towards Catholicism. Hence its reputation as a via media between Geneva and Rome. The Church of Ireland and the Episcopalians in Scotland were also Anglican. The Anglican church became established in the southern colonies from **Maryland** to **Georgia**. Its clergy came from the Church of England, the Church of Ireland and from Scottish Episcopalians until the establishment of the **College of William and Mary** in **Virginia** in 1693 provided them with a colonial seminary. The British **West Indies** were also mainly Anglican, and likewise recruited their clergy from the mother country until **Christopher Codrington** left provision in his will for the establishment of a seminary to train them in **Barbados**. Codrington College opened in 1745.

ANNE, QUEEN (1665–1714) was the younger daughter of **James II**. She was brought up as an Anglican, and remained a staunch defender of the Church of England. During the **Glorious Revolution** she deserted her father and went to Nottingham. She succeeded **William III** in 1702 as Queen of England, Scotland and Ireland. In 1707 as a result of the Anglo–Scottish Union she became Queen of Great Britain and Ireland. The Act of Union allowed Scots to trade with England's colonies, thereby merging them into the British Empire. For much of her reign her subjects were engaged in **Queen Anne's War**, which concluded in the **Treaty of Utrecht** of 1713. Although she did not take as much of an interest in America as her sister, **Queen Mary** had done, Annapolis, **Maryland**, and Annapolis Royal, **Nova Scotia** were named after her.

ANTIGUA. An island in the Leeward Islands in the **West Indies** settled by the English in 1632. Its agriculture became almost entirely devoted to sugar production. Governor Daniel Parke, an appointee of the duke of Marlborough, was murdered in 1710 after ordering troops to disperse the assembly. Parke was the only governor of a British American colony to be assassinated. In 1729 the first base for the Royal Navy in the Americas was constructed at St Johns.

ANTINOMIAN CONTROVERSY was the result of a long dispute within the dissenting community over salvation. The question was, 'how does one know if he or she is saved?' The dominant Calvinist belief was in predestination, the doctrine that God had predetermined that some, the elect, would be saved, while most would be damned. Thus only those who were elected for salvation, the visible saints, could know, through examination, who were the chosen. This precluded any notion of individual revelation. It also excluded the possibility that good works could effect salvation, which was effected only by the unearned gift of God's grace. Some **Puritans** in **Massachusetts**, however, maintained that people could prepare their hearts to receive grace. This apparent concession to the notion of good works was criticized by strict Calvinists, creating a dispute among the Independents of the Bay colony. At the center of the controversy were **Anne Hutchinson**, **John Cotton**, and **Henry Vane**, who had all emigrated to Boston from England. Their insistence that works were irrelevant to salvation struck their critics as upholding antinomianism, the doctrine that the elect could defy the ten commandments since they were not bound by the law. Moderate Calvinists insisted that although good works were not necessary to salvation they were concomitants of grace. Their views prevailed in the controversy, which ended in 1737 when Anne Hutchinson was tried for heresy, found guilty and banished from the colony.

ARGALL, SIR SAMUEL (1580–1626) was one of the early traders with **Virginia**, taking goods to Jamestown from England in 1609. He conveyed **Lord de la Warr** to the colony in 1610, and returned with him in 1611. He was back in Virginia the following year, going up the Potomac river in December, where he was responsible for the apprehension of **Pocahontas**. In 1613 the **Virginia Company** ordered him to attack French settlements in Maine and **Nova Scotia**, claiming that they infringed its privileges. Argall took prisoners he had captured on this expedition to England in 1614. In 1617 he returned to Virginia as deputy governor, a post he held for two years, during which he made many enemies, including his successor, **Sir George Yeardley**. Argall was recalled to England in 1619, and ended his days on naval service in Europe and Africa.

ARTICLES OF CONFEDERATION were the first constitution of the 'United States of America', as the first of thirteen articles styled the Confederacy. They were drafted in a committee appointed by Congress in June 1776, and presented to it on 12 July. Disagreements over such issues as the size of each state's delegation to Congress, the basis on which each paid to the common treasury, and the distribution of western lands, protracted discussions until 15 November 1777 when Congress accepted the Articles and submitted them to the states for ratification. They were expected to do so with alacrity, since 'it hath pleased the Great Governor of the World to incline the hearts of the legislatures … to approve of and to authorize the said Articles of Confederation and perpetual union'. In the event, however, the last state to ratify them, **Maryland**, did not do so until February 1781, so they did not formally come into operation until 1 March that year. Meanwhile Congress had acted in anticipation of their eventual adoption. Thus the alliance with France in 1778 was negotiated as though article nine, giving Congress exclusive authority to negotiate with foreign powers, was in effect. This was the most important of the Articles. Besides making Congress responsible for foreign affairs, provided nine states approved its actions, it also gave it the authority to adjudicate between states, for instance in boundary disputes. Provision was also made for 'a Committee of the States' to do the business of Congress between its sessions. These were to be annual, as provided for in Article five, which stipulated that it should convene every 1 November. It also stated that each state's delegation could only have one vote, resolving a dispute between large and small states in favor of the latter. Article 8 resolved that contributions to the common treasury should be made on the basis of land and property values. The vexed question of competing claims to western lands was shelved until after the war, being eventually dealt with by the North West Ordinance. Anxieties about the sovereignty of individual states being surrendered to Congress were expressed in the second Article, proposed by Thomas Burke in April 1777, 'that each state retains its sovereignty, freedom and independence and every power jurisdiction and right which is not by this Confederation expressly relegated to the United States in Congress assembled.' In this respect the Articles of Confederation created an alliance of 13 separate sovereign states. This was to create problems after the **Peace of Paris** which were eventually to lead to their replacement by the Constitution of the United States.

B

BACKUS, ISAAC (1724–1806). Born into a family of religious dissent in Massachusetts, Backus became a Baptist minister and leading proponent for religious freedom. A consequence of this was his arrest for refusing to pay the parish tax to support the established Congregational church. The revivalist activities during the period of time known as the **Great Awakening** led Backus to convert to a separatist religion and form his own congregation. In 1756 he formed the First Baptist Church of Middleborough. His arrest, as well as, that of his mother and brother for dissenting from the established church, influenced his thoughts on the separation of church and state. The Baptists created the Warren Association which Backus became involved in, collecting and presenting petitions for relief from persecution. He used the arguments of early British dissenters and Locke for relief from religious and civil oppression, but he was unsuccessful in his appeal to the **Continental Congress**.

His work, *A History of New England with particular reference to the denomination of Christians called Baptists* (1777–1796) stressed the distinction between toleration in religion and freedom of religion. Although his views paralleled those of **Jefferson** and **Madison**, he saw only partial success with the inclusion of the first amendment in the United States Constitution. Massachusetts continued to keep religious taxation on the books until 1833.

BACON, NATHANIEL (1647–1676) was born in England, and attended Cambridge University and Gray's Inn. He emigrated to **Virginia** in 1674 and became a member of Governor **William Berkeley's** council. Being from a substantial gentry family in Suffolk, and married to the daughter of a baronet, Bacon expected and obtained preferment in Virginia society. Within a year of landing in the colony he was made a member of the Council. Nevertheless, he was considered an outsider to a certain extent and his land grants only included property on the frontier rather than the tidewater. There his resentment at being cold shouldered by the tidewater elite, and the insecurity of life on the frontier, resulted in confrontations with Indians and government alike. The combination of heavy taxation, disenfranchisement of non-landowners, and a stagnant legislature which had not seen an election in 14 years resulted in **Bacon's Rebellion** in 1676. Unfortunately for Bacon, he caught dysentery and died shortly afterward. With his death, the rebellion collapsed.

BACON'S REBELLION. The outbreak in **Virginia** against the government of **William Berkeley** in 1676 is known as Bacon's rebellion because its principal leader was **Nathaniel Bacon**. Yet while he had personal reasons to resent the regime in the Old Dominion, he also brought together grievances held by many others. Berkeley ruled the colony through a tightly knit group of associates known as the Green Spring faction after his plantation. Their determination to control the political life of Virginia found expression in an Act passed by the Assembly in 1670 which took the right to vote from the freemen of the colony and restricted it to the freeholders. At the time Berkeley's grip on the assembly was so firm that there was no real resistance to this measure.

Trouble broke out in 1676 initially on the Virginian frontier, which was still east of the Blue Ridge Mountains not far beyond Richmond, then known as Henrico. Frontier settlers were attacked by the Doeg and Susquehannock **Indians**. Although the colonial militia immediately resisted these attacks, their resistance was called off by Berkeley who wished to maintain friendly relations with the Indians. The frontiersmen, led by Bacon, resented this decision and took the law into their own hands by attacking not only the Doegs and Susquehannocks but any Indians whom they encountered. Berkeley denounced their defiance of his friendly approach by declaring Bacon a traitor. This step sparked off the rebellion.

The frontiersmen were joined by sympathizers in the tide water who were themselves smarting from the Green Spring oligarchy's policies. They objected to the taxes, especially a poll tax which hit the poor harder than the rich, which were raised to pursue Berkeley's personal objectives. The governor, taken aback by the widespread support for Bacon, made concessions to the rebels, dissolving the assembly which he had controlled for 14 years, and holding an election for the first time since 1662. Bacon, who was returned to the new assembly from Henrico, dominated its proceedings. It gave the vote back to the freemen and commissioned a force to be sent against the Indians on the frontier. When Berkeley dragged his feet over issuing the commission Bacon led a body of armed men to the assembly. The governor fled to the eastern shore of **Chesapeake Bay** while Bacon published a Declaration 'in the name of the people of Virginia'.

Although this declaration has been seen as an anticipation of independence from England in fact it was an appeal to the English crown to intervene in the quarrel on the side of the rebels against the governor. In the event the king sent troops to suppress the rebellion. It ended before they arrived when Bacon suddenly took ill and died. That **Charles II** had some sympathy with his cause is implied by his observation that Berkeley executed more rebels than he had done when he came to the throne in 1660. He not only sent troops but also commissioners to enquire into the causes of the rebellion. They put the blame on Berkeley, who was recalled and replaced by **Lord Culpeper**, who had opposed the governor's policies. The removal of Berkeley and the Green Spring faction calmed the situation in Virginia, which took no active part in the **Glorious Revolution**.

BAHAMAS. A group of islands in the northern Caribbean, lying between Florida to the north and Cuba and Hispaniola to the south. Although England claimed them as early as 1629 they were not settled until 1647 when a group of English Puritans called 'the Eleutheran

Adventurers' led by William Sayles founded a colony there. During the 17th century the Bahamas became a no-man's land, notoriously providing havens for pirates until the British Crown effectively took control of them in 1718.

BALTIMORE 1ST LORD see **CALVERT GEORGE**

BALTIMORE 2ND LORD see **CALVERT CECIL**

BAPTISTS. A religious denomination whose beginnings can be traced to the early 17th century amongst the English separatist exiles in Holland. Among these were John Smyth and Thomas Helwys who disputed the practice of infant baptism, claiming that only adults could appreciate the significance of the act. After Smyth's death Helwys returned to England in 1612 and founded in London what is generally recognized as the first Baptist church in England. The original members appear to have been Arminians, and to have accepted that Christ died for all men to whom salvation was open. By 1633, however, there had emerged a significant number of Calvinists, who insisted that only the elect were predestined to be saved. This resulted in a split between General (Arminian) and Particular (Calvinist) Baptists. The latter issued a Confession of Faith in 1644. Meanwhile Baptists had joined in the Puritan migration to **New England**. Prominent among them was **Roger Williams**, who founded the first Baptist church in America at Providence Rhode, Island in 1639. Although **Rhode Island** became a haven for Baptists, New England in General, and **Massachusetts** in particular, were not congenial locations for the movement's growth. On the contrary in the 18th century one of the leading American Baptists, **Isaac Backus**, pastor of the first Baptist church of Middleborough Massachusetts from 1756 to his death in 1806, fought from the late colonial era into that of the early Republic to get the compulsory taxes to support the Congregational churches abolished. A much more fertile soil for the spread of the movement was the **middle colonies**, where the Philadelphia Baptist Association was founded in 1707. Led by Abel Morgan, who was invited to Philadelphia from Wales, many Welsh Baptists migrated to Pennsylvania. During the 18th century they dominated the expansion of Baptist churches into the back country, and eventually into the South where they were firmly rooted before the colonial period came to an end.

BARBADOS. Following its acquisition in 1625 by John Pownell, Barbados was granted by **Charles I** to the earl of Pembroke, but then the king created confusion by granting 'the Caribee islands' to the earl of Carlisle. The two earls fought over their rival claims until Charles resolved the dispute in favor of Carlisle. Barbados became the jewel in the crown of English possessions in the **West Indies**. Despite its diminutive scale – it is only 20 miles long and 14 miles wide at its longest and widest points – it was wealthier than any of the mainland colonies because of its cultivation of sugar. At first tobacco was the principal crop, but in the 1650s the much more capital intensive but profitable production of sugar took off. To exploit it **slaves** were brought to the island from Africa, and by 1684 numbered 46,500, more than twice the number of white inhabitants. An abortive slave uprising in 1692 led to draconian laws to keep them in subjection. The 18th century saw the rise of a planter aristocracy of some 30 families who between them owned most of the island and its slaves. They were among the wealthiest subjects of the British crown. The most famous of them, the **Codringtons**, established a college in the colony.

BARTRAM, JOHN (1699–1777) was born in Pennsylvania, where he was encouraged to develop an interest in botany by **James Logan**. In 1728 he bought a farm near **Philadelphia** where he cultivated the first botanical garden in the colonies. He travelled extensively throughout North America to stock it, and published in 1751 his *Observations on the inhabitants, climate, soil etc.* This gave him an international reputation, and helped to procure him the post of botanist to King **George III** in 1765.

BELLAMONT, RICHARD COOTE earl of (1636–1701) was born into an Irish family of soldiers, and like them followed a military career. He was opposed to the policies of **James II**, going to the Netherlands during his reign to command a company of English soldiers loyal to William of Orange. For this and his support of the **Glorious Revolution** he was rewarded in 1689 by being made treasurer and receiver general to Queen Mary, and promoted to the peerage as earl of Bellamont in Ireland. In the same year he was censured by James II who had him attainted by the Irish parliament which the king convened in Dublin. Since he was an Irish peer Bellamont could be elected to the English House of Commons, in which he sat as a whig member for Droitwich from 1689 to 1695. In 1695 he was appointed governor of **New York**, **Massachusetts** and **New Hampshire**, with command of the militias of **Connecticut**, **Rhode Island** and **New Jersey**, but did not take up these posts until after the **Treaty of Ryswick** in 1697. Before leaving for America he was introduced to **William Kidd**, the privateer who later turned to piracy, to whom he advanced money to finance a scheme to police the Indian Ocean to protect ships of the East India Company from pirates. Bellamont arrived in New York in April 1698. There he sided with those who sympathized with **Jacob Leisler**. As governor he arrested Captain Kidd when he arrived in New York in 1699. Bellamont used his multiple authorities in America to strengthen the defenses of the northern colonies against the French in the interval between **King William's War** and **Queen Anne's War**. Thus in 1700 he presided over a conference with the Iroquois attended by the governors of **Maryland**, **New Jersey**, and **Virginia**. He died in New York.

BERKELEY, JOHN (1607–1678) was a younger brother of **Sir William Berkeley**. He was educated at Queen's College, Oxford. After an abortive embassy to Sweden he entered the army and fought for the king against Scottish rebels in 1639, when he was knighted. Berkeley was a staunch royalist who fought for **Charles I** in the civil wars. Berkeley went into exile with the Stuarts and headed the household of James, duke of York. In 1658 he was made Baron Berkeley of Stratton. At the Restoration of **Charles II**, he became a privy councillor and was lord lieutenant of Ireland 1669–1672. Berkeley held proprietorships in the Carolinas and East Jersey, later selling his share to Quaker investors.

BERKELEY, SIR WILLIAM (1605–1677) after being educated at Oxford University, became known as a playwright. Berkeley was knighted in 1639 by **Charles I**, who appointed him governor of **Virginia** in 1641. He arrived at Jamestown in 1642. Following the king's defeat in the English Civil Wars, Berkeley invited his supporters, the so-called Cavaliers, to settle in the colony. When parliament demanded his recall in 1652 he managed to strike an agreement with it, whereby he was permitted to remain in Virginia as a private citizen on his estate at Green Spring. Upon the Restoration of the monarchy in 1660 he was reappointed as governor. He became unpopular for building up a faction which dominated the assembly and pursued its own interests to the detriment of other colonists. This resulted in 1676 in **Bacon's Rebellion**. Following its suppression Berkeley was recalled to England, where he died shortly after arriving there.

BERMUDA. In 1609 Sir George Somers was shipwrecked on an island in the Atlantic 500 miles off the coast of Virginia, where he was heading with **Sir Thomas Gates**. Initially it was named Somers Island after Sir George, who claimed it for the king of England. The **Virginia Company** set up an offshoot known as the Somers Island or Bermuda company to settle it, sending hundreds of settlers there between 1612 and 1616. The Company put the colony under the earl of Warwick, a Puritan who attracted settlers of a similar religious persuasion to the island. Tobacco cultivation was introduced and took off sufficiently to sustain about 2,000 colonists on the island by 1628, rising to around 6,000 by 1679, many of them **slaves**. By the late 17th century tobacco could not compete with competition from the Chesapeake, and Bermuda became less dependent upon it, diversifying its economy, particularly with shipbuilding and fishing. By then too Bermuda had ceased to be a puritan colony; in 1720 nearly 90 per cent of its white inhabitants were Anglicans.

BERNARD, SIR FRANCIS (1712–1779) was born and educated in England, entering the Middle Temple after attending Oxford University, and becoming a barrister in 1737. He was appointed to the governorship of **New Jersey** in 1758, and acquired a reputation for defending the interests of the Crown and colonists alike. On his appointment to the governorship of **Massachusetts** in 1760 he hoped to repeat this success. Unfortunately the policies of the Crown made it impossible. Although he privately deprecated the imposition of direct taxes on the colonies he publicly upheld them, thereby alienating powerful interests in the Bay colony. The demonstrations against the **Townshend duties** led him to call for troops to be sent to Boston. He also advocated that the Massachusetts Council should be appointed by the Crown and not elected as provided for in the 1691 charter for the colony. When these suggestions were made public there were calls for his dismissal, which led Bernard to resign from the governorship in 1769. He returned to England to spend the rest of his life there.

BLACKSTONE, SIR WILLIAM (1723–1780) was educated at Pembroke College Oxford and the Middle Temple, acquiring legal qualifications which led to his becoming a barrister in 1746. He remained at Oxford as a Fellow of All Souls and in 1758 was appointed by the University as the first Vinerian Professor of Common Law. His lectures on English law became so celebrated that **Lord Bute** persuaded him to present a copy of them to his pupil Prince George, the future **George III**. Blackstone's *Commentaries on the Laws of England*, published in four volumes between 1765 and 1769, established themselves as the most authoritative view of their subject for several generations, running into many editions on both sides of the Atlantic. They adopted a conservative view of the Constitution, reflecting the author's Tory politics. On his marriage in 1761 Blackstone had to resign his college Fellowship, and decided to pursue a political career, becoming a member of parliament. In the Commons he opposed the repeal of the **Stamp Act** and defended the government's stance on the expulsion of **John Wilkes** from the House in 1768. This led **George Grenville** to point out that he had adopted a different position on the rights of MPs in the *Commentaries*, where he had claimed that they could only be removed for treason, felony or a breach of the peace. He consequently altered the relevant passage for the second edition, adding seditious libel, for which Wilkes was removed, to the list of offenses. Discomfited by the experience, he abandoned politics for the law, becoming a judge in the court of common pleas.

BLACKWELL, JOHN (1624–1701) was a Cromwellian soldier who rose to be a deputy treasurer to the Commonwealth during the **Interregnum**. At the Restoration of the monarchy he was disabled from holding office under the Crown. In 1672 he married Frances Lambert, daughter of another Cromwellian general. In 1684 they migrated to **New England**. His financial experience led him to advance rapidly in **Massachusetts**, where he advocated an ingenious but abortive land bank. **William Penn** employed him as deputy governor of **Pennsylvania** from 1688 to 1690. The appointment was largely an attempt to circumvent **James II's** aim to centralize the colonies, including Pennsylvania, under Crown control. Penn hoped that Blackwell's military background would convince the Crown that the factious colony could be brought under control. Also, Blackwell's financial expertise would assuage London investors' concern over their colonial investments. Blackwell's tract, 'Discourse in explanation of the Bank of Credit' showed keen insight into the problems over colonial specie. Unfortunately for the new governor, his commission coincided with the overthrow of James II. The already fractious colonial government was exacerbated by Blackwell's demeanor and religious outlook. His Puritan convictions conflicted with the Quaker element. Once Pennsylvania received news of the **Glorious Revolution** and the absconding of the English king, Blackwell's credibility as deputy governor dissolved. He departed the colony, returning to Massachusetts and subsequently to England, where he died.

BLAIR, JAMES (1655–1743) was born in Scotland, and educated at Edinburgh University. He was ordained as an episcopalian minister and took up a living in Dalkeith in 1679. In 1681, however, he was removed from it when he refused to swear to recognize the Catholic James duke of York as head of the Church of Scotland should he succeed as king. Blair was in London between 1682 and 1685 where he acted as under-clerk to the master of the rolls. In 1685 he went to **Virginia** as rector of Varina (Henrico). In December 1689 the bishop of London, whose diocesan duties extended to the American colonies, appointed Blair as his deputy there. The following year Blair summoned a convention of the Anglican clergy in Virginia and recommended the establishment of a college in the colony. The Assembly took up the suggestion and in 1691 sent Blair to England to address King **William** and Queen **Mary** for a charter for the college. They accepted the request and in February 1693 issued a charter for the **College of William and Mary**. In it Blair was named President for life. To be near the new college he moved in 1694 from Henrico to Jamestown, where he was rector until 1710, when he was appointed rector of Bruton parish church in Williamsburg, where William and Mary was located. His fierce defense of the college as an institution principally for the training of Anglican ministers created critics, including three governors of Virginia, **Sir Edmund Andros**, **Francis Nicholson** and **Alexander Spotswood**. Andros suspended Blair from the Council in 1695, provoking him to go to England to protest, where he was instrumental in obtaining the governor's recall. Blair spent the rest of his life in Virginia, becoming president of the Council from 1740 to 1741. He was a life-long latitudinarian, and welcomed **George Whitefield** when he visited Virginia in 1739.

BLATHWAYT, WILLIAM (?1649–1717). After being employed as a diplomat Blathwayt was appointed as clerk in the Plantation Office under the Lords of Trade and Plantations created in 1675 to supervise the enforcement of the **Navigation Acts** in the colonies. He was also admitted to the Privy Council that year. In 1679 he was made secretary to the Lords of Trade. The following year he became Auditor General for Plantation Revenues. He held the post of secretary at war from 1683 to 1704, successfully surviving the **Glorious Revolution** as a servant of both **James II** and **William III**. William found him especially useful as he could speak Dutch, and took him on his campaigns during **King William's War**. Blathwayt made an advantageous marriage in 1686, his wife, Mary Wyntor, being heiress to a substantial estate at Dyrham Park in Gloucestershire. The couple lived there on the death of Mary's father, and Blathwayt enhanced it considerably in the 1690s, stocking the house and grounds with luxuries from the colonies. In 1696 he was appointed to the newly created **Board of Trade** and Plantations, serving on it until 1707. Blathwayt was thus at the center of colonial administration throughout his career, one of the first civil servants. His vision was to create a coherent colonial system subordinate to the Crown.

BOARD OF TRADE. In 1696 the English parliament took several steps to tighten the imperial connection between England and its American colonies. One was to pass the last of a series of **Navigation Acts**. Another was to set up a Board of Trade and Plantations to consolidate colonial administration which had previously been divided between the secretaries of state, the admiralty and other executive agencies. Initially parliament wanted the commissioners who comprised the Board to be nominated by MPs, but the ministry managed to get their nominations to be made by the king. One of the aims of the Board was to reduce all colonies to the status of Crown colonies, a policy successful in the case of **New Jersey**, whose proprietors surrendered their authority in 1702. Other proprietary colonies such as **Pennsylvania** and the Carolinas, however, successfully resisted the policy. And in 1715 **Maryland**, which had become a Crown colony in 1689, was again granted to the **Calvert** family, headed by Lord Baltimore. By then the Board's administration of the colonies was again being challenged by the secretaries of state, especially the **duke of Newcastle** who exercised most authority in colonial affairs between 1724 and 1748. Then the new president of the Board, the second **earl of Halifax**, reinvigorated its jurisdiction, particularly over the American colonies. He initiated reforms which could not be implemented until after the **French and Indian War** ended. When they were introduced by **George Grenville** they set in train a series of confrontations between the colonies and Britain which were to culminate in the **War of American Independence**. They had already provoked sufficient friction for the appointment of a secretary of state for the colonies in 1768. The colonial secretariat largely superseded the Board, which was eventually wound up in 1782.

BOOK OF GENERAL LAWS AND LIBERTIES 1648. Adapted from the 1641 Body of Liberties, it defined the powers and the functions of the Massachusetts's magistracy, while laying out the due process of law and ensuring individual liberties. This was in answer to the charge that the Puritan colony had no proper legal code. Subsequently , the magistracy, made up exclusively of Puritans, often behaved in arbitrary ways. It was also an attempt to stop Imperial intervention, ultimately a royal takeover.

BOSTON was the site chosen by the Puritans for the principal settlement in **Massachusetts** when they landed there in 1630. It was named after a town in Lincolnshire, England, the home of several of the settlers. **John Winthrop** hoped it would become 'a city upon a hill', acting as a beacon for Puritanism throughout the world. In 1640 there were only 1,200 inhabitants in the town, while by 1690 there were 7,000. This growth led to Boston becoming a commercial port whose materialism undermined the Puritan vision. Growth slowed down in the closing decade of the 17th century, and the total population might even have dropped to 6,700 by 1700. Though it grew to 15,600 by 1760 its rate of increase was outstripped by that of **New York City** and **Philadelphia**. Boston was a major flashpoint in the confrontation between the colonists and the British government during the 1760s and 1770s. Protests against the **Stamp Act** of 1765 led to the destruction of the home of lieutenant governor **Thomas Hutchinson**, while clashes between the populace and the military culminated in the **Boston Massacre** of 1770. The 'period of quiet' which followed was brought to an end by the **Boston Tea Party** in 1773. This provoked the ministry to pass the so-called **Coercive Acts** of 1774, which included one which shut up the harbor and another which transferred the seat of government from Boston to Salem. **General Thomas Gage** made the port the main base for the armed forces under his command who became involved in the skirmishes at Lexington and Concord which precipitated the **War of American Independence**. After their pyrrhic victory at Bunker Hill the British withdrew from Boston and eventually established their main base in New York City.

BOSTON MASSACRE took place on 5 March 1770. Troops guarding the customs house had been challenged by a mob for several days, but had refrained from retaliating. Taunted to open fire they now did, killing three men on the spot and wounding eight, two of whom later died of their wounds. Their commanding officer, Captain Thomas Preston, was tried for giving the troops under his command the order to fire. He was defended by **John Adams** and Josiah Quincy, and the jury acquitted him. Eight soldiers were also tried, two of whom were convicted of manslaughter, but were sentenced to being branded on the thumb rather than to death. These lenient judgments indicate that the so-called 'massacre' ended with a general wish for conciliation rather than confrontation. The troops were withdrawn from Boston to Castle William in the harbor to avoid further provocation.

BOSTON TEA PARTY was the sobriquet given to an episode which occurred in Boston harbor on 16 December 1773. Men disguised as Indians boarded ships carrying chests of tea conveyed to the port by the East India Company under the terms of the **Tea Act**. They threw 342 chests overboard, destroying their contents, weighing about 90,000 pounds, and worth approximately £9,000. Even sympathizers with the colonial cause could not justify the violent way in which the perpetrators of the 'tea party' had expressed their opposition to paying the duty on tea. Most people in Britain condemned it and supported the government's policy of punishing the culprits by passing the **Coercive Acts**.

BRADDOCK, EDWARD (1695–1755) pursued a military career, becoming lieutenant colonel in 1745, and fighting the Jacobite rebels at the battle of Culloden, which brought him to the notice of the duke of Cumberland. When news arrived in England of the defeat of **George Washington** at Fort Necessity in 1754, Cumberland recommended that Braddock, by then a major general, be sent as commander of an expedition to North America to reverse the setback. He arrived in **Virginia**, but encountered difficulties raising supplies for advancing into the interior which cost him time and made him enemies among the colonists. Eventually with 1,400 British regulars and 700 colonial troops he set out for his objective, **Fort Duquesne**. Progress was slow as they had to cut a road through the wilderness west of Carlisle, **Pennsylvania**, for their wagons. At Little Meadows he divided his forces and pressed ahead with 1,400 men, who were ambushed by French and Indian forces on the Monongahela River within eight miles of Fort Duquesne. In the ensuing rout Braddock was mortally wounded. His last words were said to be 'we shall better know how to deal with them another time'.

BRADFORD, ANDREW (1686–1742) was the son of **William Bradford**. Like his father he was a printer, and became official 'printer to the province' of **Pennsylvania**. In 1714 he published *The Laws of the Province of Pennsylvania* and on 22 December 1729 launched *The American Weekly Mercury*.

BRADFORD, WILLIAM (1590–1657) was born in England and became a member of the separatist dissenting church at Scrooby in Nottinghamshire. In 1608 he led the congregation to Leiden in the Netherlands, where there was freedom of worship. By 1620, Bradford, with others, obtained a patent from the **Virginia Company** and, along with 101 passengers, migrated to North America sailing in the Mayflower. He helped to fashion the **Mayflower Compact** while en route to America. He became the first historian of the colony which the Pilgrims established at **Plymouth**.

BRADFORD, WILLIAM (1663–1752) was born in England, where he was apprenticed in London to a Quaker printer. Bradford went to **Pennsylvania** in 1685 and set up as a printer. After a brief visit to England in 1689 Bradford was back in **Philadelphia** in 1690, where he helped set up a paper mill, the first in the colonies. He published works defending **George Keith**. He was tried and imprisoned in 1692 for printing unlicensed publications. In 1693 he was invited to New York as public printer by Governor **Benjamin Fletcher**. There he published the 'Votes' of the Assembly. In 1702 he also became public printer, and in 1710 clerk of the assembly there. Bradford launched *The New York Gazette* in 1725. His *History of New York* appeared in 1727.

BRADSTREET, ANNE (c. 1612–1672) was born Anne Dudley in England, where her father became steward to the earl of Lincoln. In 1625 he went with his family to Boston in Lincolnshire, where he was a member of the congregation of **John Cotton**. In 1628 Anne married **Simon Bradstreet**. They went to **Massachusetts** with the original settlers in 1630 and settled in Ipswich until 1644 when they moved to North Andover. Anne was perhaps the first poet in the colonies, and certainly the first to publish poems there, her *The Tenth Muse Lately sprung up in America* appearing in 1650. She herself claimed not to have authorized its publication, but added poems to it for a second edition which came out posthumously in 1678. One of the more overtly political poems, 'A Dialogue between Old England and New' betrays her Puritan sympathies for the parliamentary cause in the English civil war.

BRADSTREET, JOHN (1714–1774) was born in **Nova Scotia**, the son of an Irish officer stationed in the recently acquired Annapolis. Like his father he pursued a military career, getting his first commission as an ensign in 1735. He was captured by the French at Louisbourg in 1744, but sent to **Boston** in an exchange of prisoners. He advocated an assault on **Cape Breton** and took part in the successful siege of Louisbourg in 1745. The following year Bradstreet was promoted to the rank of lieutenant-governor of St John's Newfoundland. He took up his post there in 1747, and remained in St Johns until 1751, when he went to England. He returned to North America in 1755 and was posted to Oswego, New York. When the fort fell to the French in the summer of 1756 he withdrew to Albany. In 1757 he was promoted from lieutenant colonel to captain in the Royal American Regiment and aide-de-camp to **Lord Loudoun**. On Loudoun's recall he was promoted to lieutenant colonel and made deputy quartermaster general in America. Bradstreet's greatest feat was a raid on Frontenac in August 1758, when he led 3,100 men, only 154 of them regulars, against the French fort on Lake Ontario. Although he took it easily he realized he could not defend it against forces sent from Montreal to retake it. He therefore demolished the fort before returning to Albany. He was rewarded by being promoted to the rank of colonel. From 1758 until the end of the **French and Indian War** he resumed his duties as deputy quartermaster general in America. The outbreak of **Pontiac's War** in 1763, when all British forts west of Niagara except Pitt and Detroit were taken, led to his being recalled into active service. In the summer of 1764 he led an expedition to relieve Detroit, which was being besieged by Pontiac's forces. His handling of negotiations with Indians in the Great Lakes region, however, was inept, and provoked criticism from his superiors, who disowned the treaties he had negotiated. After relieving Detroit Bradstreet made a disastrous return journey to Oswego in which he lost many of his boats through carelessness. The disgrace led him to spend his last decade in North America fruitlessly seeking favors from the British army.

BRADSTREET, SIMON (1604–1697) was born in Horbling, Lincolnshire England. He was educated at Cambridge University and then found employment in the household of the earl of Lincoln, where he met Anne Dudley, daughter of the steward, whom he married. In 1630 he became secretary of the **Massachusetts Bay Company**, and migrated to **Massachusetts** with **John Winthrop** and his wife **Anne Bradstreet**. He served in several colonial capacities including those of Deputy Governor and Governor, a post he held first from 1676 to 1686 and again in 1689. He was instrumental in the organization of the United Colonies of New England, but refused to serve in the **Dominion of New England**. Known for his moderation and antipathy toward the oligarchical rule of the magistrates, he took a stand against the magistrates' ability to have the casting vote in a deadlock in voting, known as 'The Negative Vote', and was successful in seeing the magistrates' powers reduced. He also showed moderation in voting against fining the Presbyterians, such as Dr Richard Child, for their remonstrance against the government's arbitrary rule. After the **Glorious Revolution**, he became a royal governor until the arrival of **Sir William Phips**. During his time in office, he questioned the validity of evidence against persons accused of witchcraft and was able to save some from prosecution.

BRENT, MARGARET (c. 1601–c. 1671) was born in England and in 1638 went to **Maryland**, whose proprietor, **Lord Baltimore** was her cousin. When his deputy, Leonard Calvert, died in 1647 she became his executrix. She thus assumed responsibility for the colony's debts, which included arrears of pay for soldiers. To settle them she needed power of attorney over the absentee proprietor's estate in Maryland. Because settlement of the debts was too pressing to allow time to obtain Baltimore's permission, in 1648 the colonial court gave her this authority without it. Acting on it she asked the acting deputy governor for permission to sit in the assembly with two votes, one on her own behalf, the other as the proprietor's attorney. Although he refused, her request has been seen as an early assertion of feminist political aspirations. She proceeded to sell Baltimore's assets in order to pay his debts, thereby averting a political crisis in the colony. The assembly wrote to the proprietor commending her actions to him. He however was incensed at her acting without his authorization, and Mary felt it prudent to leave Maryland, going to **Virginia** where she died.

BREWSTER, WILLIAM (1567–1644) was born in England and educated at Cambridge University. He served as secretary to the English ambassador in the Netherlands in 1583 and to

Francis Walsingham, Elizabeth I's secretary of state, from 1585 to 1587. When Walsingham fell from favor Brewster left London for Scrooby, where his father was bailiff to the archbishop of York. In 1590 Brewster succeeded his father in that post, and a few years later became post-master for the district. The Scrooby separatists from the Church of England who became the Pilgrims who settled **Plymouth** began to meet in Brewster's house in 1606. The following year they made their first abortive attempt to escape to Holland which resulted in several of them, including Brewster, being imprisoned. In 1608 they succeeded in going to Amsterdam and thence to Leiden. Brewster made a living as a teacher. When **William Bradford** made the decision to go to America Brewster visited England in 1617 and again in 1619 to negotiate with the **Virginia Company** for a patent. Brewster sailed on the **Mayflower** to North America. In Plymouth, despite not having a degree, he became a leading elder of the Pilgrim church.

BURGOYNE, JOHN (1723–1792) was the son of a soldier and after leaving Westminster School, entered the army too, becoming a captain by 1756. In the Seven Years' War he saw active service in France and Portugal. By the end of war he had risen to the rank of colonel. Entering parliament in 1761 he opposed the repeal of the **Stamp Act** and supported the **Declaratory Act**. He also supported Lord North's **Coercive Acts** in 1774, declaring that he had heard enough of 'real and virtual representation, external and internal taxes, revenue and regulation, till one's head grows dizzy with distinctions'. The following year he went to America as a major general to support **Thomas Gage**, the commander in chief in Boston, and played a minor part in the battle of Bunker Hill. Afterwards he returned to England and presented Lord **George Germain**, the Colonial Secretary, with *Reflections upon the War in America*. This advocated isolating New England militarily by a pincer movement from Canada and New York. Burgoyne returned to North America but, disillusioned by the failure to take Fort Ticonderoga in October 1776, went back to England. He then obtained from **Lord North** the command of the British army in Canada, from where he hoped to advance south to meet up with troops under **Sir William Howe** at Albany. Burgoyne's forces marched south in June 1777, and after easily taking Ticonderoga marched on to the Hudson River through the wilderness of the Adirondack mountains, a trek that took six weeks. A detachment of troops sent to Manchester to commandeer provisions was defeated by militiamen near Bennington. Nevertheless Burgoyne continued his advance south-ward, arriving at Saratoga in mid-September. There he was confronted by 10,000 troops under Horatio Gates. The first encounter, on 19 September, proved inconclusive, though Burgoyne lost more men than Gates, who anyway could recruit to make up his losses unlike his opponent. The second battle, on 17 October, proved decisive. Burgoyne was heavily defeated, and realizing that Howe would not be coming to his relief, surrendered. Congress allowed him to go to England to answer charges against his conduct. The king denied him an audience and deprived him of his command. This treatment led him to join the parliamentary opponents of the war. When they came to power under Lord **Rockingham** in 1782 he was made commander in chief in Ireland.

BURKE, EDMUND (?1729/1730–1797) was born in Ireland, where his father, a Protestant married to a Catholic, practiced law. Burke was educated at a Quaker school and at Trinity College Dublin. In 1750, financed by his father, he went to London to prepare for a legal career at the Middle Temple. When he abandoned the law to become a man of letters his father's financial assistance came to an end. His first major publication, *A Vindication of Natural Society*, appeared in 1756. The following year he published *An Inquiry into the Origin of Our Ideas of the Sublime and Beautiful*, which had a great influence on theories of aesthetics. Burke's interest in the American colonies was also demonstrated in 1757 with the appearance of *An account of the European settlements in America*. Apparently he contemplated emigrating there himself about this time. In the event he married Jane Mary Nugent, the daughter of a Roman Catholic physician, by whom he had a son, Richard, who was born in 1758. From 1759 to 1789 Burke edited *The Political Register*. His own political career may also be said to have begun in 1759 with his appointment as private secretary to William Gerard Hamilton, who was an official on the **Board of Trade**. Hamilton served as chief secretary to Ireland from 1761 to 1764, when he had to resign. Burke, who had quarrelled with his patron, thereupon resigned as his secretary. In 1765 he was taken up by the incoming prime minister, **Rockingham**, in the same capacity. The following year he entered parliament as member for Wendover. He was thus closely involved in the repeal of the **Stamp Act** and the passing of the **Declaratory Act**. His experiences as chief spokesman for the Rockinghamites in the Commons informed his *Thoughts on the Cause of the present discontents* (1770), in which he claimed to detect a conspiracy on the part of the king's ministers to undermine liberty on both sides of the Atlantic. He maintained that the Rockinghamites were the true heirs of the whigs who had defended English liberties in the Glorious Revolution, and justified their role as a party committed to upholding whig principles. From 1771 to 1775 Burke supplemented the income paid to him by Rockingham with a salary of £500 a year he received from the colony of New York to act as its agent in England. At the general election of 1774 he was elected as MP for Bristol, a major port in the Atlantic trade, which also returned Henry Cruger, an American, as its other member. In the new parliament Burke made several speeches on the colonial crisis, two of which were published in 1775. These upheld the Rockinghamite principle that, although the British parliament had the constitutional right to tax the colonies, it should never exercise it, but return to the policy of 'salutary neglect' towards them which it had practiced before 1764. As the crisis developed into hostilities he advocated conciliation and even the repeal of the Declaratory Act which he had supported when it was passed. He also characterized the war as one in which Englishmen in the colonies were being opposed by Germans and Indians. When Rockingham formed his second administration in 1782 Burke became paymaster. He was instrumental in the passing of legislation cutting many offices and sinecures in the gift of the Crown, thereby lessening the king's ability to reward members of parliament and curbing his influence over the Commons. On Rockingham's death the incoming prime minister **Shelburne** dispensed with his services, but he was reappointed by the duke of Portland, nominal premier in the **Fox–North** coalition. Burke greeted the independence of the United States recognized in the **treaty of Paris** in 1783, observing of it that 'a great revolution has happened …. [the] appearance of a new state among mankind … It has made as great a change in all the relations and balances and gravitations of power as the appearance of a new planet would in the system of our solar world.'

BURNET, WILLIAM (1688–1729) was the son of Gilbert Burnet, a close companion of **William III** in the **Glorious Revolution** who became bishop of Salisbury. William was born at The Hague but followed his father to England. Like his father he was a staunch whig, and served as comptroller of the customs from 1714 to 1720. He succeeded **Robert Hunter** as Governor of **New York** and **New Jersey** from 1720 to 1727. Like Hunter he made powerful enemies, including the de Lanceys, who objected to his establishment of a trading post with the Indians at Tirondequot which undercut their own trading networks. They also disliked his severing of trade with Canada. In 1727 Burnet was transferred to **Massachusetts**, where again he made enemies on the General Court, disputing with them about the payment of his salary. Shortly before his death in 1729 he was appointed governor of **New Hampshire**.

BUTE, JOHN STUART, THIRD EARL OF (1713–1792) was born in Scotland but educated in England and Holland. At the age of nine he succeeded to the earldom of Bute on his father's death. He married Mary Wortley Montagu, the daughter of a celebrated 'blue-stocking' mother and a wealthy Yorkshire country gentleman, whose estates she inherited. In 1750 Frederick Prince of Wales made him one of the lords of his bedchamber. The following year, after the Prince's death, Bute became tutor to his son, the future **George III**. Although his many political opponents accused Bute of inculcating unconstitutional views into the young Prince in fact he groomed him to become a constitutional monarch. After George succeeded to the throne he made Bute secretary of state in 1761. On the resignation of **William Pitt the elder** that year Bute effectively replaced him as prime minister. In 1762 the **duke of Newcastle** left the ministry and Bute succeeded him as first lord of the Treasury. He presided over the negotiations leading to the **Peace of Paris** which ended the Seven Years' War. When this proved unpopular he was excoriated for bringing a glorious war to an allegedly inglorious end. So violent were the attacks upon him, especially those from the pen of **John Wilkes**, who sneered at his Scottish origins, that he resigned. Bute's influence with the king 'behind the curtain', however, was suspected as a sinister agent in British politics long after he ceased to have any sway with George III. He left the political scene in 1780 when he stood down as one of the 16 Scottish representative peers in the House of Lords, a position he had held since 1761.

BYRD, WILLIAM, I (1652–1704) was born in London and emigrated to **Virginia** where in 1671 he acquired estates on either side of the James River at Henrico (Richmond). In 1676 he joined in **Bacon's Rebellion**. Subsequently he managed to make his peace with **Sir William Berkeley**. From 1677 to 1682 he sat in the House of Burgesses and then took his seat in the Council. He was in England from 1687 to 1688 successfully soliciting the place of auditor general of Virginia. He was a prosperous tobacco planter and trader, trading with the Catawba Indians. By 1691 he was rich enough to move his estate to Westover, down the James from Henrico and nearer to Jamestown.

BYRD, WILLIAM, II (1674–1744) was the son of **William Byrd I**. He was born in **Virginia**, but educated in England from 1681 to 1690. After a spell in the Netherlands he returned to London where he entered the Middle Temple to study law in 1692, and was elected a Fellow of the Royal Society. Following his return to Virginia in 1696 he was elected to the House of Burgesses. In 1697 he returned to England to defend the recalled governor of Virginia **Sir Edmund Andros**. After his father's death he went back to Virginia in 1705 to take over the Westover estate. Byrd became receiver general of the royal revenues in Virginia in 1706 and was appointed to the Council in 1709. He sought to be governor of Virginia but was turned down on the grounds that governorships were reserved for military men. He was opposed to the policies of **Governor Alexander Spotswood**, going to England as agent for Virginia in 1714 to challenge them and to try to get the governor recalled. After spending the years 1714 to 1719 in England, Byrd returned to Virginia for three years but was back in London from 1722 to 1726. He spent the remainder of his life at Westover, which he considerably enhanced. Byrd kept a shorthand diary which uniquely documents the life of a leading member of the colonial elite.

C

CALVERT, GEORGE, FIRST BARON BALTIMORE (1580–1632) was the founder and proprietor of the colony of **Maryland**. He was born in Yorkshire and educated at Oxford University and Lincoln's Inn, London. Calvert obtained his influence with the early Stuart kings through the patronage of Robert Cecil, earl of Salisbury, whom he served as private secretary. **James I** appointed him one of the clerks of the privy council in 1610, and employed him on diplomatic missions. In 1617 he obtained a knighthood and in 1619 the post of principal secretary of state. He rose to be a commissioner of the treasury in 1624, but stood down on becoming a Roman Catholic. Despite his conversion he was promoted to the peerage as Baron Baltimore in 1625. James I granted him a charter for Avalon, in Newfoundland in 1623, which he visited in 1627 and again in 1628. He abandoned it, however, when he experienced its harsh climate and the hostility of the French. He sailed to the Chesapeake Bay which he preferred, but the Virginians did not make him welcome. Determined nevertheless to settle a colony there, Calvert obtained the patent for **Maryland** in 1632, but died before he could visit the colony.

CALVERT, CECIL, SECOND BARON BALTIMORE (1606–1675) was educated at Oxford University. In 1623 he announced his conversion to Catholicism, a year before his father, the **first Lord Baltimore** was converted. He inherited the proprietary colony of **Maryland** on the death of his father in 1632. He intended to go there with his wife Anne Arundel, whom he married in 1629. Opposition to the Catholic colony from Protestants in England, however, led him to stay at home to counter his critics, and he sent his brother Leonard to the colony as his deputy in his stead. Leonard went with the first shipload of colonists in 1633. The absence of the proprietor created problems with the settlers, who refused to accept laws which Baltimore sent over from England. He was anxious that the colony should not only provide a haven for Catholics but also prosper. To that end he invited non-Catholics, from Virginia and New England, to settle in Maryland. The Maryland Act of Toleration of 1649 guaranteed them religious freedom. In March 1655 some settlers from **Virginia** on Kent Island, who had tried to claim it for the Old Dominion, threw off Baltimore's proprietorship in the name of the victorious parliamentary side in the English civil war. Baltimore contrived to come to terms with Oliver Cromwell, who restored him as proprietor of Maryland before the restoration of the monarchy in 1660, which confirmed his title.

CALVERT, CHARLES, THIRD BARON BALTIMORE (1629–1715) became proprietor of **Maryland** on the death of his father the **second Baron Baltimore** in 1675. Unlike previous proprietors he visited the colony in 1684. His Catholicism caused him to be deprived of the proprietorship in 1691 following the **Glorious Revolution.** In 1711 he petitioned to have it restored, but was refused on account of being a Catholic. His conversion to Anglicanism eased the situation and he became again proprietor of Maryland shortly before his death in 1715.

CAMBRIDGE PLATFORM was the name given to the proposals for church government adopted by a Synod convened at Cambridge **Massachusetts** in 1648. Their principal proponent was **Richard Mather**. While the synod accepted the Calvinistic Westminster Confession of Faith of 1646, even though it had been drawn up by English Presbyterians, it did not adopt a Presbyterian system of church government. Instead it insisted on the autonomy of the individual Congregational churches. Its stress on the authority of the elders over the laity, however, was not universally popular.

CAMDEN, CHARLES PRATT EARL OF (1714–1794) was educated at Eton College, where he became acquainted with **William Pitt** the Elder, King's College Cambridge, and the Middle Temple. He became a barrister in 1738. His acquaintance with Pitt led to his appointment as attorney general to the Prince of Wales, the future **George III**, when his former school fellow became prime minister in 1756. The following year Pratt was made attorney general. After Pitt's resignation in 1761 he became lord chief justice of the court of common pleas. There he found himself involved in the cases arising from the publication of *The North Briton* number 45 by **John Wilkes**, and established himself as the leading liberal judge by finding in favor of the Wilkite view that general warrants were illegal. In 1766 Pratt entered the House of Lords as Baron Camden and took part in the debates on the repeal of the **Stamp Act**, echoing the arguments made by Pitt in the Commons. When Pitt, now earl of Chatham, formed a ministry on the fall of the first Rockingham administration Camden became Lord Chancellor. He supported the **Townshend duties,** but later favored their repeal, even including the tea duty which was retained, when they met resistance in America. When Chatham condemned the measures taken by the **duke of Grafton,** who acted as prime minister during his illness, Camden stood by his mentor, incurring the wrath of the king who dismissed him. He stayed in opposition throughout the ministry of **Lord North**. A speech he made against the government's American policy in February 1775 was allegedly composed after consultation with **Benjamin Franklin**. Camden asserted that 'England must one day lose the dominion of America. It is impossible that this petty island can continue in dependence that mighty continent.' During the **War of American**

Independence Camden urged conciliation rather than conflict. When **Lord Rockingham** became prime minister on the fall of Lord North Camden became president of the council, but resigned in 1783 when **Lord Shelburne**'s peace proposals were criticized in parliament.

CAMPBELL, JOHN (1653–1728) was born in Scotland and went to **Massachusetts** in the 1690s, becoming postmaster in Boston in 1702. From 1704 to 1722 he published the *Boston News Letter*, a weekly newspaper.

CANADA in the colonial era was little more than a geographical expression referring to French claims in North America including **Acadia**, Hudson's Bay, Newfoundland and **New France**. It proved relatively difficult to attract settlers from France, compared with the migration of colonists from the British Isles. Between 10,000 and 20,000 French settlers moved to Canada in the colonial period, natural increase accounting for an estimated 50,000 inhabitants there by 1760. Nevertheless Canada was perceived as a serious threat to the British colonies to the south, despite these low numbers. This was partly due to the ability of the French to recruit more **Indians** to ally with them against their neighbors, and also to the notorious difficulty in persuading them to unite against the common threat. **James II** devised the **Dominion of New England** mainly as a bulwark against French expansion south. They remained serious enemies through **King William's War**, **Queen Anne 's War** and **King George's War**. It was not until the successful outcome of the **French and Indian War** that the threat was removed when France yielded Canada to the British in the **Peace of Paris** of 1763. The European population increased rapidly thereafter, reaching about 130,000 by 1776, mainly by migration from the American colonies. The **Proclamation of 1763** projected a new British colony based on Quebec, and envisaged a colonial government with a representative assembly. By 1774, however, insufficient numbers of Protestants had migrated there to form an electorate. Consequently the Quebec Act was passed which provided for a governor who should rule through councils, and recognized the Roman Catholic Church as the established church and French civil law. It also expanded the boundaries of Quebec to incorporate the territory north of the Ohio River. The first governor of this enlarged Quebec was **Sir Guy Carleton**. Despite being petitioned by the first Continental Congress on 29 May 1775 to join the Americans in their confrontation with the British government, the Canadians remained loyal to Britain throughout the **War of American Independence**. American forces invaded Canada in September but, though they reached Quebec City, they found little support and lifted the siege at the end of December. The arrival of British troops led by **Sir John Burgoyne** in the Spring of 1776 caused the Americans to withdraw from Canada. Burgoyne established his base in Quebec in 1777 before setting out south through the Adirondack Mountains to his fatal defeat at the battle of Saratoga. This hastened the entry of the French into the war, which generated sympathy for the American cause among the inhabitants of what had formerly been New France. The failure to launch a Franco–American campaign to cash in on these sentiments, however, and the arrival of over 10,000 loyalists in Quebec, confirmed its allegiance to the British Crown.

CAPE BRETON ISLAND occupies a strategic location opposite the mouth of the St Lawrence River. It thereby guarded the gateway to **Canada**. The French built the fortress at Louisbourg on the island to protect them from attack. In 1745 an expedition from New England captured it, but it was returned to the French at the treaty of Aix-la-Chapelle in 1748. It was again taken in 1758 this time by forces under **Jeffrey Amherst**. The French ceded it to Britain along with their other territories in North America at the **Peace of Paris** in 1763.

CARLETON, SIR GUY (1724–1808) was a professional soldier who served in America in the Seven Years' War, being at the sieges of Quebec in 1756 and Havana in 1762. He was appointed governor of Quebec in 1768, and exerted considerable influence in the passing of the Quebec Act in 1774. Thus he appeared before the House of Commons in June, testifying his conviction that concessions to Roman Catholics in the province were essential to keep them loyal to Britain. His belief was tested when American troops invaded Quebec in 1775. Although he successfully repelled the invasion, for which he was promoted to the rank of general and received a knighthood, he in fact received little help from French Canadians. His failure to pursue the invaders, which contributed to the difficulties which General **Burgoyne** encountered in the Saratoga campaign, led Carleton to resign the governorship of Quebec and return to Britain in 1778. In 1782 Carleton returned to North America as commander. His principal task was to arrange the orderly dispersal of the loyalists from the former 13 colonies, which became the USA, to those in Canada and the Caribbean which remained loyal.

CAROLINAS. Between 1663–1665 **Charles II** granted land located between 36 and 31 degrees longitude, extending from the boundary of **Virginia** to Florida, to eight proprietors. These had all been directly or indirectly involved in colonial ventures. Anthony Ashley Cooper, later the first earl of Shaftesbury, had interests in Barbados and was a member of the Lords of Plantations and Trade. Sir John Colleton was a royalist during the civil wars, who migrated to Barbados after the defeat of the Crown by Cromwell. He returned to England after the Restoration of Charles II. His interest in things colonial continued with his membership of the Royal African Company. Sir William Berkeley had a more direct knowledge through his governorship of Virginia. He would have known the strategic and economic importance of extending the English empire in this part of the world more than the other proprietors. The earl of Clarendon was a valuable asset to the group by his position at court, not least as father-in-law to the duke of York, the future **James II**. Sir George Carteret was treasurer of the Navy and vice-chamberlain of the royal household. The duke of Albermarle was a survivor of the commonwealth and instrumental in bringing about the restoration of the king. The earl Craven had a more personal relationship with the king and the royal family. He was a great supporter of Charles's aunt, the queen of Bohemia, and his financial support to the exiled king was crucial during the years of the Protectorate. John lord Berkeley had interests in **New England**, **New Jersey** and the Bahamas. Together the eight proprietors proved to be a powerful group, whose main interest, aside from making money, was to further England's interests. Thus the grant of the Carolina charter was due more to their initiative than to that of the king.

The initial grant was held in free and common socage with the government based upon feudal concepts, with the proprietors as baronial lords having seignorial privileges. As a counterpoint, there was an assembly made up of freemen and freeholders. Remunerations to the Crown included 20 marks annually. As with some of the other settlements, toleration extended to religious practices. This, no doubt, was influenced by the demographic makeup of the settlers. The charter was made more precise in 1669 in the Fundamental Constitution. This document reproduced the powers of the Bishop of Durham, which gave the proprietors powers to create institutions. It made clear the powers of the proprietors and how the government should operate. Although the **Board of Trade** pursued a policy of reducing proprietary to Crown colonies, the Carolinas resisted this successfully until the reign of George I, when the governor first of **North Carolina** then of **South Carolina** became royal nominees. The two colonies then became separate entities.

CARROLL, CHARLES (1737–1832). Illegitimate son of the Carroll of Carrollton, **Maryland** and Elizabeth Brook (they later married in 1757). Charles Carroll became the only Roman Catholic to sign the **Declaration of Independence**. He was educated at the Jesuit academy of Bohemia Manor on the eastern shore of Maryland, after which he traveled to Flanders to continue his education at St Omers. When he finished at St Omers, Charles then went on to Rheims, followed by a stint at the College of Louis-le-Grand in Paris where he was influenced by the Enlightenment thinkers, particularly Montesquieu. Steeped in the theory of natural law, Carroll, besides **John Adams**, did the most to implement a government modeled on

Montesquieu's plan of mixed government with checks and balances. He continued his studies in England by studying law in 1759. There, he was able to observe the House of Commons and concluded that whatever defects England held in comparison to France, at least in England the law was applied equally to men. Nevertheless, he still favored Roman and civil law which seemed to be more systematic. Carroll never became a regular student at the Temple, but remained a lay resident. In February 1765, after failed marriage negotiations, Carroll returned home to Maryland just before the enactment of the **Stamp Act** in March. He supported the resistance to the Act, arguing for an embargo on British goods 'to make the oppressors feel it.' In 1774, as an unofficial delegate, Carroll went to Philadelphia to observe the first Continental Congress, where he was 'well received.' He served as a delegate from Ann Arundel County to the Maryland Convention and joined the committee of correspondence later the same year. This position was followed by an appointment to the committee of observation in January 1775 where Carroll helped to select delegates to the convention. He sat on the Council of Safety in 1775 which took responsibility for securing armaments for war. In 1776, he was chosen as a delegate to Congress where he arrived after the Declaration of Independence was already approved and was awaiting signatures. Carrollton was influential in the creation of the Maryland constitution, particularly with regard to the role of the Senate and the Electoral College.

CARTER, ROBERT 'KING' (1663–1733) was born in **Virginia**, where his father Colonel John Carter had gone from England and settled in the Northern Neck. When his father died in 1669 Robert was brought up by his half-brother John, who sent him to England to be educated. On his return he built a house on some land left him by his father at 'Corotoman'. On his brother's death in 1690 he inherited his considerably larger estate. Carter was elected to the assembly as a burgess in 1691, becoming Speaker of the lower house in 1696. In 1699 he was made a member of the Council. Following the death of his first wife he married again in 1701, this time to Elizabeth Landon Willis, by whom he had ten children. During the rest of his life Carter accumulated an estate in Virginia of some 300,000 acres worked by 1,000 slaves. This made him one of the wealthiest men in colonial north America. He acquired the nickname 'King' as a derogatory title alluding to his imperious manner.

CARTERET, GEORGE (c. 1610–1680) was born on the Channel Island of Jersey. He pursued a naval career, rising to become a vice-admiral in 1637. **Charles I** prevented him serving parliament in that capacity when the civil war broke out in 1642. Instead he supplied the royalists with arms by sea. In 1643 he became bailiff and lieutenant governor of Jersey. Charles I made him a baronet in 1645. When **Charles II** visited Jersey while in exile in 1649–1650 he stayed with Carteret. As a reward for his services the king gave him an island in the mouth of **Chesapeake Bay** which Carteret intended to call **New Jersey**, but he never established his claim successfully. Parliament captured Jersey in 1651 and Carteret went into exile with the king and his brother James duke of York. At the Restoration he was made treasurer of the navy, a post he exchanged in 1667 for that of vice-treasurer of Ireland. Threatened with impeachment for not providing proper accounts for his period as naval treasurer Carteret resigned in 1669. He served as a commissioner of the navy from 1673 to 1679. His interest in colonial affairs led to his employment as a member of the councils of trade and plantations. In 1663 he became one of the proprietors of the **Carolinas** and proprietor of East Jersey. At his death, Carteret's widow sold his Jersey proprietorship to a group of Quaker investors.

CARVER, JOHN (d. 1621) was one of the Pilgrims who went with **William Bradford** and **William Brewster** to Holland in 1608. Like Brewster he was involved in the negotiations with the **Virginia Company** which obtained a grant of land in America. He sailed in the Mayflower in 1620 and after signing the **Mayflower Compact** was made governor of the new colony. Carver survived the first winter in Plymouth but fell ill in April 1621 and died.

CEDED ISLANDS. Dominica, Grenada, St Vincent and Tobago, islands in the **West Indies** ceded to Britain by France in the **Peace of Paris** in 1763.

CHAIN OF FRIENDSHIP 1701 was the product of **William Penn**'s attempt to stabilize his proprietorship of **Pennsylvania** and to reinforce his purchase in the north of the colony. He was able to effect a treaty in 1701 with the Susquehannocks whereby they agreed not to ally with any tribes opposed to England. To some extent, this treaty encroached upon the **Covenant Chain** established by **Edmund Andros**. However, Penn still needed to secure his claims at the other end of the Susquehanna down to the **Chesapeake Bay**. To do this, he concluded a treaty with ten 'Kings and chiefs,' whereby they agreed to keep peace and be bound by the colony's laws. Also, agreement was made within the treaty not to ally with any other nation that was not friendly towards England. Thus the treaty had international repercussions as well as intercolonial ones.

CHARLES I (1600–1649) succeeded his father **James I** in 1625 as King of England, Scotland and Ireland. His promotion of Arminians to bishoprics and other livings in the **Anglican Church** culminating in his appointment of William Laud as archbishop of Canterbury in 1633, was criticized by **Puritans**. Attacks upon Arminianism in parliament were partly responsible for the king's decision not to call it after 1629. During the 11 years' personal rule many Puritans left England for New England, starting with those who went to **Massachusetts** with **John Winthrop**. Some were persecuted for nonconformity, but most went because they felt that the king was not promoting godly rule, especially when he issued the *Book of Sports* in 1633 which promoted recreations they considered to be sinful. They were also suspicious of his indulgence towards Catholics, encouraged by his French wife Henrietta Maria. This led him to grant a charter to **George Calvert**, first Lord Baltimore for a Catholic colony, **Maryland**. Charles provoked resistance in Scotland when he extended his religious policies to the northern kingdom, resulting in the so-called bishops' war in 1638. This forced him to call parliament in 1640. Relations between Charles and the members were so strained that it was soon dissolved but the need for money obliged the king to call another which passed an Act whereby it could not be dissolved without its own consent. This Long Parliament tried to impose restrictions on the royal authority which Charles would not accept, leading in 1642 to civil war. During the war the migration to New England slowed down, and some colonists actually returned to England hoping that their religious aspirations would be met. Some who played a prominent part in the proceedings of the Long Parliament had been involved in other colonizing activities during the 1630s, such as the Providence Island venture. Although parliament was victorious in the war, deadlock over the terms of a settlement could only be resolved by the king's trial and execution, leading to the **Interregnum**.

CHARLES II (1630–1685) dated his reign from the death of his father **Charles I** in 1649, though he was not restored to the throne until 1660, after the **Interregnum**. The Restoration came about because Charles seemed to offer an alternative between anarchy and absolute monarchy. In the Declaration of Breda of 1660 he offered attractive proposals as conditions of his restoration, including liberty for tender consciences. The king seems to have been sincere in his protestations of religious toleration. He rebuked the General Court in **Massachusetts** for its persecution of Quakers, insisting on their ending it. Charles used colonial grants as a cheap way of rewarding those who had been loyal to the Stuart cause during the civil wars, or to win over some who were suspicious of his intentions. Thus he granted New Netherland to his brother **James duke of York**, though he had to wrest it first from the **Dutch**. He gave a charter for the **Carolinas** to several proprietors. The largest proprietary grant of all, **Pennsylvania**, went to **William Penn**. The king's colonial policies provoked resentment as well as gained supporters. His generous award of the quit rents of the northern neck in Virginia to Lords Arlington and Culpeper was resented by the Governor **Sir William Berkeley**, and contributed to the outbreak of **Bacon's Rebellion.** Charles continued the policy started during the **Interregnum** of using **Navigation Acts** as a means of making colonial commerce profitable to the mother country and the crown. He sent **Edward Randolph** to the colonies to investigate breaches of the Acts. It was on the basis of Randolph's report about flagrant disregard for them in **Massachusetts** that Charles revoked that colony's charter in 1684.

CHARLES TOWN was so styled in honor of **Charles II**, an echo of Jamestown in **Virginia** which was named after that king's grandfather **James I**. It did not become known as Charleston until after the colonial period. Charles Town was the main settlement in the **Carolinas,** established at the confluence of the Ashley and Charles rivers in 1680. There were only about 300 original residents. The estimated total grew to 2,000 by 1,700 and 8,000 by 1760. This made Charles Town the only city in the southern mainland colonies to compete in size with the northern ports of **Boston, New York** and **Philadelphia**. It was of great strategic significance, especially before the settlement of **Georgia** when it was on the frontier between the English colonies and the Spanish in Florida. During **Queen Anne's War** it was heavily fortified to resist invasion, which it did successfully in 1706.

CHARTER COLONIES is a term used by historians to distinguish those which were virtually self-governing from those governed directly by the Crown or Proprietors. The term is not entirely satisfactory as the Crown issued charters to its own colonies as well as to proprietors. However it was used by contemporaries, the **Board of Trade** distinguishing between Crown, 'proprieties and charter governments' in 1698. By then, although in its very early years, **Virginia** had been a company chartered colony, there were only three charter colonies left, **Massachusetts**, **Rhode Island**, and **Connecticut.**

CHARTER OF PRIVILEGES 1701 was the final revision of the **Pennsylvania** frame of government. It retained broad political toleration as in the previous frames, albeit allowing only Protestants to hold office. The number of representatives from each county was reduced to four each. The charter also laid out the division between **Delaware** and Pennsylvania, offering the former its own independent assembly. The significance of the charter was to devolve more power to the colonial legislature by giving it the right to initiate legislation. This became a bone of contention in the struggle for power between England, the proprietor and the colonists.

CHESAPEAKE BAY is the largest expanse of water on the eastern coast of North America. Its length extends 200 miles from the mouth of the Susquehanna River to the opening to the Atlantic Ocean at Cape Henry, while its mouth is over 20 miles wide. The eastern shore is flat and sandy, with relatively few rivers, such as the Choptank, whereas the western shore is riddled with rivers and inlets, which provided opportunity in the 17th and 18th centuries for directing shipping of tobacco and other products from plantations dotted along the waterways. The rivers James, Rappahannock and Potomac became major conduits for trade, along which plantations were established. (The York, although called a river, is in reality little more than an inlet, and could never be exploited in the same way). The Bay was also the environment which nourished the cultures of **Maryland** and **Virginia**. Plantations that developed along the waterways were primarily self sufficient and this reduced the need for towns. It was not until towards the end of the 18th century that Baltimore developed as a major port.

CHILD, ROBERT (1613–1634) was educated at the Universities of Cambridge, Leiden and Padua. He visited **Massachusetts** twice, first from 1638 to 1641, and secondly from 1645 to 1647. On the second visit he challenged the authority of the Puritan dominated colony by charging them with infringing the rights of Englishmen. His *Remonstrance and Humble Petition* accused the colonial government of abusing its powers by using its charter for purposes not originally intended. Therefore, the laws of the colony were not in line with English law. Also, because the church excluded most of the inhabitants from the sacrament, for example Presbyterians like Child, the church needed reform. In November 1646 he was brought to trial for criticizing the government and church, and when he refused to retract his 'contemptuous speeches' fined £50. In 1647 he was imprisoned for attempting to leave the colony with a petition to parliament against its leaders. When he was set at liberty he sailed home. His condemnation of them caused the colonial leaders, **John Cotton** and **John Winthrop**, to draw up a 'Body of Liberties' that more precisely defined the powers of the magistracy.

CLAIBORNE, WILLIAM (1600–1677) was born in England and educated at Cambridge University. In 1621 he was appointed surveyor of **Virginia** by the **Virginia Company** and went to the colony. When it became a Crown colony Claiborne rose to prominence there, serving as a councillor from 1624 to 1661 with a break from 1638 to 1642; as secretary from 1626 to 1634 and again from 1652 to 1661; as treasurer from 1642 to 1660; and as deputy governor from 1652 to 1660. He was a wealthy merchant who acquired Kent Island in the upper **Chesapeake Bay** as a trading post in 1631. When **Lord Baltimore** was granted **Maryland** two years later he laid claim to the island too. Claiborne went to England to protest this claim in 1637, but it was upheld by the court of admiralty. Colonists from **Maryland** forcibly seized the island the following year. Claiborne returned to Virginia where as major general of the militia from 1644 to 1646 he had to deal with a serious uprising of the Indians against the colony. During the **Interregnum** when the Catholic proprietor of Maryland was deprived of his colony Claiborne again laid claim to Kent Island. He had to relinquish it, however, when Baltimore regained the proprietorship in 1658.

CLARKE, JOHN (1609–1676) was born in England and in 1637 went to **Massachusetts**. There he took the side of **Anne Hutchinson** in the **Antinomian Controversy** and went with her into exile, settling in **Rhode Island**. Despite having no medical qualifications he practiced medicine, and though he had never been ordained he became preacher of the church at Newport. In 1644 the congregation agreed that infant baptism had no scriptural sanction and it thereby became effectively a Baptist church. Clarke went to London as agent for Rhode Island in its dispute with **William Coddington**, which he resolved to the colony's satisfaction. While in England he published *Ill News from New England* (1652). Subtitled 'a narrative of New England's persecution' it criticized the intolerance of the saints in Massachusetts and called for religious toleration there. Clarke also got caught up in the radical politics of England during the **Interregnum**. After the Restoration of **Charles II** Clarke obtained from the king a new charter for Rhode Island in 1663, replacing one granted by parliament in 1644. He subsequently returned to the colony as minister in the Newport church until his death.

CLINTON, GEORGE (c. 1686–1761) was the second son of the sixth earl of Lincoln, brother of the seventh earl, and uncle of the ninth, and consequently a member of one of the families which made up the powerful political connection of the **duke of Newcastle**. Clinton entered the navy in 1708, rising to the rank of captain in 1716, commander-in-chief of the Mediterranean Squadron in 1737, vice-admiral in 1743 and admiral in 1747. Always in financial difficulties Clinton used his Newcastle connection to try to relieve them with colonial offices. In 1731 he obtained the governorship of Newfoundland, but later in the 1730s sought the more lucrative post of governor of **New York**, to which he was appointed in 1741. Arriving there in 1743 he immediately ran into difficulties with the assembly over his salary. He had to accept an annual rather than a permanent grant, and his concessions on other matters, including appointments to colonial offices previously made by governors but now wrested from him by the assembly, seriously undermined gubernatorial authority in New York before he was replaced in 1753.

CLINTON, SIR HENRY (1730–1795) was the son of **George Clinton**, governor of **New York**, where Henry was taken at the age of 11. He entered the army as a lieutenant in an infantry company there, but returned to England in 1748. There the influence of his father's patron, the **duke of Newcastle**, obtained for him a lieutenancy in the Coldstream Guards. During the Seven Years' War Clinton served as aide-de-camp to Sir John Ligonier in Germany. At the outset of the **War of American Independence** he went to Boston, and in 1776 to **South Carolina**. When General **Howe**, against Clinton's advice, went to the Chesapeake in 1777 rather than join **Burgoyne** in the Hudson River Valley, he left Clinton behind in New York City. On hearing of Burgoyne's defeat at Saratoga Clinton offered his resignation. Instead he was made commander-in-chief in North America, and ordered to remove the base of British operations from Philadelphia to New York. After France entered the war on America's side he also had to contend with French operations. In 1780 he launched an attack on Charles Town, which he took after a long siege. He then left **Cornwallis** in charge there and returned to New York. Clinton disapproved of Cornwallis withdrawing from the lower south to the Chesapeake, and failed to detach a fleet in time to prevent the blockade of the Bay by the French and the American victory at Yorktown. The disaster led Clinton to return under a cloud to England.

CODDINGTON, WILLIAM (c. 1601–1678) was born in England and subscribed to the **Massachusetts Bay Company** in 1629, going there with the first voyage in 1630. In 1637 he took the side of **Anne Hutchinson** in the **Antinomian Controversy** and went into exile with her in **Rhode Island**. There **Roger Williams** helped him acquire land from the Narragansett Indians where he founded Portsmouth. He served as chief magistrate there for only a year, being ousted in 1639 following a dispute with Anne Hutchinson. The following year he moved to Newport. When Newport united with Portsmouth in 1640 to form a single polity Coddington became its governor. His authority was extended to include Warwick when it joined Newport and Portsmouth in 1647. Other settlers in Rhode Island disputed Coddington's claims to this jurisdiction and sent **John Clarke** to England to challenge them. In 1654 Coddington had to abandon his independent rule and agreed to serve under the terms of the charter granted to Rhode Island in 1644. Thereafter he played a less prominent part in the colony's affairs until 1674 when he was elected deputy governor, becoming governor in 1678 the year of his death.

CODRINGTON, CHRISTOPHER (1640–1698) was born in **Barbados** where his father had gone as one of the first settlers in 1627. He inherited a considerable estate when his father died in 1656, and added to it during his own lifetime. By the 1680s he owned 618 acres in Barbados and 380 in Antigua. He cultivated sugar on his estates, which made him one of the wealthiest planters in the English West Indies. His wealth brought him power, and he served as governor of Barbados from 1669 to 1672, thereafter sitting in the assembly, of which he was Speaker between 1674 and 1682. In 1689 he was appointed governor of the Leeward Islands, which he governed during **King William's War**. At its outset the French took St Kitt's, which Codrington regained in 1690. However the French were granted part of the island in 1697 at the Treaty of Ryswick. Codrington himself lost land there when it was partitioned between France and England.

CODRINGTON, CHRISTOPHER (1668–1710) was born in **Barbados** but educated in England where he went to Christ Church, Oxford, and was elected a Fellow of All Souls in 1690. He spent the next decade in Europe apart from taking part in the attack on Martinique in 1693. On his return he served as a soldier in **King William's War** becoming lieutenant general in 1695 in recognition of his valiant conduct at the siege of Namur. He returned to England in 1698. When he learned of his father's death he determined to go to the West Indies. Before going he obtained the post of governor general of the Leeward Islands. Shortly after his arrival there he became involved in a case in Nevis when two settlers there complained to the Council that Codrington had abused his powers and evicted them from their lands. In 1702 the case was taken to the House of Commons, which exonerated Codrington. During **Queen Anne's War** he commanded a fleet in the West Indies which made an abortive attack on the French island of

Guadeloupe in 1703. That same year he suffered a prolonged illness which led him to request the **Board of Trade** to relieve him of his governorship. He spent the rest of his life on his estates, dying in Barbados. In his will he left his Barbados estate, estimated to be worth £30,000, to the **Society for the Propagation of the Gospel**. The Society arranged for the foundation of Codrington College in Barbados, which opened in 1745.

COERCIVE ACTS (or Intolerable Acts) was the name given to statutes passed by the North ministry in response to the **Boston Tea Party**. They included the Boston Port Act, the Massachusetts Government Act and the Administration of Justice Act. They first closed Boston harbor until compensation was forthcoming for the destruction of the East India Company's tea. The second changed the Charter of 1691 whereby the Bay Colony's Council had been elected by the Lower House of Assembly. Now it was to be selected by the king. Town meetings were also restricted to one session a year. The third empowered the governor to transfer cases to another colony or even to Britain if he felt a fair trial could not be held in Massachusetts. Colonists who opposed this legislation also lumped with it the **Quebec Act**, though it was a coincidence that this was passed in the same parliamentary session as the others and was not intended to accompany them.

COLDEN, CADWALLADER (1689–1776) was born in Ireland and educated at Edinburgh University. He went to London in 1705 to study medicine and in 1710 emigrated to **Philadelphia**. After eight years in **Pennsylvania** he moved to **New York**, the colony with which he became closely associated. Thus he held the posts of surveyor general, councillor and lieutenant governor. He was a Renaissance scholar, writing on history, mathematics, medicine and philosophy, and corresponding with other scholars including **Benjamin Franklin**. Colden published a *History of the five Indian nations depending on the province of New York* (1727), and tracts on medicine and physics.

COLLEGE OF WILLIAM AND MARY was established in Williamsburg, **Virginia**, in 1693, being the second institution of higher education in the colonies, the first being **Harvard**. There had been proposals to found one in Virginia in the 1620s, but these appear to have come to nothing. In 1691 Lieutenant **Francis Nicholson** persuaded the assembly to petition **William III** and Queen Mary for a charter for the proposed college. The king and especially the queen welcomed this initiative, granting not only a charter in 1693 but £2,000 and 20 acres of land for the purpose. The college was intended to train **Anglican** clergyman, the first president being **James Blair**.

CONGREGATIONALISTS or Independents as they were originally called, emerged in England in the early 17th century. The main body of Congregationalists who went to colonial America were the **Puritans** who migrated to **Massachusetts**. Initially they claimed that they were not separating from the Church of England, unlike the Pilgrims who went to **Plymouth**. On the contrary, they insisted that they remained Anglicans, but had withdrawn from the Church in England until it was more thoroughly reformed. Thus they objected to some Anglican rites, clerical vestments, the Book of Common Prayer, and any central authority such as bishops, which they claimed were remnants of Roman Catholicism. Once established in New England, however, they did develop along separate lines, until they felt the need to define their doctrinal position in the Synod of Cambridge in 1648. Although these discussions and agreements were not binding, the **Cambridge Platform**, as it became known, defined congregational worship and church organization.

CONNECTICUT was a colony of 5,009 square miles of land in the New England region which included the area around the Connecticut River Valley to the Long Island Sound. It did not include **New Haven** until 1665. Prior to **Thomas Hooker's** migration to Hartford, it was populated by Dutch as well as the English. Migration was mainly from Massachusetts and for reasons from expanding the fur trade and acquiring farm land to seeking religious toleration. In 1687 it was incorporated into the **Dominion of New England**. When the Dominion disintegrated in the **Glorious Revolution** Connecticut regained its independence.

CONTINENTAL CONGRESS originated as a result of events and growing tensions between Britain and its North American colonies. A primary catalyst for the meeting of the first Continental Congress was the **Coercive Acts** of 1774. These created a realization that a unified political effort was required to oppose British policy. Delegates from each colony (except **Georgia**) were sent to Philadelphia in 1774 to 'attend a Grand Congress'. The first Continental Congress set out three objectives: to draw up a clear statement of colonial rights; to specify the Acts of Parliament that violated those rights; and to propose measures to secure repeal of the offending legislation. The first objective was less a success than the other two primarily because the colonies could not decide in unison what those rights were. The second Continental Congress met in 1775 after the war broke out in Massachusetts and continued to serve as the 'United States in Congress Assembled' throughout the war. There was an attempt to give the Congressional powers some substance with the drafting of the **Articles of Confederation**, but there was resistance initially because opinion was still split over whether there should be complete independence or reconciliation with Britain. There were additional issues surrounding the extent to which the congress should hold authority over the colonies.

COODE, JOHN (1648–1709) was born in England and attended Oxford University, where he received ordination as an Anglican minister. He went to **Maryland** in 1672, and left the ministry on his marriage to a wealthy heiress. He then became a captain in the militia and a member of the assembly. His involvement in a plot against the proprietary government of the **third Lord Baltimore** in 1681 led to his being deprived of his captaincy. Coode led the Protestant Association in Maryland during the **Glorious Revolution**. After its success he was effectively the governor of the colony from 1689 to 1690 when he was replaced by Lionel Copley. He went to England to justify the Protestant Association's actions against Baltimore, but returned in 1692 with no new commission. Following the arrival of **Francis Nicholson** as governor in 1694 he was given a commission in the militia, but later incurred the enmity of Nicholson, who charged him with corruption while he presided over the affairs of Maryland. Coode fled to Virginia to escape the charges, but was eventually forced to appear in court to answer them. He was found guilty and fined, though Nicholson's successor pardoned him.

CORNBURY, EDWARD HYDE, VISCOUNT (1661–1723) was the heir to the earldom of Clarendon. He was educated in Oxford University and Geneva before becoming a professional soldier, rising in the officer ranks from colonel to general. He became notorious as the first English officer to defect from **James II's** army to join that of the invading William of Orange in the **Glorious Revolution** of 1688. His notoriety was not confined to that desertion, for as governor of **New York** 1701–1708 (to which **New Jersey** was added in 1703) he was accused of corruption, incompetence and above all of cross-dressing. These charges have been attributed to the machinations of his political enemies in the colony, who wished to ruin his reputation. But there can be little doubt that Cornbury was guilty of peculation, while suspicion still lingers that he did dress as a woman at public functions, justifying it on the grounds that he was the representative of a queen. Although he was recalled in 1708 he remained in New York as a prisoner for debt until his accession to the earldom of Clarendon in 1709.

CORNWALLIS, CHARLES MARQUESS (1738–1805) pursued a military career, serving in Germany during the Seven Years' War, rising to the rank of lieutenant colonel. Succeeding his father as Earl Cornwallis in 1762 he entered the House of Lords. His 'Country' suspicions of the Court led him usually to side with the Rockinghamites, opposing the **Stamp Act** and voting for its repeal, though he voted against the **Declaratory Act.** He went on to support the Chatham administration, and was made vice treasurer of Ireland in 1769. Although he had opposed the measures which provoked Americans to resist the Crown, he volunteered to serve in the forces sent to the colonies when resistance turned to rebellion. He arrived in the Spring of 1776 and fought in the battle of Long Island that summer. His failure to follow it up by pursuing Washington's army vigorously led to charges of incompetence, and even of continuing sympathy for the colonists' cause. Cornwallis redeemed his reputation at the battle of Brandywine after which he returned to England. He went back briefly in 1778 but had to return home when his wife fell ill. After her death he sailed once again across the Atlantic to join **Sir Henry Clinton** in the so-called 'southern strategy'. After their successful siege of **Charles Town** Clinton went back to New York while Cornwallis went on to defeat General Gates at Camden. Thereafter he headed north to the Chesapeake Bay, establishing a base at Yorktown where he was decisively defeated by **Washington** and Rochambeau. Cornwallis returned to England and in 1786 started another, more successful career as governor general of India.

COSBY, WILLIAM (c. 1690–1736) married the sister of the **earl of Halifax**, which connected him to the governing elite associated with the powerful **duke of Newcastle.** After an army career which culminated in the governorship of Minorca he was appointed as governor of **New York** and **New Jersey** in 1731. His office was characterized by corruption, such as the appointment of his son to be secretary of New Jersey. This led him to be attacked in the press by **John Peter Zenger**.

COTTON, JOHN (1595–1652) was born in Derby, England and educated at Trinity College, Cambridge. Cotton became vicar of St Botolph's Church in Boston, Lincolnshire. In 1630, he preached a sermon to departing Puritans for America who included **John Winthrop**. The sermon entitled 'The Divine Right to Occupy the Land', emphasized the view that it was God's will that Puritans should 'inhabit all the world'. Shortly after, in 1632, when the English ecclesiastical courts sought to indict Cotton for unorthodoxy, he migrated to **Massachusetts**. During his time as minister there, he was involved in a number of crises that threatened the hegemony of the Puritans. The colony was charged by Dr **Robert Child** with abusing its charter for the sole benefit of the Congregational church and to the exclusion of other churches. In this case, Child, a Presbyterian, charged that Massachusetts laws were not in line with English law. In essence, there was no proper legal code. Cotton and Winthrop drew up a code of laws which eventually evolved into what became known as The Body of Liberties and finally *The Book of General Lawes and Libertys*. Politically, it was an attempt to ward off metropolitan interference. Cotton was also implicated in the **Antinomian Controversy** when **Anne Hutchinson** claimed that he was one of only two preachers in the colony who upheld the covenant of grace and not the covenant of works. He distanced himself from her by denying her claim and thereby avoided her fate. Subsequently he became the most powerful minister in Massachusetts, insisting that only the regenerate should be allowed to participate in communion services. **Thomas Hooker** protested against this rigid rule, and led the migration from Massachusetts to **Connecticut,** where all were admitted to communion.

COUNCIL FOR NEW ENGLAND 1620–1635. The Council evolved out of the **Virginia Company of Plymouth. Sir Ferdinando Gorges** obtained the grant for it in 1620. Initially there were 38 members, all peers, knights or Esquires. Later merchants were admitted to it on payment of a 'fine' of £100. In 1623 a group of 'adventurers' from Dorchester, led by the Reverend John White, obtained a patent from the Council for a plantation and established a settlement at Cape Ann, but abandoned it in 1626. Some of the settlers moved to Naumkeag, which **John Endecott** renamed Salem when he arrived there in 1628. They were also joined by members of the New England Company, established that year by patent from the Council. In 1629 the Company severed its link with the Council and relaunched itself as the **Massachusetts Bay Company.**

Gorges protested against this and asserted the claims of the Council, but was unable to enforce them. In 1635 it was dissolved.

COVENANT CHAIN was a number of loosely connected treaties created by governor of New York, **Sir Edmond Andros** in an effort to stabilize relations between settlers and **Indians**. He negotiated the first and most important of these compacts with the five nations of the Iroquois in August 1675. This covered the vast area from the Mohawk River valley in upper New York to the Ohio River in the west. In June 1676 they met again at Albany to forge the chain between Andros, the Indians and 'the great King Charles who liveth over the Great Lake'. The Covenant was to endure beyond the death of **Charles II** into the 18th century. It broke down, however, with the start of **the French and Indian War**, when the Iroquois either stayed neutral or sided with the French. The congress which met at Albany in 1754, more celebrated for the **Albany Plan of Union**, was convened to try to renegotiate the Covenant.

COVERTURE was a term describing the legal status of women whose rights over their possessions were subsumed under the male head of the household . This applied particularly to married women. Widows and other single women had more control, although it was highly unlikely they were heads of their households because typically they lived with relatives. Before 1680, there was more flexibility in this situation, in individual colonies. Whether they lived in a rural or urban environment also affected the stringency of the law. After 1680, laws were more rigorously enforced primarily by defining women as femes covert. By disallowing women to act as femes sole, their legal rights were restricted to that of their husbands.

CROWN COLONIES. Colonies that came under the direct control of the Monarch. **Virginia** started out as a **charter colony**, but after failing to become economically viable, largely through mismanagement, the colony was taken over in 1624 by King **James I**. New York was another colony that moved from being a **proprietorship** under the duke of York, to a crown colony when he became **James II**. **New Hampshire** was originally a proprietary colony but was assumed by the Crown in 1676. Massachusetts, from being a charter colony which elected its own governor under the charter of 1629, had to accept a royal nominee to its governorship under the new charter of 1691. From 1689 to 1715 the proprietary colony of Maryland became a Crown colony. After 1696 the **Board of Trade** pursued a policy of bringing all proprietary colonies under the Crown. It was successful in the short run only with **New Jersey**, which became a Crown colony in 1702. However, in the long run the **Carolinas** were also transformed from proprietary to Crown colonies. **Georgia** was launched under trustees in 1733, but it was intended to become a Crown colony from the outset, which it did in 1738.

CULPEPER, JOHN (1644–1694) settled in **Charles Town**, **South Carolina** in 1671. He was a mapmaker who drew one of the first plans of the city and became surveyor general of the colony. For unknown reasons he left South Carolina for Albermarle county in **North Carolina**. There he became known as the leader of a group of malcontent planters who, in 1677, revolted against customs duties imposed by the proprietor's government in implementation of the Plantations Duties Act of 1673. The result was the overthrow of the government with Culpeper taking charge. Though the government was eventually restored, while he himself faced charges of treason in England, the proprietors defended him and he returned to North Carolina.

CULPEPER, THOMAS, SECOND BARON CULPEPER (1635–1689) was born in England and went into exile with the Stuarts after the civil wars. At the Restoration he was granted substantial lands in the Northern Neck in **Virginia**, to the chagrin of **Sir William Berkeley** the Governor of the colony. He was even more chagrined when Culpeper was offered the succession to the governorship by **Charles II**. He was formerly appointed in 1677, but did not arrive in Virginia until l680. Culpeper attained popularity by pardoning those who had taken part in **Bacon's Rebellion**.

Following his return to England, however, there were disorders in Virginia caused by the low prices being obtained for tobacco. Some planters destroyed the tobacco of others in a desperate attempt to reduce supply and thereby increase prices. Charles II ordered Culpeper back to the colony to suppress the disturbances. On his second visit from 1682 to 1683 he dealt severely with those who had been involved in the destruction of tobacco, condemning several to death. When he returned to England again in 1683 the king deprived him of the governorship of Virginia and replaced him with Lord Howard of Effingham. **James II**, however, who succeeded to the throne in 1685, confirmed Culpeper in his ownership of lands in the Northern Neck which Charles II had granted him in 1673.

D

DALE, SIR THOMAS (d. 1619) was a soldier who had served in Ireland and the Netherlands before he was sent to **Virginia** in 1610 to impose order after the ravages of starvation and disease. He put the colony on a military footing and codified its laws in *Lawes Divine Morall and Martiall* (1612). His suppression of disorder was draconian, involving capital punishment for theft, those condemned being tied to trees and starved to death. He dealt with the disease-ridden environment at Jamestown by settling Henrico up the James River on the present site of Richmond. Dale was relieved by **Sir Thomas Gates** only to succeed him in 1614 as governor again. In that year he made peace with the **Powhatan Confederacy** cementing it with the wedding of **John Rolfe** to **Pocahontas.** In 1616 he ended his stint in the American colonies and returned to England. Dale took charge of a fleet under the East India Company and saw action against the Dutch in the East, where he died in 1619.

DARTMOUTH, WILLIAM LEGGE, SECOND EARL OF (1731–1801) inherited the title in 1752 and entered the House of Lords. His widowed mother married the earl of Guildford, father of **Lord North**. Dartmouth and North were both educated at Trinity College, Oxford and went on the Grand Tour together. After his return to England Dartmouth married a wealthy heiress, Frances Catherine Nicholl. The pair became devout adherents of the Countess of Huntingdon's Methodist connection. In 1765 Dartmouth joined the first **Rockingham** administration as President of the **Board of Trade**. This put him at the forefront of the dispute over the **Stamp Act**, the passage of which he had disapproved. Although he supported its repeal he was also firmly behind the **Declaratory Act**. He was out of office from 1766 to 1772 when Lord North persuaded him to become Colonial Secretary left vacant by the resignation of **Lord Hillsborough**. His appointment was welcomed by **Benjamin Franklin** and other Americans as the replacement of a hard liner by a friend of the colonists, a view which found expression in the founding of Dartmouth college, New Hampshire, which was named after him. Nevertheless, Dartmouth supported the **Coercive Acts** passed in reaction to **the Boston Tea Party**. His hopes that these would bring the colonies to heel were dashed, and he shrank from the measures which North felt were necessary to deal with armed rebellion. In November 1775 Dartmouth was moved from the Colonial Secretaryship to the post of Lord Privy Seal, an office he held until the fall of the North ministry in 1782.

DAVENPORT, JOHN (1597–1670) was born in England and educated at Oxford University. He became curate of St Lawrence Jewry, a church in the City of London, moving to St Stephen, Coleman street in 1625. The following year he became one of the feofees for impropriations, a Puritan body which sought to buy up church livings in order to appoint to them godly preaching ministers. This was regarded as subversive by the Arminian archbishop of Canterbury, William Laud, and the feofees were suppressed by the court of high commission in 1633. Davenport fled to Holland until 1636, when he decided to go to **Massachusetts.** There he was involved with the trial of **Anne Hutchinson**. In 1638 he moved with his congregation to Quinnipiac, later named New Haven, in order to preserve the strictest rules of church membership, confining it exclusively to visible saints. He was opposed to the more liberal attitude of **Thomas Hooker** who established a church with a much broader membership in Connecticut. Largely for that reason Davenport unsuccessfully opposed the absorption of New Haven into **Connecticut** in 1662. In 1667 he returned to Massachusetts to be pastor of the First Church in Boston, where he died.

DAYE, STEPHEN (1594–1668) was born in England where he was employed as a locksmith in Cambridge. In 1638 he went to Boston, his passage paid by the Rev Joseph Glover, to whom he bound himself for two years after landing in America. Glover intended setting up as a printer, for he took a press with him. He died, however, on the voyage. His widow nevertheless set up a printing business in Cambridge, **Massachusetts** in 1639. Daye managed it, thereby becoming the first printer in the English colonies in North America. Mrs Glover married Henry Dunster, President of **Harvard College**, in 1641. Thereafter the press printed publications for the college as well as for the colony. Daye continued working for it after his bond expired, though he preferred other more remunerative jobs.

DEANE, SILAS (1737–1789) was born in Groton, **Connecticut** and attended **Yale College**. He practiced law upon graduation. His second marriage, to Elizabeth Saltonstall Ebbets, who belonged to the powerful Saltonstall family, provided a boost to his political career. He served as assemblyman for Weathersfield, Connecticut from 1768–1769 and again from 1772–1775. He belonged to the Susquehannah Company which sent settlers to the Wyoming valley to claim the territory for Connecticut in contest to Pennsylvania's claim. As the troubles with Britain grew, Deane became more prominent in the growing resistance by the colonists. He was appointed secretary of the Connecticut Committee of Correspondence. In 1774, he was chosen as one of Connecticut's delegates to the first two Continental Congresses. In 1776, he was chosen to represent the colonies in France in order to solicit arms and supplies. He was partly successful in getting clothing and arms to the colonies through a company, Hortalez & Co. headed by Pierre Augustin Caron de Beaumarchais, which was a front to conceal aid from the French government. In the end, he had trouble paying the French which led to some compromising his secret position and earned him charges of embezzlement of funds that were to be paid to the French by Arthur Lee, brother to Richard Henry Lee who was living in London. The dispute between Arthur Lee and Deane resulted in a split in Congress between the supporters for each. Eventually, both were recalled to America.

DECLARATION OF INPENDENCE, after accusing **George III** of tyrannical rule, concluded that 'these colonies are, and of right ought to be, free and independent states'. Drafted by **Thomas Jefferson**, it was approved by the **Continental Congress** on 4 July 1776.

DECLARATORY ACT 1766 was passed immediately after the repeal of the **Stamp Act** to reassert the right of the British parliament to legislate for the colonies 'in all cases whatsoever'. It thereby repudiated the claim of the **Stamp Act Congress** that its legislative power over them did not extend to raising revenue, a position which **William Pitt** upheld in the debates in the House of Commons.

DEERFIELD is located on the Connecticut River in western **Massachusetts**. In 1704 the town had 260 inhabitants. On 29 February Deerfield was subjected to attack by between 200 and 300 French and Indian troops. Fifty-three of the townsfolk, men woman and children, were massacred, while 109 were taken captive, 88 of them, including the minister **John Williams**, being taken to **Canada**.

DELAWARE. Bordering the Delaware Bay and **Pennsylvania** to its northwest, the colony was first inhabited by the Dutch, Finns, and Swedes. In 1663 and subsequently by the Treaty of Westminster in 1674, Delaware became part of a larger grant to the English duke of York, James Stuart. From 1681, the colony, along with Pennsylvania, came under the proprietorship of **William Penn**. The grant, however, was questionable because it was given by the duke of York and not by the king, who had the final authority over grants. This caused conflict between Penn and the proprietor of **Maryland** for many years in their dispute over the Maryland-Pennsylvania border. Since Pennsylvania initially had three counties, while Delaware was also divided into three, New Castle, Kent and Sussex, the area was originally referred to as the Lower Counties. Unlike Pennsylvania, which was dominated by Quakers, Delaware was primarily Anglican. This caused political as well as religious tension with the inhabitants of Pennsylvania, enough to finally force the proprietor to cede to Delaware the right to its own assembly in the **Charter of Privileges** of 1701. In 1704 the Lower Counties took advantage of Penn's offer to secede from the assembly in Philadelphia and to set up their own. Hence, it became politically separate from Pennsylvania. Noted for its accessibility to the sea via the Delaware River and Bay, the colony's main produce was grain and, later, tobacco and corn. However, its livelihood depended on its importance as a port and gateway to the Delaware region.

DE LA WARR, LORD see **WEST THOMAS**

DICKINSON, JOHN (1732–1808) was born in **Maryland** but moved to **Delaware** with his Quaker parents in 1741. After studying law at the Middle Temple in London he began to practice as a lawyer in Philadelphia. He also started a career in politics, becoming speaker of the Delaware assembly in 1760. Two years later he was elected to the Pennsylvania assembly siding with the anti-proprietary members. He parted from them, however, when they sought to persuade the Crown to take the colony out of the proprietorship of the Penn family and into its own. Dickinson was prominent in the Stamp Act Congress, helping to draft its resolutions against taxation without representation. His most conspicuous contribution to the colonial cause was his *Letters from a Farmer in Pennsylvania* published in response to the **Townshend Duties**. These effectively refuted the British contention that the Americans would accept indirect taxes. Dickinson was a leading figure in Philadelphia among those who opposed the Tea Act and the **Coercive Acts**, urging support for the town of Boston. He attended the first continental congress as a representative for Pennsylvania and greatly influenced its firm stance against the British government. When his hopes of reconciliation were dashed with the outbreak of open hostilities in 1775 he enlisted as an officer in the forces raised to resist the British. His insistence on negotiations rather than confrontation led him to lose his influence in the second continental congress, especially when he opposed the Declaration of Independence. The new Pennsylvania state legislature dismissed him as its delegate to the congress. He resigned from the army and retired to Delaware. That state's assembly returned him to the continental congress in 1779, but after serving one session he ceased to attend it. In 1781 he was elected governor of Delaware and the following year he became president of the Pennsylvania council.

DOMINION OF NEW ENGLAND. In 1687 **James II** incorporated the colonies of **Connecticut**, **Massachusetts, New Hampshire** and **Rhode Island** into one government, thereby superseding their colonial charters and removing any representative institutions which could challenge his authority. This became known as the Dominion and Territory of New England, usually abbreviated to the Dominion of New England. The fuller title is the more accurate as the king sought to extend his control over land rights as well as the administration of the area. In 1688 it was extended to incorporate **New York** and **New Jersey**. The governor, **Sir Edmund Andros** was assisted by a Dominion Council based in Boston. Council members included Robert Treat and John Allyn of Connecticut, and Colonel **Francis Nicholson** of New York. Nicholson also became Lieutenant governor under Andros. The council had a more direct impact on Massachusetts, for obvious reasons, than it had in the colonies further afield such as New Jersey and New York. The Dominion created much resentment which found expression in the **Glorious Revolution**.

DONGAN, THOMAS (1634–1715) was an Irish Roman Catholic who pursued an army career. From 1677 to 1680 he was lieutenant governor of Tangier. The Duke of York appointed him to be governor of his proprietary colony of **New York** in 1683. On his arrival there Dongan convened the first assembly in the colony, which passed the 'Charter of Liberties'. Dongan caused the duke of York's arms to be exhibited in Iroquois villages. The duke continued him in office when he became king as **James II** in 1685. In the years 1687 to 1688 Dongan raised a force for the defense of Albany. When New York was attached to the **Dominion of New England** in 1688 Dongan was dismissed as lieutenant governor of New York and was thus not in office at the time of the **Glorious Revolution**. Nevertheless his Catholicism was cited as evidence of an intent to empower 'Papists' by revolutionaries such as **Jacob Leisler**. In 1691 Dongan returned to England. He succeeded his brother as earl of Limerick in 1698.

DUDLEY, JOSEPH (1647–1720) was the son of **Thomas Dudley**, the second governor of **Massachusetts**, where he was born at Roxbury. In 1665 he graduated from **Harvard College**. He was a member of the General Court from 1673 to 1676 and of the Council from 1676 to 1684. Anticipating the revocation of the Massachusetts charter Dudley went to England in 1682 to try to forestall it. Following the nullification of the charter he was made president of the Council and governor of Massachusetts and New Hampshire in 1686. On the appointment of **Sir Edmund Andros** as governor of the **Dominion of New England**, Dudley became chief justice. When the Dominion fell in the **Glorious Revolution** he was imprisoned until William III ordered his release. Although he was pursued by the new rulers of Massachusetts who indicted him on 119 charges, he was acquitted. Dudley was then appointed as head of the Council of New York, in which capacity he presided over the trial of **Jacob Leisler**. In 1692 he resigned and went to England, where he became an **Anglican**. He served as governor of Massachusetts from 1702 to 1715.

DUKE'S LAWS. A code of law based upon New England practices instituted by **New York** governor **Richard Nicolls** in order to attract settlers into the new English colony after the second Anglo–Dutch war. They contained civil and criminal codes of law. The law allowed for towns to have self-governing privileges including elected town officials, and the right to their own choice of church. While it allowed the proprietary government a certain amount of political freedom, it did not include an elected assembly. Ultimately the laws were constrained by the executive power concerning trade and taxes.

DULANY, DANIEL I (1685–1753) was born in Ireland, and settled in **Maryland** in 1703. He trained as a lawyer as a clerk in a law office. On a visit to England from 1716 to 1717 he was admitted to Gray's Inn. Dulany resided in Annapolis in 1720, and was elected to the assembly from 1722 to 1742, when he was appointed to the Council. He served as the colony's attorney general from 1721 to 1725. Dulany defended the colonists against the proprietor Lord Baltimore in *The Rights of the Inhabitants of Maryland to the benefits of English laws* (1728). When Baltimore visited Maryland from 1732 to 1733 he conferred the offices of judge in the vice-admiralty court and attorney general on Dulany.

DULANY, DANIEL II (1722–1797) was the son of **Daniel Dulany I** who sent him to England to be educated at Eton College, Clare College Cambridge and the Middle Temple. After becoming a barrister Dulany returned to **Maryland** in 1747 to practice law. He was elected as a member of the Maryland lower house of assembly from 1751 to 1757, when he was appointed to the council by the proprietor. Following another visit to England from 1761 to 1763 he became deputy secretary of the colony. In 1765 he published an influential pamphlet against the **Stamp Act**, *Considerations on the propriety of imposing taxes on the British colonies for the purpose of raising a revenue*. During the 1770s Dulany became involved in a public debate over the rights of the proprietors of Maryland, which he defended. This identified him with the loyalists in the American Revolution, and though he insisted he was neutral much of his property was confiscated in 1780.

DUMMER, JEREMIAH (1680–1739) was born in Boston and educated at **Harvard College** Dummer practiced law in England, where he became agent for **Massachusetts** in 1710 and **Connecticut** in 1712. He helped Elihu **Yale** as benefactor of the College named after him, giving over 1,000 books to its library. In 1721 he published a *Defence of the New England Charters* claiming that colonies were more important than corporations.

DUTCH. The Dutch East India Company commissioned Henry Hudson to explore the upper reaches of the river which bears his name to search for a North West Passage. Hudson established a trading post on the site of Albany in 1613 which was called Fort Orange. In 1624 the Dutch West India Company, which had taken over the North American activities of the East India Company, sent a party of settlers to the fort. The Company also established an outpost on the Delaware near the site of **Philadelphia** which they called Fort Nassau. A third fort, New Amsterdam, was established in 1626 at the southern tip of Manhattan Island. There was also a fort on the Connecticut River where Hartford was to be founded. This network of forts protected a trading venture of the West India Company which was known as New Netherland. To it in 1655 was added New Sweden, a colony on the Delaware established by Swedes since 1637. By then the Company had largely lost interest in its North American venture, being more concerned with a vain attempt to hang on to Brazil which it had seized from the Portuguese.

The Company were also disappointed that few colonists had been attracted to settle in New Netherland. In an attempt to entice them the Company launched a scheme to grant large patroonships in the Hudson River valley. But although several patroonships were issued only one was seriously implemented, that given to Van Rensselaer near Fort Orange. By the time Peter Stuyvesant took over the direction of New Netherland in 1646 there were fewer than 10,000 Europeans in the colony. By no means all were Dutch. Even those from the Netherlands tended to come from the outer provinces rather than from the core maritime states of Holland and Zealand. They were mingled with Germans, Norwegians, Swedes, Finns and even French Huguenots. The resulting babel of tongues was matched by the variety of religions, with Jews joining the Christians in 1657, lured to New Netherland by the practice of religious toleration there. Stuyvesant tried to encourage others to emigrate to the colony, relaxing the authoritarian regime which the West India Company had inaugurated. Thus New Amsterdam acquired municipal government. He also endeavored to make the colony less dependent upon the fur trade with the Indians, which was experiencing diminishing returns as the peltry moved westward, and become more reliant upon agriculture. There were signs that these measures were beginning to be effective on the eve of the English conquest in 1663 which was to turn New Amsterdam into **New York**. Even after the colony was transferred from the Netherlands to England Dutch influence remained prominent, especially in the upper Hudson and Mohawk valleys.

DYER, MARY (d. 1660) was born in England where she married William Dyer in 1633. They went to **Massachusetts** in 1635. There Mary became acquainted with **Anne Hutchinson** whom she publicly defended at her trial during the **Antinomian controversy**. Together with her husband she then escaped to **Rhode Island**. Meanwhile **John Winthrop** tried to discredit her by exhuming the body of a still born child she had borne which was reputedly a monster. In the early 1650s Mary went back to England where she became a Quaker. She returned to Boston in

1657, though Massachusetts banned Quakers from bearing witness in the colony, with capital punishment being the penalty for a repeated offense. Mary was immediately imprisoned and subsequently banished. In 1659 she returned despite the death penalty for so doing and faced trial again. She was sentenced to execution but reprieved literally at the last moment. She went back to Rhode Island but appeared again in Boston in 1660 and was once more sentenced to death. This time she was hanged. Her martyrdom as a Quaker was instrumental in persuading **Charles II** to require the colony to relax its persecution of religious dissenters.

E

EATON, THEOPHILUS (1590–1658) was born in England where he served an apprenticeship to a London wool merchant. After completing it he joined the Eastland Company and traded with Denmark. Eaton attended the church of St Stephen, Coleman Street in the City of London. There he was acquainted with **John Davenport**, with whom he went to **Massachusetts** in 1637. Finding the **Antinomian controversy** at its height they moved westward and established a settlement later known as **New Haven**. Eaton was elected as its first governor, and served until his death. He presided over a colony riven with religious disputes. His own wife was excommunicated in 1645 for not attending services. Eaton introduced a legal code into New Haven with his *New Haven's settling in New England* (1656).

ECONOMY. The colonies were overwhelmingly rural, and many farming communities were practically self-sufficient, creating a domestic market which was not reliant upon overseas trade. They did not operate in an entirely subsistence economy, however, for they supplied surplus produce to local outlets. Thus **New England** farmers sold livestock, especially hogs and cattle, for meat, while those in the middle colonies, especially **Pennsylvania**, sold wheat to be made into flour. It is hard to measure this domestic market by contrast with the data available for trans-Atlantic commerce, and it might have been seriously underestimated in calculations of colonial economic activity. At the same time the economy of colonial America cannot be considered in isolation from that of Great Britain since trans-Atlantic trade, which the British government tried to control through the **Navigation Acts**, was a crucial component in the economic life of the colonies. Indeed there was not a single American economy in the colonial period, as different regions developed distinct economies. Economic historians distinguish between the staple and non-staple regional economies. Thus the staples of rice, sugar and tobacco underpinned those of **South Carolina** and **Georgia**, the **West Indies** and the **Chesapeake Bay**. **North Carolina**, sandwiched between the Chesapeake and lower south, lacked a staple in the colonial era, and economically was more like the colonies north of Maryland. Their economies too were based on the exploitation of primary products, such as timber, flour, fish and fur, rather than on manufactures. Until the rise of Baltimore in the middle of the 18th century, the major ports other than **Charles Town** were in the north, led by **Philadelphia**, **New York** and **Boston**. These were primarily centers of distribution, though they also produced manufactured articles, such as ships, rum and increasingly consumer goods which were originally supplied from the mother country. Many British commodities continued to be consumed in the colonies, such as books, furniture and other luxuries. The British government tried to uphold a system whereby the colonies provided raw materials in return for manufactured items. Thus the **Hat Act** was passed in 1732 to prevent the making of fashionable fur hats in the colonies, requiring pelts to be sent to England for that purpose. In 1750 the **Iron Act** attempted to restrict the exploitation of iron resources in the colonies to the extraction of pig or bar iron to be sent to England to be forged. This measure proved ineffective in preventing the growth of a colonial steel industry. Nevertheless the exchange of primary produce for manufactures continued throughout the colonial period, producing a boom in Atlantic trade which was profitable to both sides. The most lucrative for the colonies was the export of sugar from the West Indies to Britain, which increased from 22,017 tons in 1700 to 41,425 tons in 1748. Its share of the Atlantic commerce rose from 10 to 20 per cent in the colonial period, to the great enrichment of the white inhabitants of **Barbados**, **Jamaica** and the other British islands in the Caribbean. It has been estimated that on the eve of the Declaration of Independence they owned 25 times more wealth than the white colonists on the mainland. At that time too the average wealth of the American colonists measured by probate inventories was only about a third of that of their counterparts in Britain. Again those in the southern 'staple' colonies were wealthier than their northern neighbors. The cash crops of rice and tobacco, and the **slaves** who tended them, gave the southern colonists an economic advantage over the northern, especially those in New England. At the same time artisans and laborers, who were not likely to leave probate inventories, were probably better off than their equivalents in the mother country, as there was a shortage of labor, especially skilled, in the colonies. Pennsylvania was known as 'the best poor man's country'. The gap between rich and poor, though it was apparently widening in the 18th century, especially in New England, was not as wide in the colonies as it was in Britain. Nevertheless, overall standards of living improved over the colonial period.

EDWARDS, JONATHAN (1703–1758) was born in East Windsor, **Connecticut**. His father was a clergyman and his mother was the daughter of another, Solomon Stoddard. From 1716 to 1720 he studied at **Yale College** for his BA, and after graduation stayed on to take an MA. While studying for his Master's degree he underwent a religious experience in the summer of 1721 comparable to a 'new birth'. It profoundly affected his beliefs and actions for the rest of his life. As a scholar he achieved a synthesis of Protestant theology with Newtonian physics and Lockeian psychology. Where Newton and Locke seemed to him to explain natural phenomena in purely mechanistic terms he insisted that they required a divine explanation. His scholarly achievements led the great historian of Puritanism Perry Miller to describe Edwards as the first American philosopher. His career as a clergyman began in 1722 when he went as pastor to a congregation of English Presbyterians in New York. The following April he returned home to complete his master's thesis on 'a sinner is not justified in the sight of God except through the righteousness of Christ obtained by faith'. Following its completion in 1723 he became pastor of a church in Bolton Connecticut. From 1724 to 1726 he was a tutor at Yale College, then between 1726 and 1729 he assisted his grandfather Stoddard in his Congregational ministry in Northampton **Massachusetts**. In 1728 he was ordained and on Stoddard's death the following year Edwards succeeded him as minister in Northampton. Where Stoddard had allowed the unregenerate to take part in the communion service, Edwards insisted that only those who had provided evidence of saving faith should be communicants. Many of his congregation gave satisfactory accounts of their new births, giving rise to spectacular conversions in the mid-1730s, and again after 1740, which are cited as significant elements in the **Great Awakening**. Edwards himself gave an account of them in his *Faithful Narrative of the surprising work of God* (1737) and *Some Thoughts concerning the present Revival of Religion in New England* (1742). His most famous sermon *Sinners in the hands of an angry God* (1741) emphasized the sovereignty of God, the depravity of humankind, the reality of hell, and the necessity of rebirth. Some members of his congregation, however, objected to the severity of his demands upon them and demanded his dismissal. In 1750 he agreed to the adjudication of a council of churches, which found against him. The following year he moved to Stockbridge in western Massachusetts, where he became prominent as an outspoken critic of Arminianism. Edwards was appointed as President of the new College of New Jersey (later Princeton) in January 1758, but died that March of a fever following inoculation against smallpox.

ELIOT, JOHN (1604–1690) was born in England and educated at Cambridge University. He became acquainted with **Thomas Hooker**, who employed him as a teacher in his academy at Chelmsford in 1629. When Hooker fled the ecclesiastical authorities, and the school was closed, Eliot decided to go to **Massachusetts** where he arrived in 1631. He became a staunch supporter of **John Winthrop**, defending the banishment of **Roger Williams** in 1636 and cross examining **Anne Hutchinson** at her trial the following year. His main claim to fame was his proselytizing mission to the Indians, which he launched in 1646. For this purpose he learned the Algonquin language and translated the Bible and other texts. He also promoted 'praying towns' – communities where converted Indians could practice Christianity. The first was established at Natick in 1651. By 1674 there were 14 such towns inhabited by 1,100 Indians. The experiment, however, received a grave setback with **King Philip's War**.

ELIZABETHTOWN GRANT. As part of the plan to draw settlers south from New England, in 1664 Governor Richard Nicolls of **New York** granted an area east from the Passaic river to the Raritan river for this purpose. This area later became known as **New Jersey** but at the time was part of the newly acquired New York.

ENDECOTT, JOHN (d. 1665) was one of the patentees of the New England Company who in 1628 invested £50 in a venture to settle at Cape Ann. When he arrived as governor there in September the settlers had moved to Naumkeag, which he later named Salem. The Pilgrims at Plymouth got him to chop down the maypole which **Thomas Morton** had erected at Merrymount. In 1629 New England was placed under the auspices of the **Massachusetts Bay Company**, which enrolled Endecott in its service. The Puritans, however, were suspicious of his relations with Plymouth College, accusing him of seeking separation from the Church of England. He defended the church at Salem from these charges. When **John Winthrop** arrived in the Bay in 1630 he assumed the governorship, and Endecott became an assistant. He provoked a crisis in 1634 when he cut the cross of St George from the English flag, claiming it was a Popish symbol. Though Winthrop privately agreed with him, publicly he felt bound to rebuke him. Endecott was on active service during the **Pequot War**. On Winthrop's death in 1649 Endecott was elected governor of **Massachusetts**, a post he had previously held in 1644. He was to hold it for a total of 13 years before his death. He thus presided over a period of persecution for religious dissenters, especially Quakers. **Mary Dyer** the Quaker martyr was first reprieved from execution by him but subsequently hanged. This moved **Charles II** to require Endecott to relax the colony's harsh laws against dissent.

F

FLETCHER, BENJAMIN (1640–1703) was appointed Governor of **New York** by King **William** and Queen Mary in 1691. He tried to establish control after the rebellion of **Jacob Leisler** by granting political hegemony to the colony's elite Anglo–Dutch families. This served to cause tension within the colony, but it also reflected the struggle between the Tory and Whig parties in England. For Fletcher was a Tory, a client of the Earl of Nottingham who was William III's secretary of state. As Governor of New York Fletcher issued a proclamation of war against the French in 1693. In pursuit of the war he tried to enlist the **Connecticut** militia but his jurisdiction over it was denied by its officer. He replaced **William Penn** as Governor of **Pennsylvania** in 1692 because William III did not trust Penn or the Quakers in the colony's assembly to prosecute the war against France. Penn was suspected of being a Jacobite, while the predominantly Quaker assembly opposed any financial support for military defense. Penn persuaded the king that he was loyal to him in 1694, and was reinstated as governor of Pennsylvania. In 1698 Fletcher was replaced as Governor of New York by a whig, **Lord Bellamont** who reversed his anti-Leislerian policies.

FLORIDA. There was a strong Spanish presence in North America before the English settled there. Spain had constructed a fort at St Augustine on the Atlantic coast of Florida before the 'lost colony' was settled on Roanoke Island. Indeed Sir Francis Drake destroyed it in 1586 to protect the new settlement. There was friction between the English settlements and the Spanish in Florida throughout the colonial period. The defenses of Jamestown, the first permanent colony in **Virginia**, were constructed to protect it against possible attacks up the James river from Florida rather than down the river from Indians. The settlement of the **Carolinas**, near to the border with Florida, increased the tension in the late 17th century. The second charter of 1665 even extended the southern boundary to include St Augustine. This was revised when Spain protested but agreed to recognize England's claim to the Ashley and Charles Rivers, the site selected for the building of Charles Town. Open hostilities broke out in **Queen Anne's War** when the Spanish colonies recognized the Bourbon claimant to the throne of France and became one of Britain's enemies. South Carolina launched an attack on St Augustine in 1702 which took the town but failed to take the fort, which had been reconstructed from cocina, a hard local stone. After seven weeks the siege was raised. There was uneasy peace between the Spanish and English colonies after the treaty of Utrecht in 1713 until the settlement of **Georgia** in 1733. This was specifically to defend the southern flank of the English settlements and provoked Spanish protests. When the war of Jenkins's Ear broke out in 1739 the governor of Georgia, **James Oglethorpe** attacked St Augustine but was repulsed. He successfully held off a Spanish counter-attack in 1742, defeating them in the battle of Bloody Swamp. During the French and Indian War Spain remained neutral until 1762, when it was drawn into the conflict. As a result Florida was acquired by the British at the **Peace of Paris** in 1763. **The Proclamation of 1763** divided it into two colonies, East and West Florida. During the **War of American Independence** they remained loyal to the Crown, and East Florida was used as a refuge by southern **Loyalists**. Notwithstanding their loyalty in the **Peace of Paris** of 1783 Florida was returned to Spain.

FORT DUQUESNE. Situated at the confluence of the Allegheny and Monongahela Rivers, which join to form the Ohio River, Fort Duquesne was the main link in the chain of forts which the French built between **New France** and Louisiana in the late 1740s and early 1750s. The British disputed the French claim to the territories on which the forts were built, and had actually built a fort on the site themselves which the French demolished in 1754 to construct theirs. Forces were sent under **George Washington** and **Edward Braddock** to challenge them. Their defeats led to the onset of the **French and Indian War**. Following the defeat of the French in that conflict and their surrender of territory in North America at the **Peace of Paris** in 1763, Fort Duquesne was renamed Pittsburg.

FORT WILLIAM HENRY. There were other forts so named, but the most well known, being immortalized in James Fennimore Cooper's *The Last of the Mohicans*, was constructed in 1755 at the southern end of Lake George at the outset of the **French and Indian War**. In August 1757 it was captured by a French and Indian force. Although the French promised the English garrison a safe passage, the Indians ignored this and massacred most of them, though some escaped to **Boston**.

FOX, CHARLES JAMES (1749–1806) was the second son of Henry Fox, Lord Holland, who served as paymaster general from 1757 to 1765. The son, after being educated at Eton, Oxford and on the Grand Tour, followed in his father's footsteps by supporting the Court after his return to parliament in 1768, when he was still a minor. Thus he voted for the expulsion of **John Wilkes** from the House of Commons, and upheld the measures of **Lord North**, with whom he became personally acquainted. This laid the foundations for their later coalition. North gave him the post of commissioner of the Admiralty in 1770, and although he resigned it for personal reasons in February 1772, he was appointed as a commissioner of the Treasury in December. When he resigned in February 1774, again for personal reasons, he was still inclined to support the government. However, he soon went into opposition over the ministry's policy of coercion of the American colonies. During the **War of American Independence** he kept in touch with such colonial leaders like **Benjamin Franklin**, whom he met on a visit to Paris in late 1776 and early 1777, and **Thomas Jefferson**. Fox gravitated towards the Rockingham whigs, a process encouraged by **Edmund Burke** who assisted in Fox's conversion to the whig principles of the Rockinghamites. Thus Fox approved the motion of the Rockinghamite Dunning in 1780 that 'the influence of the Crown has increased, is increasing and ought to be diminished.' In the general election of that year Fox stood successfully as a whig candidate in Westminster, a popular constituency which he was to represent with only one break until his death. Fox was instrumental in bringing about the fall of Lord North in 1782, and when **Rockingham** formed his second ministry he became foreign secretary. When Rockingham died suddenly that summer, and **Shelburne** succeeded as prime minister, Fox resigned. In February 1783 he led the opposition to the peace terms which Shelburne had presented to the Americans, and when they were defeated in the Commons the prime minister resigned. Fox now entered into a coalition government with Lord North which has tended ever since to be castigated as a sinister, opportunist alliance. But apart from their disagreements over the American issue, which was now over, they had always been friendly. They tried to negotiate better terms for the loyalists than Shelburne had achieved but accepted the **peace of Paris** on virtually the same basis as their predecessor's preliminaries. The Fox–North coalition came to grief not on an American but an Indian issue, their provisions for the administration of India being defeated by the intervention of the king in December 1784. Fox was out of office for the next twenty years, becoming foreign secretary in 1804 on the eve of his own death. The king disliked not only his politics but his dissolute life style. Fox was a compulsive gambler, heavy drinker and notorious womanizer, whom George III held responsible for the dissoluteness of the Prince of Wales. Yet he had his passionate admirers too, who called themselves Foxites and enrolled in the Fox Club in the 1790s. These members expressed their leader's support of America by sporting buff and blue, the colors of the uniforms worn by **George Washington**'s troops.

FRANKLIN, BENJAMIN (1706–1790) was born in Boston where he served an apprenticeship as a printer, before moving to Philadelphia in 1723. He went to England in 1724 for 18 months, where he gained notoriety with his published rejoinder to William Wollaston's *Religion of Nature Delineated, A Dissertation on Liberty and Necessity, Pleasure and Pain*. He returned to **Pennsylvania**, where he set up in business as a printer. In 1729 he began to edit a newspaper, *The Pennsylvania Gazette* . His most celebrated work, *Poor Richard's Almanac*, was launched in 1732. His editorials on domestic issues, such as the 1747 piece on Polly Baker, who was prosecuted for having five illegitimate children, reached international notice. Also, his political tracts found their way in print such as *Rattlesnakes for felons*, written in 1751 as a response to the British Acts of Trade and Navigation, and in 1754, his editorial *Join or Die* which urged the unification of the colonies, to facilitate a common defense against French troops and their Indian allies.

Franklin was chosen clerk to the Pennsylvania assembly in 1736, and became public printer for the colony. The following year he was made deputy postmaster in America, becoming joint postmaster in 1753. Franklin was a moving spirit in the American Enlightenment. In 1728 he established a Junto club in Philadelphia to debate morals, politics and science. In 1731, he founded the Library Company of Philadelphia and five years later, he organized Philadelphia's first fire company. His scientific interests led him to become internationally renowned for his experiments with electricity and his invention of a heating stove. Franklin's scientific achievements were impressive enough for the British Royal Society to present him with the Copley medal in 1753. Three years later, he became a member of the London Society of Arts. Franklin wrote and published *A Proposal for Promoting Useful Knowledge* which laid the basis for the **American Philosophical Society**. He was also involved in establishing a lending library in Philadelphia, the first in the colonies. Another initiative was the establishment of the Academy of Philadelphia in 1751, the first secular college for higher education in the colonies, which was to become the University of Pennsylvania. Franklin wrote the curriculum for the new Academy.

During his second visit to Britain, Franklin made political and scientific connections by attending two clubs. The Club of Honest Whigs met once a week and included James Boswell, **Joseph Priestley** and **Richard Price**. The other was a weekly meeting of scientists, philanthropists, and explorers. He also attended the Royal Society and the Society of Arts. His work there was impressive enough for him to be awarded an honorary degree of doctor of laws from St Andrews and an Oxford doctorate of civil law.

His own religious outlook, though he had been brought up as a Presbyterian, was that of a deist. In politics he took a stance against the pacifism of the dominant Quaker party. In **King George's War** he published a tract, *Plain Truth* (1744) calling for the establishment of a militia. At the outset of the **French and Indian War** Franklin took part in the **Albany Congress** to which he presented his plan of Union. He equipped **Edward Braddock** with supplies for his disastrous expedition in 1755. The following year he took part in the coup on the assembly, which replaced pacifists with men prepared to engage Pennsylvania in the hostilities which had ravaged the colony's frontier.

In 1757 the assembly sent Franklin as its agent to London to petition the king to protest at alleged abuses of their authority by the proprietors of Pennsylvania, whom they accused of exempting themselves from taxation in the colony. His efforts were unavailing, as they were to be again in 1764 when the colony charged him with urging the British government to change Pennsylvania from a proprietary into a crown colony. Franklin thus found himself advocating an increase in the king's power in the colonies at the time when many colonists were protesting that he was abusing it by supporting arbitrary taxation. So far from adopting a radical stance he was prepared to accept office for his son William as a distributor of the stamps to be introduced into America by the **Stamp Act** of 1765. It took nimble footwork on Franklin's part to get on the colonial side of the dispute with **George III** and to earn a reputation as one of the Founding Fathers of the American Republic. He gave evidence against the Stamp Act, warning Parliament that if it tried to enforce the Act with military force, they would only succeed in starting a rebellion. His efforts to forestall military conflict failed. Franklin returned to America in 1775 ultimately serving on the committee to draft the Declaration of Independence. Franklin was instrumental in the formation of the **Articles of Confederation**, although his idea of proportional representation was voted down. He also became, in effect, the first secretary of state in which capacity he dealt with foreign affairs. He was elected as Pennsylvania's president to the state convention and drafted, unsuccessfully, the Pennsylvania declaration of rights.

The Continental Congress appointed Franklin, along with **John Adams** and Edward Rutledge, to meet with **Lord Howe** to negotiate peace terms, but the talks broke down and the Americans left. Once hostilities commenced, Franklin, Arthur Lee, and Silas Dean were appointed to the commission to France to gain French aid. In 1781, he was on the commission to negotiate peace with Great Britain. His ability to maintain friendships in Britain throughout the war probably helped to ease the conclusion of the 1783 Peace Treaty. Franklin's international reputation and respect was so great that at his death, France went into official mourning for three days.

FREE SOCIETY OF TRADERS was organized by **William Penn** in the first years of **Pennsylvania**'s establishment. Although it failed by 1685, its uniqueness lay in its membership. Shareholders of the company were made up of investors regardless of their religious affiliations. Quakers as well as Anglicans were involved in the venture. The impact of the company on early Philadelphia is still apparent in the area of Society hill, which is named after it.

FRELINGHUYSEN, THEODORE (1691– c. 1748) was born in Germany, the son of a Dutch Orthodox clergyman. After holding livings in Friesland, in 1720 he went to Raritan, **New Jersey**, at the invitation of the **Dutch** churches there. His ministry was marked by his insistence upon strict Calvinism, making him a major figure in the **Great Awakening**.

FRENCH AND INDIAN WAR is the name given in North America to the hostilities known in Europe as the Seven Years' War. It is a more appropriate name for the conflict in North America, since it broke out in 1754, two years before the opening of the European war, which lasted from 1756 to 1763. News that the French were building **Fort Duquesne** led Virginia to send a force of militiamen led by **George Washington** to attack them. They defeated a French force in the Great Meadow and then built Fort Necessity there to use as a base for an advance on Fort Duquesne. They were however obliged to surrender to superior French and Indian forces on 3 July 1754. When the British government learned of this it despatched an expedition under **General Edward Braddock** to take Fort Duquesne. It arrived in America in 1755 and after gathering supplies made its way towards the Monongahela, arriving there with nearly 1,500 men in July. On 9 July, when he was within eight miles of Fort Duquesne, Braddock was attacked by a French and Indian force, defeated and killed. His men fled, nearly a thousand being killed in the flight. The rest retreated all the way to **Philadelphia**, leaving western Pennsylvania exposed to the enemy. Campaigns against the French in other theaters went badly too. Thus an attempt to take Crown Point was unsuccessful, leading the British to fall back to the southern end of Lake George, where they built **Fort William Henry**. The campaign went badly for the British in North America for the next three years. In August 1756, when war had already broken out in Europe, the French took Oswego on Lake Ontario from them. The following year they took fort William Henry. In July 1758 General **James Abercromby** was defeated at Ticonderoga. That same month, however, British forces captured Louisbourg on **Cape Breton Island**. This marked a turning point in their fortunes. In November they finally acquired Fort Duquesne, where they built Fort Pitt, later to be known as Pittsburgh. 1759 was the 'wonderful year' which saw the success of British arms against France throughout the globe. In the Caribbean they acquired Guadeloupe. In North America they took Crown Point in August and Quebec in September. The capture of Quebec by **James Wolfe** was the supreme achievement of the French and Indian War. It led to the fall of Montreal to British and American forces in 1760. The following year they took Martinique. After the entry of Spain into the war in 1762 a force made up mostly of veterans of the campaigns in North America took Cuba, albeit at horrendous cost in lives lost, not to enemy action but to disease. The **Peace of Paris** signed in 1763 gave Cuba back to Spain in exchange for **Florida**. In compensation the French, who lost all their settlements in North America east of the Mississippi to Britain, gave Louisiana to the Spanish.

FUR TRADE. North America east of the Rocky Mountains was the natural habitat for hosts of animals whose pelts were in great demand from the European settlers of the region. Beaver fur was especially valued for making hats, which sold in Europe as well as in the colonies. Before the development of staples in the south fur was the main commodity in trans-Atlantic trade. It was supplied to the Europeans by the **Indians**, who exchanged it for European goods such as weapons, implements and, notoriously, alcohol. So great was the demand that the eastern seaboard was effectively denuded of beavers by the late 17th century, and the peltry moved west, particularly to the Great Lakes region.

G

GAGE, THOMAS (1720–1787) was born in England and educated at Westminster School, after which he obtained a commission in a foot regiment and commenced a military career. During **King George's War** he saw active service at Fontenoy and Culloden. In 1754 he accompanied **Edward Braddock** to America and was present at the general's disastrous defeat near Fort Duquesne. Unlike Braddock Gage escaped to fight another day, at Ticonderoga in 1758. After the fall of Montreal he became its military commander and at the end of the Seven Years' War he succeeded **Amherst** as commander-in-chief in North America, based in **New York**. After a brief sojourn in England in 1773 he returned to America as governor of **Massachusetts** to confront a deteriorating situation in the colony. In April 1775 he sent troops to Concord who encountered stiff resistance at Lexington and required reinforcements to accompany them back to Boston. Gage's wife, a wealthy New Jersey heiress, was sympathetic to the colonial cause. It is possible that she tipped off the militiamen about her husband's dispatch of troops to Concord. Following the pyrrhic victory at Bunker Hill Gage returned to England.

GASPEE INCIDENT took place in June 1772. The *Gaspee* was a schooner operated by the Customs in **Rhode Island**. Its captain had become notorious for his zeal in enforcing the **Navigation Acts**. When it ran aground on a sandbank some of those who regarded themselves as his victims went aboard, made him and his crew go ashore, and burned the boat to the waterline. The captain got no support, being court martialled for losing the vessel and tried for seizing ships arbitrarily, of which he was found guilty. In 1773 a royal commission was set up to enquire into the affair, with a view to bringing the perpetrators to justice, but nobody was ever brought to trial.

GALLOWAY, JOSEPH (1731–1803) was the son of a wealthy landowner in **Pennsylvania** and **Maryland**, where he was born. He became a successful lawyer in Philadelphia, and was returned to the Pennsylvania assembly in 1756. Following his support for **Benjamin Franklin**'s abortive mission to England to try to transform Pennsylvania from a proprietary to a Crown colony Galloway failed to gain re-election in 1764. His anti-proprietary stance had brought him into public dispute with **John Dickinson**, a prominent supporter of the proprietors. Galloway defeated Dickinson in the 1765 elections to the assembly, of which he became speaker from 1766 to 1775. As a delegate to the first continental congress he advocated a Plan of Union which would have set up a Grand Council to represent all the colonies, to which the king would appoint a President General. This body would be responsible for internal colonial affairs but would join with the British parliament to regulate imperial concerns. When the congress rejected his plan Galloway became disillusioned with the colonial cause. He declined an invitation to sit in the second continental congress and published *A candid examination of the mutual claims of Great Britain and the colonies*. In December 1776 he enlisted with the British army and served under General **Howe** as Civil Administrator of Philadelphia from 1777 to 1778. When **Washington** retook the city Galloway fled, first to New York then to England. There he published *Letters to a Nobleman on the conduct of the War in the Middle Colonies* (1779), which was critical of the Howe brothers. He also published *Political Reflections on the Rise and Progress of the American Rebellion* (1780). Meanwhile his property in the USA had been confiscated, he was refused permission to return to Pennsylvania, and spent the rest of his life in England.

GATES, SIR THOMAS (d. 1632) was knighted in 1596 during active service as a soldier in Spain. He also served in the Netherlands before being commissioned to go to **Virginia** in 1609. En route he was shipwrecked in a violent storm – which possibly inspired Shakespeare's play *The Tempest* – on **Bermuda**, along with Sir George Somers. After staying there for several months Gates succeeded in reaching Virginia in 1610. There he found the settlers in Jamestown determined to quit the colony, and even to burn the town. He persuaded them not to destroy the settlement but agreed to leave with them. As they sailed down the James River, however, they encountered **Lord de la Warr** arriving with reinforcements and supplies from England. Gates returned with them to Jamestown. De la Warr sent him to England to persuade the Virginia Company to send further supplies and settlers. Gates successfully pleaded the case for continuing to support the colony and returned to it in 1611, when he succeeded **Sir Thomas Dale** as governor. He continued the martial law implemented by his predecessors, and also extended the settlement to the falls of the James River, where he founded Henrico. Gates returned to England in 1614 intending to return to Virginia, but never did.

GEORGE I (1660–1727) succeeded **Queen Anne** as monarch of Great Britain in 1714, even though many others had a stronger hereditary claim. Thanks to the Act of Settlement of 1701 they were overlooked because they were Catholics. The succession was placed in the Protestant house of Hanover of which, as elector of Hanover, George was the head. Among the Catholic claimants disbarred by the Act was the head of the exiled house of Stuart, James Edward, the son of **James II**. His supporters, known as Jacobites, styled him James III, while Hanoverians called him the Pretender. In 1715 Jacobites fomented a rebellion against George I which was not suppressed until 1716. Religion also played a part in the restoration of **Lord Baltimore** to the proprietorship of Maryland in 1715. The **Calvert** family had been deprived of succession largely because they were Catholics. Their conversion to Anglicanism helped them to regain the colony. In 1717 George issued a Proclamation offering pardons to pirates who gave themselves up. Many based in the Bahamas took advantage of the offer. This brought an end to the classic age of piracy which had done much to add a disruptive, if colorful, element to colonial life. In 1718 the king gave his assent to an Act of parliament allowing judges to sentence felons to transportation rather than to death. Previously this alternative to capital punishment could only be granted by the crown exercising the prerogative of mercy. The result of delegating the pre-rogative to judges was a massive increase in the number of convicts transported to the colonies, especially to the West Indies and the southern mainland. In 1719 George took the Carolinas out of the hands of their proprietors, appointing governors to **North and South Carolina**. This paved the way for them to become Crown colonies. Speculation in the stock of the South Sea Company, whose main commercial activity was trade with Spanish colonies, led to its price on the exchange to soar rapidly in 1720, then to collapse, resulting in the South Sea Bubble. The regime survived the crisis largely thanks to the financial acumen of Sir Robert Walpole, who began his career as the longest serving British prime minister. Under him administration of colonial affairs shifted from the **Board of Trade** to the principal secretary of state, the **duke of Newcastle**.

GEORGE II (1683–1760) succeeded his father **George I** in 1727 as king of Great Britain. Sir Robert Walpole survived an immediate attempt to dislodge him to remain as prime minister until 1742. Despite his presiding over the classic period of so-called 'salutary neglect' of the colonies, nevertheless there were some developments in colonial affairs. In 1729 the propri-etors of **North and South Carolina** finally resigned their rights of government to the king, making them Crown colonies. In 1732 the king granted a royal charter to the trustees of **Georgia**. Further to regulate colonial commerce, George gave the royal assent to the Hat Act in the same year and to the Molasses Act in 1733. The first prohibited the colonies from manufac-turing beaver hats, requiring the pelts to be sent to England. The second placed a heavy duty on sugars bought in the French islands e.g. Guadeloupe and Martinique, in order to protect the British planters in the West Indies. Another colonial staple, tobacco, was involved in Walpole's abortive Excise Scheme of 1733, which, had it succeeded, would have lifted the import duties on the plant, requiring importers to store it in bonded warehouses. When it was brought out of them it would have paid an excise duty instead. Between 1728 and 1735, three dockyards were built in the British West Indies: English harbor on Antigua; Port Antonio and Port Royal on Jamaica. As a result of friction between Britain and Spain in the West Indies and the southern mainland colonies George declared war on Spain in 1739. In 1740 he sided with Austria against Prussia in the War of the Austrian Succession. These wars are collectively called **King George's War**. He fought in person at the battle of Dettingen in 1743, the last British king to lead troops into action. France declared war on Britain the following year. This led to the Jacobite rebellion of 1745, when the rebels succeeded in taking Edinburgh and got within a day's march of London before being forced back to Scotland, where they were defeated at the battle of Culloden in 1746. The war also led to hostilities in North America which culminated in the taking of Louisbourg in 1745. This was handed back to the French in the treaty of Aix-la-Chapelle which ended the war in 1748. In 1749 George granted a charter to the Ohio Company giving it rights over 500,000 acres in the Ohio River Valley, which was claimed by France. The king gave the royal assent to the Iron Act in 1750, restricting the production of iron in the colonies, and to the Currency Act in 1751 which forbade Massachusetts from issuing paper money. Georgia became a Crown colony in 1752. Friction on the frontier led to the **French and Indian War** in 1754. George lived to see the 'wonderful year' of 1759, when his forces were triumphant on three continents. He died in 1760, and was succeeded by his grandson George III, his eldest son Frederick, who gave his name to many colonial towns, having died in 1751.

GEORGE III (1738–1820) succeeded his grandfather **George II** as King of Great Britain and Elector of Hanover in 1760. He earned the resentment of the Whigs who had been ruling Britain since the accession of the house of Hanover in 1714 by dismissing the Whig prime minister, the **duke of Newcastle**, in 1762 and replacing him with his own tutor, the **earl of Bute**. Bute took over the negotiations which led to the peace of Paris in 1763, ending the **French and Indian War**. The king was accused of making unnecessary concessions to the French, throwing away the fruits of glorious victories. Among his many critics the most outspoken was **John Wilkes**, who attacked the king's speech to parliament introducing the terms of the peace in the forty-fifth number of his paper *The North Briton*. Bute was so unnerved by the chorus of criticism that he resigned in April 1763. The king appointed **George Grenville** as Bute's successor. In October 1763 George III responded to the news of the outbreak of **Pontiac's war** by issuing a **Proclamation**. This restricted settlements to the crest of the Appalachians. The Proclamation also created four new British colonies; East and West Florida; Grenada and Quebec. This use of the royal prerogative encouraged colonists who disputed the sovereignty of the king in parliament over them to argue that there were in fact two distinct constitutions. One was the constitution of Great Britain, over which the king and parliament were indeed sovereign. The other was the constitution of the British empire, with the Crown at its head but with the colonies subordinate to it and not to parliament. George showed that he did not share this assumption when he agreed with Grenville on the need to make the American colonies pay some contribution to the national debt, which had soared during the war. 'I am fighting the battle of the legislature' he was to observe later, after the rift occurred. He accordingly gave his assent to the **Sugar** and **Stamp Acts.** Grenville suspected that Bute continued to influence the king's decisions, while George was offended by the prime minister's handling of the Regency crisis of 1765. A regency seemed to be necessary to take over some of the duties of the king when he succumbed for the first time to the effects of porphyria, a disease which was to recur in 1788, and then at intervals until George finally did require a Regency from 1810 until his death. In 1765 the attack was short lived, but before it ended Grenville incurred the king's wrath by excluding his mother, the Queen dowager, from those named as regents in the bill presented to parliament. Outraged at the prime minister's inept behavior George dismissed him.

Instead of asking Bute to suggest a successor George sought advice from his uncle the duke of Cumberland. Although this indicated that his favorite's influence was diminishing, Bute was still held to be a secret adviser 'behind the curtain' for many years. Cumberland advised his nephew to bring back the Whigs who had supported the duke of Newcastle and who were now led by the **marquis of Rockingham**. The short lived Rockingham ministry repealed the **Stamp Act** and passed the **Declaratory Act**. George was unhappy with this decision. He agreed that something had to be done in response to agitation against the Stamp Act, which as it stood was unenforceable. But he thought amendments to it were preferable to repeal, which was a hostage to fortune. He later regretted acceding to the repeal, claiming it was the origin of all his problems with the American colonies. As long as Rockingham was in power, though, he felt obliged to give him his full backing and did not oppose repeal. The death of Cumberland, however, left Rockingham without a major patron at Court, and in 1766 George replaced him with **William Pitt**, whom he ennobled as earl of Chatham. Chatham's mental state, however, prevented him from being an effective prime minister, and he resigned in 1768. Meanwhile the burden of conducting the ministry's affairs fell to the **duke of Grafton**, who became effective premier before formally replacing Chatham in 1768. The decision to place duties on American imports in 1767 was taken by the chancellor of the exchequer **Charles Townshend**. The **Townshend duties** provoked further demonstrations in the colonies until in 1769 the Grafton ministry agreed to repeal all of them except those on tea. When **Lord North** succeeded Grafton as prime minister in 1770 he implemented the repeal.

This brought a brief period of quiet in the disputes with the colonies. George expressed indignation whenever the peace was disturbed, as in the **Gaspee incident** of June 1772. And when news reached him of the **Boston Tea Party** he gave Lord North his full backing in the passage of the **Coercive Acts.** When he learned in November 1774 that the colonies had elected the first Continental Congress he observed that 'blows must decide whether they are to be subject to this country or independent'. That was a remarkably shrewd observation to make before actual fighting broke out in April 1775. But then George usually had a clear view of the issues at stake. Not for him the fudging of the Rockinghamites, admitting that the king in parliament had the right to legislate for the colonies but urging that it should never be exercised. To the king a right was not worth claiming unless it were exercised. George was more hawkish too than his prime minister. North appeared timid to him, making gestures of conciliation to the colonies. When the second continental congress sent him the Olive Branch Petition in 1775 George rejected it, and instead on 23 August proclaimed the colonies to be 'in open and avowed rebellion', adding 'the die is now cast. The colonies must either submit or triumph'. It became clear that the king was not part of the solution but the main problem for the Americans. **Thomas Paine** expressed the feelings of many when he called George 'the royal brute' in *Common Sense*. This prepared the ground for the Declaration of Independence, which placed the blame for the rupture squarely on the king's shoulders. No fewer than 18 charges were levelled against him to demonstrate that he had 'in direct object an absolute tyranny over these states'. Today these charges tend to be dismissed as propaganda. George is generally regarded as a constitutional monarch who saw his role as defending the sovereignty of parliament against that of the people. Yet if he did not in any sense act tyrannically then the Declaration was at best based on an unfortunate misunderstanding and at worst on a deliberate lie. In fact to levy taxes on a people who were not represented in the legislature which taxed them was to say the least arbitrary. Though this was perceived as tyranny by the colonists George does not appear to have understood their point of view at all. His thinking was clear because it was shallow. George was determined to impose his will on them. Even when all was lost at Yorktown he did not immediately come to terms with it. When North offered his resignation he told him that he would lose his confidence if he did. The king was as good as his word, for North forfeited his support when he nevertheless resigned in 1782. George was so shaken that he even penned an abdication speech, but then thought better of it. He did eventually accept the inevitable, and recognized the independence of the United States. When **John Adams** presented his credentials as the first American ambassador to the Court of St James in 1785 the king received him with refreshing candor saying 'I was the last to consent to the separation'; 'but the separation having been made, and having become inevitable, I have always said, as I say now, that I would be the first to meet the friendship of the United States as an independent power.'

GEORGIA came into existence as a result of the philanthropic efforts of **James Oglethorpe**, the earl of Egmont and others who sought to establish a settlement in America where 'worthy poor' could be given an opportunity to make a fresh start in life. They had in mind not only poor people in general but insolvent debtors languishing in jail in particular. In 1732 they obtained a charter from **George II** to establish a Trust to pay off the debts of such prisoners in return for their transportation to the new colony. There they were provided with 50 acres of land and sufficient resources to exploit them for one year, after which they were expected to be self-sufficient. The colony was granted to Oglethorpe, Egmont and 19 others for 21 years, when it was to be taken over by the Crown. Defense against Spanish Florida to the south was a major incentive in the king's agreeing to the scheme, and Oglethorpe, an army officer, went out to

Georgia with the first party of settlers in 1733 to defend it. When war broke out with Spain in 1739 this became a vital role. Oglethorpe led a raid against Florida in 1741, and had to fight off a reprisal raid in 1742. The Trustees had intended to keep the colony free of **slaves**, more out of fear of their threat to social stability than through any qualms about the morality of slavery. But this led to difficulties in developing the economy of Georgia, which had to compete with the rice growing region of neighboring **South Carolina**, which relied on slave labor. Pressure from the settlers forced the trustees to rescind the ban in 1751, after which the colony began to prosper. In 1754 it duly became a crown colony. Many colonists were attracted to Georgia by its practice of religious toleration. Oglethorpe himself took Austrian Lutherans from Salzburg, while Moravians went there with their leader Count Zinzendorf, though as pacifists they went to Quaker dominated **Pennsylvania** when war with Spain broke out in 1739. The religious revival known as the **Great Awakening** received a boost from the visits to Georgia of **George Whitefield**. During the **War of American Independence** Georgia played a key role in the British southern strategy of 1778–1779, when **Sir Henry Clinton** took it and held Savannah as a base from which to launch campaigns against South Carolina.

GERMAIN, GEORGE SACKVILLE (1716–1785) was the younger son of the first duke of Dorset and baptized with his father's name of Sackville. After attending Westminster school and Trinity College Dublin he commenced a military career, obtaining a commission as captain in 1737. He rose rapidly in the ranks during **King George's War**, becoming aide-de-camp to the king in 1743 to the end of the war in 1748 serving in Scotland as a colonel from 1746 to 1748. Meanwhile he had also entered politics, being elected a member of parliament for various boroughs from 1740 to 1782. At the outbreak of the **French and Indian War** he was major general and lieutenant general of the Ordnance. In 1758 he became commander of the British forces in Europe on the unexpected death of the duke of Marlborough. The commander-in-chief of the allies in the European theater was Prince Ferdinand of Brunswick, who was to accuse Sackville of disobeying orders at the battle of Minden in August 1759. Sackville went back to England in disgrace, ignominiously discharged from all his offices by the king. Although the court martial he demanded virtually acquitted him he was ever after known as 'the coward of Minden'.

Sackville remained in disgrace until 1765 when he was appointed to the lucrative post of vice-treasurer of Ireland by the **marquis of Rockingham**. When Elizabeth Germain left him a fortune in 1770 provided he adopted her name he did so. It was as George Germain that he succeeded the **earl of Dartmouth** to the secretaryship of state for the American colonies in 1775. As the minister responsible above all for the conduct of military affairs in the **War of American Independence** Germain obtained a reputation for being the leading hawk in the cabinet of **Lord North**. He even maintained that Britain should carry on the conflict after Yorktown, insisting that 'we can never continue to exist as a great or powerful nation after we have lost or renounced the sovereignty of America'. His was a very isolated voice in 1782, when he left office along with North. By way of compensation he was elevated to the peerage as Viscount Sackville.

GERMANTOWN was originally a 25,000 acre tract of land northwest of Philadelphia purchased by a German agent for the Frankfurt Company, Daniel Pastorious. In 1686, Pastorious arrived with his fellow German pietists along with some Quakers from Germany to settle the area. Germantown became known for its fine linen production. It remained a predominantly German speaking 'urban village' into the 18th century, though the growth of Philadelphia threatened to absorb it into the suburb it became in the 19th century.

GLORIOUS REVOLUTION. The Revolution of 1688 in Britain, which overthrew **James II** of England and VII of Scotland, had repercussions in the American colonies which are generally referred to as the Glorious Revolution in America. James alienated his British subjects by trying to empower his fellow Catholics, which was seen as a threat not only to Protestants but also to liberty, since in pursuing his aim he strengthened the power of the Crown at the expense of the checks on royal authority provided by parliament and statute law. In America too he was seen as acting arbitrarily in pursuit of his goals. Three areas of the American colonies were actively involved: **New England**; **New York**; **and Maryland**. New England had experienced the impact of James's policies even before he became king, when as duke of York he persuaded his brother **Charles II** to revoke the charter of **Massachusetts** in 1684. After he succeeded to the Crown in 1685 James devised a scheme to incorporate all the colonies in the area – **Connecticut, New Hampshire and Rhode Island** as well as the Bay colony – into the **Dominion and Territory of New England**. In 1686 this scheme was implemented when **Sir Edmund Andros** was appointed as governor of the Dominion. As in England, where James ruled without parliament after 1685, Andros dispensed with representative assemblies. He raised taxes by decree. He also introduced religious toleration into New England, where previously it had only been a reality in Rhode Island. Thus the Congregational churches of Connecticut and Massachusetts were effectively disestablished.

A major aim of the Dominion was defense against the French. When they attacked Indians friendly to the English in the Mohawk river valley in 1687 James decided to extend the Dominion to include New York and **New Jersey**. Andros remained governor of the whole, while **Francis Nicholson** became his deputy in New York and New Jersey. The Dominion of New England demonstrated that James II sought to increase the power of the Crown as well as to empower Catholics, since its government was arbitrary, while there were few Catholics to favor. Although this did not prevent the king's opponents of accusing Andros and Nicholson of favoring 'papists' as they were pejoratively called, there was little substance in the charges when compared with the prevailing polity in Maryland, where the proprietor, **Lord Baltimore**, was a Catholic. His deputy, William Joseph, was also a Catholic, and ruled the colony with a Council dominated by his co-religionists, even though there were four times as many Protestants as Catholics in Maryland. When in January 1689 the Council ordered the militia to hand in their arms Protestants were convinced it was to disarm them. They formed a Protestant Association led by **John Coode** to resist Lord Baltimore's appointees in the colony. On 16 July 1689 they apprehended Joseph and convened an assembly. Coode took over the government of Maryland, which became a crown colony when **William III** deprived Baltimore of his proprietorship.

Meanwhile Andros had been seized by insurgents in **Boston** on 18 April, who set up a Council of Safety. The council handled Massachusetts affairs for a couple of months until confirmation came from England of the new regime of William and Mary. On May 22, the council, led by **Simon Bradstreet**, voted to return the colony to its former government before the Dominion of New England subsumed it. The Dominion had collapsed. This was a signal for the other New England colonies incorporated in it to assert their independence, reinstating their old charters. Although the **Puritans** in Massachusetts also hoped to regain the charter granted to the colony in 1629, many of those who took part in the rebellion against the Dominion did not want the return of the rule of the 'saints'. They welcomed the new charter granted by William III in 1691. This gave the right to vote for the General Court to the freemen at large, where before it had been restricted to full members of the Congregational church. It also made Massachusetts a crown colony, for where before the governor had been elected now he was to be appointed by the king.

While there was no question that the king could appoint the governors of New York and New Jersey, there was about whom he would appoint in the aftermath of the overthrow of the Dominion of New England. Francis Nicholson, Andros's deputy, continued to act as the lieutenant governor after learning that James II had been overthrown. Thus he dismissed Catholic officials and convened a general convention to take stock of the situation. His right to take these steps was challenged by **Jacob Leisler**, who argued that the government of the colony had been dissolved with the king's downfall. When Leisler seized control of the fort Nicholson decided to go to England, leaving him in effective charge of New York City. In December a letter arrived from the king addressed to Nicholson or 'in his absence to such as … take care for the preservation of the peace'. Leisler presumed that he fulfilled those requirements and assumed the title of lieutenant governor. William III, however, refused to recognize him as such, and appointed Henry Sloughter as governor of New York in 1690. It was not until March 1691 that Sloughter arrived in New York, whereupon he arrested Leisler who was tried for treason and executed on 17 May 1691.

Where the revolutions in Maryland and New England were relatively simple replacements of one regime by another, clearly events in New York were more complex. The causes are to be found in the more diverse ethnic and religious elements in the colony. The fact that it had been **Dutch** before it became English, and even experienced a reversal of fortunes in 1673 when New Netherland was temporarily restored, goes far to explain them. Leisler, although German himself, had married a Dutch wife and appealed to those elements which had enjoyed temporary restoration of status during the Dutch reconquest. The English, however, wanted to restore the situation which had existed before the Dominion of New England, when they had wrested from James the right to be represented in an assembly. These tensions between Leislerians and anti-Leislerians were to polarize politics in the colony long after Leisler himself had been executed.

GORGES, SIR FERDINANDO (1568–1647) was born in England and pursued a military career, serving France, where he was knighted in 1591, and the Low Countries. From 1596 to 1629 he was commander of the fort in Plymouth, Devon, except for the years 1599 to 1603 when as a client of the earl of Essex he was implicated in Essex's rebellion. Although he turned Queen's evidence against the earl he spent a spell in prison until he was pardoned in 1601. On the accession of **James I** he was reinstated as commander in Plymouth. In 1605 he was presented with three Indians brought from America by Captain George Waymouth. This aroused his interest in colonization. Gorges campaigned for the charter granted to the Virginia Company in 1606. He became involved in the Plymouth Company set up under the charter and encouraged expeditions to New England to settle a colony there. When these failed and the Company was wound up in 1619 he helped set up the Council for New England, to which the king in 1620 granted the region between the Delaware Bay and Newfoundland. In 1622 Gorges and John Mason were allotted the area which became Maine and **New Hampshire**. Gorges, as governor general, went out for a few months to establish a settlement at Wessagusset, which was later renamed Weymouth. In 1635 the Council for New England was dissolved and Gorges was appointed as governor-general of New England by Charles I. The grandiloquent title was also an empty one as he did not go to America. Instead he sent a cousin Thomas Gorges as governor of Maine after receiving a charter for the colony in 1639. Even this failed, as Thomas returned to England in 1643 and eventually Maine merged with Massachusetts.

GORTON, SAMUEL (1593–1677) was born in Gorton Lancashire and moved to London where he worked as a clothier. He also acquired heretical views, for instance doubting the reality of heaven and hell. In view of this it seems odd that he chose to go to New England in 1636 where he settled in Plymouth. He was banished from the colony for his defiance of its jurisdiction. He then went to **Rhode Island**, where he fell foul of **William Coddington** in Portsmouth and **Roger Williams** in Providence. He was clearly a difficult man to get on with, as the Indians found when he settled among them at Shawomet. They claimed that he had cheated them of their lands. Gorton was summoned to Boston and when he defied the summons he was forcibly transported there. Gorton was sentenced to a few months' hard labor in 1644. After his release he went to England to complain to the Court about his treatment by the authorities of Massachusetts. The court instructed them to stop molesting him and his fellow settlers at Shawomet. On his return there in 1648 he renamed it Warwick after the earl of Warwick who had taken his side against Massachusetts.

GRAFTON, HENRY FITZROY, THIRD DUKE OF (1735–1811) inherited his title on the death of his grandfather, the second duke, in 1756, his uncle, the duke's elder son, and his father, a younger son, having both died in the 1740s. Shortly after becoming a peer he was appointed as a lord of the bedchamber to the Prince of Wales, the future **George III**. Although Grafton was an adherent of the **duke of Newcastle**, his chief political mentor was **William Pitt**. Thus he opposed the terms of the **peace of Paris** as a betrayal of British victories achieved when Pitt was prime minister. When **Rockingham** formed his first administration in 1765 Grafton became secretary of state, on condition that Pitt should be encouraged to join the ministry. The consequent negotiations broke down, upon which Grafton resigned. Pitt, now earl of Chatham, appointed Grafton as first lord of the treasury when he succeeded Rockingham as prime minister. Chatham's frequent absences from London through illness obliged Grafton to take on his duties as prime minister. He thus had to deal with the objections of **New York** to the Mutiny Bill and the general discontent in the colonies caused by the **Townshend duties**. On Townshend's death in 1767 Grafton appointed **Lord North** to the vacant chancellorship of the exchequer. Chatham's resignation in October 1768 led the king to formally appoint Grafton as prime minister. He recognized the seriousness of the deteriorating relations with the colonies by creating the post of colonial secretary, appointing **Lord Hillsborough** to it. The return of **John Wilkes** to parliament at the general election of 1768 precipitated a political crisis which reflected badly on Grafton. His reputation was also impugned by savage anonymous attacks upon him in the *Letters of Junius*. The continuing resistance in the colonies to the Townshend duties led the cabinet to discuss their repeal in May 1769. It was resolved to drop all except the duty on tea, a resolution to retain that being passed by five votes to four. Grafton voted against the resolution. In January 1770 he resigned from the ministry, having arranged for Lord North to succeed him as prime minister. Out of office Grafton supported North until 1775, when he opposed his colonial policies. He became lord privy seal in the second Rockingham administration, holding the post until 1783.

GREAT AWAKENING is the title given by most historians to the religious revivals which occurred in the colonies in the 1730s and 1740s. It began in New England and the Middle Colonies where the ministries of **Jonathan Edwards** and **William Tennent** stressed the necessity for a 'new birth' and witnessed many conversions. It was co-ordinated and galvanized by the barnstorming tours through the colonies of **George Whitefield** following his first arrival in **Georgia** in 1739. In 1742 Jonathan Dickson observed 'He must be a stranger in Israel who has not heard of the uncommon religious appearances in the several parts of this land'. It was not only a uniting phenomenon, creating a sense of American identity which superseded the colonial, but also a force for disunity, dividing religious denominations. Thus the Congregationalists split between the 'new lights' who insisted on strict Calvinism, and the 'old lights' whom they accused of Arminianism. A similar division occurred between the 'old' and 'new' sides in the Presbyterian churches.

GRENVILLE, GEORGE (1712–1770) was educated at Eton, Christ Church Oxford and the Inner Temple, where he commenced a legal career, being called to the bar in 1735. Instead of continuing to practice law, however, he became a politician, entering parliament in 1741 as MP for Buckingham. He owed his seat to his maternal uncle Richard Temple, Viscount Cobham, a leading light in the opposition to **Sir Robert Walpole**, whose protégés were known as 'Cobham's cubs'. In 1744 he entered the ministry as a lord of the admiralty and became a lord of the treasury in 1747. On the death of **Henry Pelham** in 1754 Grenville was made treasurer of the navy. The following year he and **William Pitt**, another of Cobham's cubs, were dismissed for opposing what they perceived to be the pro-Hanoverian policies of Pelham's successor as prime minister, **the duke of Newcastle**. When Pitt replaced Newcastle and formed a government headed nominally by the duke of Devonshire, Grenville regained the treasurership of the navy, a post he retained when Pitt and Newcastle combined at the head of the ministry in 1757. He did not resign when Pitt left office in 1762, a sign that their political ties had weakened. Pitt resented Grenville's remaining in the ministry. When **Bute** became prime minister Grenville was promoted to a secretaryship of state. His lukewarm support of the terms of the **peace of Paris**, however, led to him being demoted to the first lordship of the admiralty. Upon Bute's resignation he succeeded him as prime minister. The king's reluctance to part with Bute and his continued reliance on his favorite's private advice led Grenville to protest that he should have the support of the Crown. Grenville bore the brunt of the criticisms of general warrants levelled at his ministry for their use in the case of **John Wilkes**. He weathered that storm and proceeded to play a prominent part in colonial affairs with his measures to raise a revenue in America, sometimes anachronistically called 'the Grenville programme'. The first of these was the **Sugar Act** of 1764. When introducing it he announced that he would be imposing stamp duties on the colonies the following year. The **Stamp Act** was duly passed in 1765. By then **George III** had wearied of Grenville's pitiless verbosity and was determined to get rid of him. The prime minister's objection to the queen dowager being named in a Regency bill stiffened his determination. There was some delay in dismissing him until the duke of Cumberland persuaded the king to replace him with the **marquis of Rockingham**. In opposition Grenville denounced the repeal of the Stamp Act, encouraged **Townshend** to levy the duties associated with his name, and withdrew from the House of Commons when their partial repeal was moved in 1770. Shortly afterwards he died.

H

HAKLUYT, RICHARD (?1552–1616) was educated at Westminster School and Christ Church, Oxford, where he became a fellow, or 'student' as fellows are called in that college. He became famous as a geographer whose work *Divers Voyages touching the Discovery of America*, published in 1582, got him noticed by Lord Howard of Effingham, then Lord Admiral. Hakluyt held the posts of chaplain to the English ambassador to France, rector of a living in Suffolk, prebendary and archdeacon of Westminster. His main interests, however, lay in the navigations to the new world. An investor in the **Virginia Company** he was involved in petitioning for the new colony. His principal contribution to English colonization in America was his *Discourse of Western Planting* of 1584, subtitled 'a brief collection of certain reasons to induce her Majesty and the state to take in hand the western voyage and the planting there'. This is traditionally regarded as the classic statement of the advantages of colonization. Yet it has curiously little to say about religious motivation, stressing the economic gains to be obtained, such as giving employment in the colonies to unemployed men at home. It also pointed out the prospect of stopping Philip II of Spain from effectively claiming more territory in America. Elizabeth in fact paid little heed to his advice, colonizing activities in her reign being the work of private individuals rather than of the state. Hakluyt's most famous work was his *Principall Navigations voyages traffiques and discoveries of the English nation* published in 1589, a second edition, in three volumes, appearing between 1598 and 1600.

HALF-WAY COVENANT. In order to hold public office in colonial **Massachusetts** it was necessary to be a full member of the Independent (**congregational**) Church. This in turn required a test of 'saving faith' on the part of aspirants for membership, whereby they became 'visible saints'. Only these were admitted to communion in the Bay colony. By the second generation there was a fall in the numbers applying to be church members. Some **Puritan** preachers attributed this to a declension from the spiritual values of the original settlers. It led to vacancies in public offices, and in 1648 the **Cambridge Platform** allowed lesser offices such as constables and jurors to be held without the requirement of full church membership. By 1662 the numbers of full church members had fallen even more. There was concern among those who did not enjoy such membership that they could not even have their children baptized. A special synod was convened to address this question. It decided that the adult children of full members could have their own children baptized even if they themselves were not 'visible saints'. It took time for this 'half-way covenant' to become generally acceptable in the Bay colony.

HALIFAX, GEORGE MONTAGU DUNK SECOND EARL OF (1716–1771) succeeded to the earldom on the death of his father in 1739. He sided with the opposition to **Sir Robert Walpole** in the House of Lords, and snubbed the former prime minister when he entered the upper chamber as earl of Orford after his fall from power in 1742. Halifax was appointed President of the **Board of Trade** in 1748, a post he held until 1761, his tenure of it broken only briefly between June 1756 and October 1757. He undertook to retrieve for the Board its control over colonial affairs which it had lost since its creation in 1696. One way was to enhance the post of President by making it a cabinet office, but although he was supported by the **duke of Newcastle** the king, **George II**, refused to give it that distinction until 1757. Halifax still contrived to enhance the Board's authority, ensuring for instance that it nominated colonial governors in Crown colonies. He advocated a separate secretaryship of state for the colonies, which the king also resisted, leading to Halifax resigning temporarily from the Board in 1756. Although he was appointed to the cabinet on his return to office the following year a secretariat for the colonies had to wait until 1767. Halifax's association with the colonies was manifest when the principal town in **Nova Scotia** was named after him.

In 1761 he moved from the Board of Trade to become lord lieutenant of Ireland, a post he held until September 1762 when he was made secretary of state. As secretary he had to deal with the issue of general warrants raised by the case of **John Wilkes**. He supported the **Stamp Act** and opposed its repeal, stating that 'it is not the Stamp Act that is opposed but the authority of this legislature'. On **Lord North**'s becoming prime minister in 1770 Halifax was made lord privy seal, and the following year secretary of state. Shortly after his appointment he died.

HAMILTON, ALEXANDER (1757–1804) attended King's College (Columbia University) in 1773 and was very active in the lead up to the **War of American Independence**, writing pamphlets between the period of 1774–1775. During the war, his republican sentiments were articulated in his work on Republicanism and signing himself as Publius. Hamilton praised those who served for the common good and criticized the revolutionary congressmen for not rising to greatness. He joined the army in 1776 and became **Washington**'s secretary and aide-de-camp. After the war, Hamilton urged a strong central government politically and especially economically. His *Continental Letters*, 1781–1784, lay out the argument for a strong fiscal government. He championed the political central control of Congress from its inception and was vindicated in later debates during the creation of the Constitution.

HAMILTON, ANDREW (d. 1703) was born in Scotland, and moved to **New Jersey** where he became deputy governor 1692 to 1697. He then moved to **Pennsylvania**, where he was deputy governor 1701–1703. From 1692 to 1703 he was deputy postmaster general for the colonies, in which post he achieved fame by establishing the colonial postal system.

HAMILTON, ANDREW (c. 1676–1741) was born in Scotland and went to **Virginia** around 1698, where he set up as a lawyer. He moved his legal practice to **Maryland** in 1708. Hamilton attracted the notice of **William Penn**, who was in dispute with **Lord Baltimore** over the border between Maryland and **Pennsylvania.** Penn persuaded him to go to Gray's Inn where he was called to the bar in 1713. He returned to America, settling in Philadelphia. He became attorney general of Pennsylvania in 1717 and a member of the colony's council in 1720. Hamilton went to London in 1725 to assist the Penn family in its dispute with Baltimore. Back in Pennsylvania by 1727 he served as recorder and a member of the colony's assembly as well as that of the Lower Counties (**Delaware**). He became prominent in colonial North America by his defense of **John Peter Zenger** in his dispute with **William Cosby** the governor of **New York**. Following his triumphal return to Philadelphia after his success in the Zenger case Hamilton became a judge of the vice-admiralty court there in 1737.

HANCOCK, JOHN (1737–1793) was adopted by his uncle Thomas at the age of seven. He inherited not only his uncle's wealth, but his love of extravagant living. The family wealth was derived from canny mercantile investments resulting in the 'House of Hancock.' The Hancocks became the major suppliers to England in the **French and Indian war**. After finishing at **Harvard** in 1754, John spent time in London, Amsterdam, and Hamburg establishing ties with Hancock agents, paying and collecting debts. He also established contacts with the British Board of Ordnance and signed a contract making the House of Hancock primary American suppliers for the British contractor for all troop supplies in Nova Scotia. Although described by his uncle in his letters of introduction as a 'sober, modest sound gentleman' the young Hancock did not neglect London's social events dressed in the latest fashions. The cost of his visit resulted in a rebuke by his uncle. Hancock returned to Boston in the fall of 1761 and two years later became a full partner in the House of Hancock. His elevation coincided with the end of the Seven Years' War and the opening up of the Canadian territory. With increased migration to the new territory, local property values dropped. One of Hancock's first acts as a partner was to buy as much property as possible in **Massachusetts** and **Connecticut**. He also capitalized on shortages caused by the war such as whale oil. In 1764, with the death of his uncle, the young Hancock became a merchant king at the age of 27. Although the end of the war provided some economic opportunities, mostly it had the effect of depressing commerce, and the Hancock enterprise was not immune to it. The timing of the **Stamp Act** with the post war economic stagnation was enough to cause colonial merchants to react against it. While the earlier molasses duties enacted by Parliament did not alienate them, the Stamp Act undoubtedly did. Hancock wrote to his agent in London asking him to lobby on his behalf against the passage of the Stamp Act saying that it would ultimately harm Great Britain because the colonies would not be able to carry on trade with such a burden. In reality, Hancock and his colonial peers suspected ulterior motives on the part of the British government. That fear was reinforced when the **Quartering Act** was passed forcing colonists to accommodate British troops. Still, Hancock thought that he, as a member of the merchant elite, could influence parliamentary action against the tax, but to no avail. Hancock's refusal to react as violently as other merchants cost him the election to the lower house in favor of **James Otis** and **Samuel Adams**. News of the repeal of the Stamp Act was greeted with relief only to be replaced with outrage at the news of the **Declaratory Act**. While Hancock maintained a low profile over the Stamp Act, he went into action against its successor calling for a partial boycott of British luxury goods and urging colonists to produce their own goods such as clothing and cheeses. This was in direct opposition to English law. To make his position clear, Hancock refused to allow English customs commissioners to board his ships. His popularity was further enhanced when, after the **Boston Tea Party**, he was charged with high treason and high misdemeanours. By 1774, Hancock became one of the leading proponents of the colonial cause. In 1775, the first Continental Congress named Hancock as its president where he mediated the creation of the **Articles of Confederation**. In 1776, he became the first signer of the Declaration of Independence. Although his comment that his signature was intended to be large so that the King can read it without his spectacles may be apocryphal, nonetheless, the description was in keeping with his flamboyant nature. In a show of confidence, Massachusetts elected Hancock as governor in 1781. With the end of the war and **the Treaty of Paris**, Hancock assured the ratification of the Constitution by proposing nine Conciliatory Amendments which became part of the Bill of Rights.

HARVARD COLLEGE. The need for an educated and trained ministry for the Independent churches of **Massachusetts** led to the founding of the college by the General Court in 1636. It was named after a benefactor, John Harvard, who left his library and some property to the new institution. When its courses commenced in 1638, besides theology the college also provided instruction in the arts and sciences.

HAT ACT 1732 was passed to prohibit the manufacture of hats, particularly from beaver fur, in the colonies. Instead the pelts were to be exported to England to be made into hats there. The Act is often cited as a perfect example of mercantilist theory informing commercial relations with the colonies by using colonial raw materials for manufacture into consumer goods in England. In practice it proved almost impossible to enforce.

HAYNES, JOHN (1594–1654) was born in England, the son of a country gentleman and became a landowner himself, acquiring an estate in Essex in 1625. After the death of his wife he went to **Massachusetts**, accompanying **Thomas Hooker** there in 1633. They settled in Cambridge, then called Newtown. Haynes rapidly rose to prominence in the Bay Colony, serving as governor from 1635 to 1636. When Hooker left it to settle in the Connecticut River valley at Hartford, however, Haynes again went with him. He was instrumental in the adoption of **Connecticut**'s Fundamental Orders in 1639, and was elected governor of the colony, a post he held several times. In 1649 he went to England on an abortive mission to obtain a charter for Connecticut.

HEADRIGHT was a system devised by **Thomas Dale**, governor of **Virginia** to encourage migration to a colony where land was abundant and settlers were much in demand by the Virginia Company. He granted Virginian land in perpetuity to settlers on the following criteria: the original settlers got 100 acres after their terms of service were finished or if they had financed their own way to the colony. An additional 100 acres were given to shareholders in the Company who settled there. Anyone arriving after 1616 was allocated an headright of 50 acres on the same basis.

HENRY, PATRICK (1736–1799), the son of a Scottish-born tobacco planter, was born in Hanover county, **Virginia**. He was schooled locally and taught by his father, a former student of King's college, Aberdeen. Henry became a successful lawyer, winning most of the many cases within the first three years of his practice. His most celebrated success was in the **Parson's Case**. In 1763, Henry represented Louisa county against a suit brought by the clergy and won when the jury awarded the clergy only token damages. His success led to his election in 1765 as assemblyman for the county. His entrance into politics coincided with the passage of the **Stamp Act**. His impressive oratory and passionate defense of English liberties led to the adoption of five of his seven proposed resolutions denying Parliament's authority to levy taxes in the colonies. **The Virginia Resolves** led the way for a colonial wide boycott of British goods, eventually forcing parliament to repeal the act. Henry was also joint author of the Virginia Resolutions of 1773 which laid the basis for the emergence of the committee of correspondence. He became a Virginia delegate to the first Continental Congress. Representing Hanover county in 1776, Henry urged the securing of French support before declaring independence, but gave way when the scheme did not prove practical. He proposed a motion to renounce allegiance to the king making the colony the first to commit to political separation from Britain. In 1774 Henry advocated placing the Virginia militia on a war footing. He subsequently led an armed force after the Royal Marines seized the arsenal at Williamsburg. Consequently, the government paid restitution for the seized munitions, but Virginia's governor declared Henry an outlaw. His popularity was so great that a succession of county militias made sure his safe arrival to the continental congress in May 1775 and his eventual election as governor of Virginia in 1777 and again in 1784. He effectively stopped Britain from retaining any territory south of the Great Lakes by financing and equipping the troops so that they could consolidate their control over the Ohio Valley.

Patrick Henry was famous for his firebrand and passionate oratory for which he was supposed to have claimed, 'Give me liberty or give me death.'

HILLSBOROUGH, WILLS HILL, FIRST EARL OF (1718–1793) inherited the Irish title of Viscount Hillsborough from his father in 1742. The family had extensive estates in County Down, Ireland. As an Irish peer Hill was not only entitled to sit in the House of Lords in Dublin but was eligible for election to the British House of Commons. He did in fact represent Warwick from 1742 to 1756, when he was elevated to the peerage of Great Britain as Baron

Harwich and took his seat in the Upper House in Westminster. In 1763 he became President of the **Board of Trade** and was thus directly involved in colonial affairs. His experiences in Ireland were relevant to his dealings with the colonies. Although he claimed to have advised against the **Stamp Act** he did not resign from the government of **George Grenville**. When it fell Hillsborough lost his post, only to be re-appointed to it by **William Pitt** in 1766. At the end of that year, however, he was made post-master general, and thus escaped direct responsibility for the colonies during their reaction to the **Townshend duties**. When the **duke of Grafton** persuaded the king to create a secretaryship of state for the colonies in 1768 Hillsborough was the first incumbent of the new post. Shortly after his appointment to it the General Court of **Massachusetts** issued a circular letter to other colonies to urge them to consent only to taxes voted by their assemblies. Hillsborough countered this by requiring colonial governors to prorogue or dissolve assemblies which defied parliament's right to tax them. He also demanded that Massachusetts rescind the circular letter, a demand rejected by 92 votes to 17 in the lower House. In June 1768 he ordered **General Gage** to station troops in Boston, a move which intensified the dispute. Premises of those suspected of supporting the British government were painted with a mixture of dung and urine known as 'Hillsborough paint'. The partial repeal of the Townshend duties in 1770, however, relaxed the tension temporarily. During the ensuing 'period of quiet' Hillsborough became enmeshed in a project to found a new colony to be called Vandalia. His opposition to the project led him to resign in 1772. Out of office he supported the policy of coercion rather than conciliation of the colonies. He rejoined the government in 1779 as secretary of state, and held out against recognizing American Independence.

HOOKER, THOMAS (1586?–1647) was born in England and educated at Emmanuel College, Cambridge, a noted Puritan stronghold, of which he became a Fellow in 1611. He obtained livings at Esher in Surrey and Chelmsford Essex. His Puritan preaching brought him to the attention of the ecclesiastical authorities. He was twice cited to appear before the court of high commission. On the first occasion, in 1629, the case against him was dropped when many parish clergy supported him. On the second, however, he decided to go to Holland rather than appear before the court. He stayed there until 1633, when he went to **Massachusetts**. In 1636 he became the leading minister of the migration from Massachusetts to Hartford in the Connecticut River Valley. He and his followers disagreed with the arbitrary way in which the Massachusetts general court acted in the **Antinomian controversy.**

HOWE, RICHARD (1726–1799) began a career as a sailor in 1735 on board a merchant ship, joining the Royal navy in 1739. During **King George's War** he served in the West Indies and South America, and at the start of the **French and Indian War** was sent to North America, though later he returned to European waters. In 1757 he became an MP and sat in the House of Commons until 1782. When his elder brother George Augustus was killed near Ticonderoga in 1758 he inherited his title of Viscount Howe in the Irish peerage. Howe served on the Admiralty Board under **Grenville** and as treasurer of the navy under **Rockingham** and **Pitt**. In 1770 he was given the command of the Mediterranean fleet. His sympathy for the American colonists and his friendship with **Benjamin Franklin** were well known. His family name too was respected in the colonies. His brother, George Augustus, had so endeared himself to them that Massachusetts had commissioned a monument to his memory in Westminster Abbey. Nevertheless this did not prevent Howe accepting the appointment of commander in chief of the navy in North America on 1 February 1776. On the contrary the sympathies of the colonists were regarded as assets since he was also sent as a commissioner for peace. He felt that his main task was to support the army commanded by his brother **William Howe**. Thus he conveyed it from **New York** to the top of the **Chesapeake Bay** enabling it to defeat **Washington** at Brandywine Creek and capture Philadelphia in 1777. On hearing the news of **Burgoyne**'s defeat at Saratoga both Howe brothers offered their resignations and returned to England in 1778, after spending an extravagant winter in Philadelphia for which they were much criticized in the

British press. Despite approaches from **Lord North** to offer him a ministerial post Howe went into opposition. When the **marquis of Rockingham** formed a ministry in 1782 he made Howe and admiral and he also obtained an earldom for him.

HOWE, WILLIAM (1729–1814) began his military career as a cornet of dragoons in 1746 and rose rapidly through the ranks to become a lieutenant colonel by 1757. The following year he went to North America and played a distinguished part in the taking of Quebec, Montreal and Havana. By the start of the **War of American Independence** he was a major general. In 1775 he was appointed second in command to **General Thomas Gage** whom he succeeded in October. Howe moved the base of British operations to New York City, where he was joined by his brother **Admiral Richard Howe** in July 1776. The brothers had the twin tasks of defeating the rebels and negotiating a peace with them, which made their position difficult if not impossible. The tension between them partly accounts for Howe's failure to pursue **Washington** effectively across Manhattan and **New Jersey**, and for his decision to take Philadelphia rather than to join up with **General Burgoyne** in 1777. He thereby contributed indirectly to the defeat of the British at Saratoga and the entry of the French into the war on the side of the Americans. In 1778 he was replaced by **Sir Henry Clinton** and returned to England. Both Howe brothers were members of parliament and raised the case for an enquiry into their conduct in the House of Commons, which they were convinced would clear their names. When the ministry of the **marquis of Rockingham** succeeded that of **Lord North** in 1782 he was made lieutenant general of the ordnance, a post he held until 1804.

HUDSON'S BAY in **Canada** was disputed between England and France in the 17th century, since both claimed territorial rights there. The English launched the Hudson's Bay Company in 1670 to exploit these. The French regarded the company as a provocation to their claims, and there were armed reprisals against it during the 1680s even when England and France enjoyed amicable relations in Europe. When open hostilities broke out between them in **King William's War** and **Queen Anne's War** the region became involved in them. At the **Treaty of Utrecht** in 1713 France ceded Hudson's Bay to Britain.

HUGUENOTS were French Calvinists who emerged as a Protestant sect in France in the mid-16th century. They were subjected to persecution by the dominant Catholics, notably in 1572 in what became known as the St. Bartholomew's Day Massacre where over 8,000 Huguenots were killed. The Edict of Nantes was issued in 1598, granting them freedom of worship, guaranteed by giving them a number of towns for security, among them La Rochelle. During the early 17th century they came to be regarded as a state within a state and were subjected to renewed repression. When they allied with the English in 1628 the French authorities besieged La Rochelle and forced it to surrender. Thereafter the concessions of Nantes were increasingly eroded until in 1685 the Edict was revoked. Although they were prohibited from leaving the country many did, finding their way to England and the Dutch Republic. Some of those who escaped France also went to the colonies, principally to the **Carolinas**.

HUNTER, ROBERT (1666–1734) was born in Scotland, and went into the army. He protected Princess Anne, **James II's** daughter in the **Glorious Revolution**, afterwards receiving a commission from **William III**. He fought in Flanders in **King William's War** and under the duke of Marlborough, when he took part in the battles of Blenheim and Ramillies, during **Queen Anne's War**. He served as lieutenant colonel from 1704 to 1706, when he left the service following a dispute with Marlborough over his own role in the taking of Antwerp. While in London he associated with Joseph Addison and Richard Steele, contributing articles to their journal *The Tatler*. He also became acquainted with Jonathan Swift. In 1707 he was appointed as lieutenant governor of **Virginia**. Hunter never reached the colony, however, as his ship was captured by a French privateer and he was taken to France. After returning to England following an exchange of prisoners he was appointed governor of **New York** and **New Jersey** in 1709. He arrived in New York in 1710 with about 3,000 German refugees from the Palatinate who were sent over in a scheme to settle them in the Mohawk River valley. Hunter claimed that the funds raised in England were insufficient and that he had to spend his own money on them, incurring debts to the amount of £21,000. He cooperated in the defense of the northern colonies with the governor of **Massachusetts, Joseph Dudley**. Hunter continued his work as an author, writing a farce *Androborus* which was the first play written and printed in the American colonies. Its satirical treatment of former governors of New York, including **Lord Cornbury**, made Hunter popular in the colony. He had became involved in disputes with the assembly over finance, but in 1716 his popularity led to his supporters winning the elections to the lower house. He then enjoyed good relations with it until ill health led him to resign the governorship and return to England in 1719. He recovered his health sufficiently to go as governor to **Jamaica** in 1727, where he managed to persuade the assembly to vote a permanent revenue for the governor. Hunter was unique among colonial governors in obtaining this concession. He died fighting the maroons.

HUTCHINSON, ANNE (1591–1643) was a Puritan controversialist who became a catalyst in the **Antinomian controversy** in **Massachusetts** from 1636 to 1638. Hutchinson claimed that those in the covenant of free grace did not need to commit themselves to a covenant of works. She was influential enough to hold meetings in her home where men as well as women came to hear her. Her pronouncements ran counter to the general synod in Boston for a number of reasons. Her philosophy disrupted and challenged its authority as did the fact that her gender caused an affront to the order of society. Eventually, she was brought before the general court where she claimed that her views were due to personal divine revelation. It was determined that she be banished. Along with her husband, Hutchinson moved to Rhode Island. After her husband's death, Anne moved on to **New York**. It was there that she and all but one of her children were murdered by **Indians**.

HUTCHINSON, THOMAS (1711–1780) was born in Boston, **Massachusetts** and attended **Harvard College** from 1723 to 1727. He was elected to the assembly in 1737 and served as speaker from 1746 to 1748, when he failed to secure re-election. This was due to the unpopularity he had incurred from his support of measures to stabilize the colony's paper currency. His house was burned down, probably by an arsonist. Nevertheless the measures succeeded, giving Massachusetts the soundest colonial currency. In 1749 Hutchinson was elected to the council. At the **Albany Congress** in 1754 he helped **Benjamin Franklin** draft his **Plan of Union**. Hutchinson became lieutenant governor of Massachusetts in 1758 and two years later the governor, **Sir Francis Bernard**, made him chief justice of the superior court. As a judge he incurred unpopularity by supporting the customs officials who issued writs of assistance to search for contraband goods. Although in private he expressed disapproval of the **Stamp Act** he felt obliged to support it in public. Once again he provoked hostility leading to his house being burned down, this time by an angry mob. The manuscript of his authoritative *History of the colony and province of Massachusetts Bay*, the first volume of which had appeared the year before, was thrown out of the window with other effects in August 1765. Enough of it was salvaged for him to bring out a second volume in 1768 and *A Collection of Original Papers* in 1769. When Bernard went to England in 1769 Hutchinson became acting governor of the colony. He played a crucial role in keeping order at the **Boston Massacre**, protecting the soldiers who had fired from the anger of the crowd and escorting them to prison, at the same time ordering other troops to withdraw from the town. After his appointment as governor of Massachusetts in 1771 he became involved in a dispute with the assembly over the right of parliament to tax the colonies. He insisted that the only alternative to parliamentary sovereignty was complete independence, a polarization of the issues which was not welcome to the imperial authorities. When East India Company tea arrived in Boston in 1773 Hutchinson, whose sons were consignees, insisted that it be unloaded and sold. His insistence helped to provoke the **Boston Tea Party**. He apprehended that the **Coercive Acts** would further inflame the situation and went to England in June 1774 to make his objections felt. Unfortunately letters he had written to Thomas Whateley castigating radical colonists fell into his opponents' hands and were published, to his discredit. Hutchinson stayed in England although he disliked it and longed to return home. He died in London, one of the more prominent **loyalists**.

I

INDENTURED SERVANTS were a broad category of servitude that involved some kind of bondage by a person to a land owner, proprietor, or company, for a definite period of time. Servants in husbandry were often hired for a year by farmers in England. In the case of colonial indentured servitude, individuals would agree to work for a longer period of time in order to pay their way to North America. The length of time could extend anywhere from four to seven years. Usually, the servant held a skill, whether it was as an artisan, craftsman or housemaid. Often it was a way to spend a kind of apprenticeship in which the servant would perfect their skill. At the end of the service, the servant could gain land, usually 50 acres, and freedom to start a new life. The preponderance of indentured servants depended upon region and time. As the standard of living improved in England during the 17th century, people were less inclined to migrate. At the same time, the southern colonies were experiencing a boom in tobacco growing which required more intensive labor. The demand for servants was outstripping the supply so much so that eventually, increasing numbers of **slaves** were imported to do the job.

INDIANS. Indigenous people of North and South America, so called because Columbus believed he had sailed to the East Indies. They kept this name throughout the colonial period even after it had been established that the early European explorers had in fact encountered a continent previously unknown in Europe. Because of this misnomer some modern scholars prefer to call them Native North Americans. This is a clumsy expression too, however, for by 1763 most white inhabitants of the north American continent were natives, or Creoles. Moreover the term clearly does not apply to the aboriginal peoples of the Caribbean. Many ethno-historians therefore prefer to retain the older term, a practice followed here.

A major problem in dealing with Indian history is that the only written records were produced by Europeans or whites of European origins. These tended to treat the Indians they encountered as obstacles in the way of settlement. Efforts to comprehend their way of life led to their being ascribed to 'tribes' with distinct names such as Mohawk and Cherokee. It has been established by recent scholarship that this is a very Euro-centric way of labeling Indians, who did not necessarily live in self-contained 'tribes'. Yet the nomenclature is so ingrained in the literature that it is almost impossible to escape from it. Thus the first settlers at Jamestown are usually referred to as settling in the region of 'Powhatan's Empire', while the **Covenant Chain** is described as a treaty between the English and the Iroquois. This European terminology has led some historians to despair of ever writing an objective history of the Indians, which they dismiss as a hopeless task. Others reject such defeatism, and try with the aid of anthropology, archaeology and other methodologies to supplement the written records and to tease out of them astonishing insights into Indian culture. Their views on religion, time, history and the environment have all been shown to differ from those of Europeans. Ecological historians, for example, have argued that they did not see man as superior to other creatures but as one who lived in symbiosis with them. Their adoption of European attitudes led to the exploitation of **the fur trade** to the virtual extermination of some species.

Such investigations into Indian culture since the 1970s led many to conclude that the arrival, or 'invasion' as it was dubbed, of Europeans marked an unmitigated disaster for North American Indians. Thus they brought with them diseases, such as smallpox and measles, from which the natives they encountered had acquired no immunity. The result was a demographic catastrophe. It has been estimated that in 1600 there were about 500,000 Indians living in the areas along the eastern seaboard which the English were to occupy in the ensuing century. By 1700 their numbers had been reduced to around 250,000. The decline was due to disease rather than to armed conflict.

Concentration on the conflicts which marked the encounters between the colonists and the Indians can convey the impression that their relations were marked by ceaseless strife. There were indeed bloody episodes in the 17th century, from attempted massacres of settlers in **Virginia** in 1622 and 1644 and the **Pequot War** in **Connecticut** in 1637 to **King Philip's War** in New England from 1675 to 1676, led by an Indian known to contemporary Europeans as King Philip and to modern historians as Metacom. The 18th century also witnessed violent struggles between the two peoples, though these tended to be assimilated in the wars between Britain and France, when both countries sought and found Indian allies. At the end of the colonial period one of the bitterest conflicts between Indians and British colonists was fought after the **peace of Paris** eliminated the French from the equation in 1763, when Pontiac, who had allied with France, continued fighting until 1765. A narrative of relations with Indians structured around these conflicts seems to substantiate the view that the Europeans invaded and conquered north America.

Yet side by side with this chronicle of carnage another story could be woven around peaceful interactions. The Indians whom the first English settlers encountered in Roanoke Island in the 1580s appear to have been friendly. So far from being stereotypical 'savages' they also apparently enjoyed a fairly civilized life, judging from the pictorial representations of them by John White, which show them living in villages and cultivating crops as well as hunting and fishing. The celebration of Thanksgiving Day, though it has been overlaid with legend, is not entirely mythical, and does record amicable relations between the Pilgrims and the Indians of the Cape Cod area. **John Eliot's** attempt to convert natives in Massachusetts, gathering them into 14 'praying towns' between 1650 and 1675, although it has been condemned as cultural hegemony, was based on humane intentions. Early **Pennsylvania** witnessed genuine attempts to establish a symbiosis with the Indians, so much so that even Francis Jennings, who coined the term 'invasion' to describe European settlement, had to admit that he liked **William Penn**.

Such interactions have led other historians more recently to prefer the idea of 'the Middle Ground' to the notion of invasion. In the view of those who advocate that America was invaded the Indians are seen as victims, their culture being destroyed by that of the Europeans. But, while many were indeed victims, others were able to deal with the white settlers on more equal terms. They established commercial, diplomatic and other relations with them. Some aspects of the trade between them, especially that in alcohol, were detrimental to their well being. But they benefited from the exchange of fur for clothing and utensils. Indian women participated in this commerce, though how far their roles in their own communities were adversely affected by it is a matter of debate. To some feminist historians Indian society was largely matriarchal before the encounter with Europeans. Thereafter contact with white settlers led to the adoption of their views of male supremacy. Others insist, on the other hand, that the Indians held on to their cultural traditions throughout the colonial period, and that it was not until after American Independence and the drive west which was enshrined as 'manifest destiny' that the Indian way of life was destroyed or confined to reservations.

INTERREGNUM. The period between the execution of **Charles I** in January 1649 and the Restoration of the monarchy in 1660, during which England became a republic. From 1649 to 1653 it was ruled by the Rump Parliament, so called because it was the remnant of the Long Parliament left after the Commons had been purged to ensure there was a majority in favor of the trial and execution of the king. The Rump abolished the House of Lords in 1649, making England a unicameral republic. In 1651 it passed the Navigation Ordinance, the first of the **Navigation Acts**. Commissioners from the Rump installed parliamentary governors on **Virginia**

and **Maryland** which had declared themselves loyal to the Stuarts. In 1653 the Rump was dissolved by Oliver Cromwell. After a brief experiment with a nominated parliament Cromwell accepted the Instrument of Government in 1654, which appointed him as Lord Protector. The Protectorate launched the 'western design' in 1655 to take Hispaniola in the West Indies from Spain. Although the design failed in its objective it succeeded in taking **Jamaica**. The Protectorate was more tolerant than the Rump. For example, in 1656 **Lord Baltimore** was restored to his proprietorship of Maryland. When Cromwell died in 1658 his son Richard became Protector. It was clear that his government was weak and that anarchy threatened, playing into the hands of Royalists. In the colonies the restoration of the crown seemed inevitable. In Virginia **Sir William Berkeley** was elected governor in March 1660, anticipating the restoration of **Charles II**.

IRON ACT 1750. An Act of Parliament prohibiting the colonies from producing steel. However, they could export pit or bar iron to England without paying duties. Like the **Hat Act** it proved almost impossible to enforce.

J

JAMAICA was acquired by the English in 1655. It was the largest of the islands settled by England in the **West Indies**. It rapidly developed sugar production which led to the introduction of **slave** labor. By 1696 there were 30,000 slaves on the island and only 10,000 whites. In 1715 the ratio was 7,000 whites to 55,000 blacks. Both populations failed to increase naturally as the death rate from malaria and yellow fever was higher than the birth rate. The numbers of whites shrank as they were not replaced by new immigrants, whereas the numbers of blacks increased through constant shipments of slaves from Africa. Males vastly outnumbered females among the whites throughout the 18th century, leading to sexual relations between white men and black women. In 1733 the Jamaican Assembly recognized the consequences of this by passing a law whereby mulattoes were held to be legally white after three generations. Slaves by contrast were subjected to brutal laws subjecting them to their masters. This led to rebellions and runaways, slaves finding sanctuary in the mountains of the islands where they became known as maroons. The maroons fought the whites constantly between 1700 and 1739. There was a temporary respite when the Jamaican government recognized their independence. In 1760, however, there was the biggest confrontation of the century in Tacky's rebellion, when 400 blacks and 90 whites were killed. Jamaica remained loyal to the British Crown during the **War of American Independence**. It was threatened with attack from the French navy after the battle of Yorktown, but was saved by Admiral Rodney at the battle of the Saintes in 1782.

JAMES I (1566–1625) reigned as King James VI of Scotland after 1567 and James I of England following the death of Queen Elizabeth in 1603. He also inherited from the Queen the problem of the **Puritans**. In 1604 he convened the Hampton Court Conference to thrash out the dispute between them and the more conservative members of the **Anglican Church**. The outcome was largely in favor of the latter, though few Puritans left the established church, most preferring to wait a more favorable opportunity for reform. Among those who became separatists, however, were the **Pilgrims** led by **William Bradford**, who left for Leiden in Holland in 1609, despairing of a godly thorough reformation in England. When the Pilgrims went to Plymouth in 1620 they did so as separatists from the established Church, and without a royal charter. Instead they had a patent from the **Council for New England** which the king had permitted to settle lands north of the 40th parallel in North America. James had granted a charter to the Virginia Company in 1606 which led to the first permanent English settlement in America at Jamestown, named after the king, in 1607. In 1609 the Company received a second charter increasing its authority over **Virginia.** In 1622 the Council of New England gave **Sir Ferdinando Gorges** a patent for land in the area of future Maine and New Hampshire. The following year it granted land from Maine to Rhode Island to 20 patentees, including merchants from Dorchester who settled at Gloucester on Cape Ann. In 1624 the Virginia Company was dissolved and the colony taken over by the Crown. James appointed Sir Francis Wyatt as the first royal governor of Virginia.

JAMES II (1633–1701) as duke of York went into exile during the **Interregnum**. On the Restoration of his brother **Charles II** he was made lord admiral and acquired a keen interest in colonial affairs. In 1663 Charles granted him a proprietorship over land which stretched from Maine to the Delaware Bay. Much of it was occupied by the **Dutch**. Their colony of New Netherland was acquired for James by **Richard Nicolls** in 1664, and renamed **New York** after James's duchy. Nicolls, who acted as his deputy, introduced the so-called 'Duke's Laws' into the colony, which made the proprietor virtually absolute with no provision for an elected assembly. The Dutch retook the colony during the second Dutch war of 1672 to 1674, but gave it back to the English at the peace treaty of Westminster. By then James had been obliged to resign from his post as lord admiral, since the Test Act of 1673 required those who held offices under the Crown to take communion in the Church of England. As a Roman Catholic James could not do so. His surrender of the post was the first public acknowledgment of his Catholicism. He never-theless continued to exercise his prerogatives as proprietor of New York and **New Jersey**. Thus he appointed **Edmund Andros** as his deputy in New York, whose arbitrary rule provoked calls for an assembly there. James only reluctantly conceded one in 1683. Meanwhile he had ceded New Jersey, which he had also acquired from the Dutch, to **John Lord Berkeley** and **Sir George Carteret**. In 1681 he reluctantly gave land across the Delaware to **William Penn** to form the lower part of **Pennsylvania**. Charles II put pressure on his brother to do this in an attempt to appease members of the opposition, known as Whigs, who were demanding that James should not succeed Charles since he was a Roman Catholic. This had given rise to the Exclusion Crisis between 1679 and 1681, during which three successive parliaments dominated by Whigs had tried to exclude James from the throne. Charles seized the initiative from the Whigs by not summoning another parliament between 1681 and his death in 1685. He also took over Whig strongholds in the corporations by use of the writ **Quo Warranto**. Besides boroughs in England one of the corporations subjected to the writ was the colony of **Massachusetts**, which had to surrender its charter to the Crown in 1684. James was very active in promoting this policy. When he succeeded his brother as James II in 1685 he showed his inclinations towards abso-lutism both in England and in the colonies. In England he promoted Catholics to offices under the Crown, including commissioned officers in the army, despite the Test Act. When parlia-ment refused to endorse this policy he dismissed it in 1685 and never summoned it again. Although his avowed aim was for religious toleration, which he sincerely extended to Protestant dissenters, he also sought to put the Catholic church on an even footing with the Anglican. This required him to increase the powers of the Crown in ways which were regarded as arbitrary, and thereby provoked the **Glorious Revolution** forcing him into exile in France where he died. In the colonies his arbitrary methods of government were even more blatant, as exemplified by the **Dominion of New England**. When news of his flight to France reached the colonies it precipi-tated the Glorious Revolution in America.

JAY, JOHN (1745–1829) was descended from French Huguenots on his father's side and the Dutch Van Cortlandts on his maternal side. His marriage allied him with the New Jersey Livingstones. Jay attended King's College in 1764 (later Columbia University) studying law and was admitted to the bar in 1768. He became known for his moderation and willingness to com-promise and effective negotiation skills. As tensions between the American colonies and Great Britain reached a flash point, Jay was chosen as a member of the Committee of Correspondence in 1774 and as delegate to the first Continental Congress. Though Jay opposed moves toward independence from Britain, he was responsible for drafting congress's justification, *Address to the People of Great Britain*, which declared Parliament's acts unconstitutional. However, he continued to resist calls for independence until the Declaration was signed. From that point forward, he fully backed the war efforts. When the colonies formed their constitutions, Jay helped to draft that of New York in which he was able to reconcile opposing views. But the issue of religious freedom was somewhat of a sticking point for him. His family background may have influenced his views. His paternal grandfather suffered from the French government by being imprisoned for his faith. Eventually, he was able to escape and emigrated to America. Consequently, Jay distrusted the Catholic church and the French government. He tried at one point in the New York Convention to deny civil freedoms to anyone who swore allegiance to a priest or the pope or any foreign power. Yet, before the outset of the war, he tried to entice Canada to join the cause saying that the fate of the colonies, whether they were Catholic or Protestant, were linked.

Elected as Chief Justice of New York's supreme Court, he was simultaneously chosen as a delegate to the **Continental Congress** where he was also selected as its President. Thereafter, he was selected as U.S. representative to Spain in order to participate in the peace negotiations at the end of the war where he was unsuccessful at getting Spain to cooperate in the negotiations. Jay was called to France to help **John Adams** and **Benjamin Franklin** in their negotiations with the French. Jay was instrumental in outmaneuvering the French after suspecting them of secretly treating with Britain. He was able to convince Adams and Franklin to open up direct discussions with Britain. Consequently, France and Spain were forced to sign the **Peace of Paris**, thus formerly acknowledging the United States as an independent nation. After the treaty was signed, Jay returned to the U.S. to become Secretary of Foreign Affairs.

JEFFERSON, THOMAS (1743–1826) was born into an already prominent family in **Virginia** where his father was an office-holder and large landholder in Albermarle county. Upon his father's death, Jefferson inherited an estate which included more than 5,000 acres of land, numerous **slaves**, a library and an influential position in local society. His education was impressive, one that was grounded in the Classics. After being educated privately, Jefferson studied at William and Mary College in Williamsburg from 1760–1762. He was introduced to the eminent lawyer George Wyeth and Governor Francis Fauquier by the Scottish mathematician, William Small, whom Jefferson later dubbed, 'a partie quarre'. The Enlightenment, as reflected by these men, greatly influenced Jefferson's political outlook, specifically in his pamphlet, *The Summary View of the Rights of British America*, written in 1774. In the debate over the imperial constitution, Jefferson's principles were grounded in British Enlightenment thought. Most importantly, the implication of the *Summary View* was one of a contract between the king and his subjects. It is these principles that guide Jefferson throughout his political career.

Jefferson married Martha Wyles Skelton who was the daughter of another prominent Virginian whose main wealth was connected to the slave trade. At his father-in-law's death in 1773, Jefferson inherited 135 slaves and transatlantic trade connections. The timing of Skelton's death also entangled Jefferson in the debt incurred with the British merchants over trade. Jefferson was appointed as justice of the peace to the county court and as lieutenant of the county militia and in 1769, he was elected to the Virginia House of Burgesses. During his time in the assembly he headed the reform and codification of the Virginian laws. Although his proposals were not completely successful, such as provisions for universal education and gradual emancipation of his colony's slaves, he was able to get the law of primogeniture abolished, while guaranteeing religious freedom.

In 1775 Jefferson was elected to the second Continental Congress, mainly due to his ability to argue the colonial case so eloquently. He is credited with the original draft of the 'Declaration of the causes and necessity of taking up arms', in July of the same year. The following year, he drafted the Declaration of Independence. The Declaration, with its assertion that all men are created equal, and governments derive their powers from the consent of the governed, is a summation of enlightenment thought whence Jefferson transfers the idea of natural and contractual rights of the people.

In 1779, Jefferson was elected as governor of Virginia. No sooner had he got into office, his state was invaded and its government was driven out of Richmond. Jefferson barely escaped from his home in Charlottesville. He left public office and returned to a private life only to be thrust back into the public arena with the death of his wife in 1781. Between 1783 and 1784 Jefferson represented Virginia in Congress, after which he was appointed as American minister to France. Jefferson returned to the U.S. in 1790 to become Secretary of State in **Washington**'s administration. In 1796, he came runner-up to **John Adams** in the Presidential race. His opposition to Adams' federal policy and favoritism toward Britain over France, put him in a weak position as vice-president. Events within the country, rather than outside conspired to elevate Jefferson to the Presidency in 1800.

JOHNSON, SAMUEL (1696–1772) was born in **Connecticut**, where he was taught at home until the age of 11, showing precocious learning which prepared him to enter the collegiate school at Saybrook in 1710. He became a tutor there in 1716, and moved with it to New Haven where it became **Yale College**. In 1720 he was appointed Congregationalist minister at West Haven, but converted to **Anglicanism** in 1722. After visiting England for ordination he was sent back to America by the **Society for the Propagation of the Gospel** to set up an Anglican church at Stratford, Connecticut in 1724. His interest in Enlightened thought led him to publish an *Introduction to Philosophy*. When King's College was established in New York in 1754 he was appointed as its first president, a post he held until 1763.

JOHNSON, SIR WILLIAM (1715–1774) was born in Ireland, and moved to **New York**, settling in the Mohawk valley around 1738, where he managed his uncle's estate. He enjoyed good relations with the Mohawk Indians, with whom he traded. Johnson acquired sufficient knowledge of them that he became superintendent of Indian affairs in 1756, a position he held for the rest of his life. During the **French and Indian War** he took over the command of British and Indian troops at the battle of Niagara in 1759 when the commander was killed, and led them to victory. Johnson managed to prevent most of the Iroquois from taking part in **Pontiac's War**.

JONES, JOHN PAUL (1747–1792) was born on the Solway Firth in Kircudbrightshire, Scotland. His early career as a British merchant captain did not presuppose later fame. Early on, he was accused of murdering his own men, ostensibly for neglect and mutinous behavior. On the second charge, he absconded to America where he added the surname of Jones to John Paul. Notwithstanding his questionable behavior as commander of a ship, he was fearless and at the outbreak of the **American War of Independence** Jones was given a first lieutenancy on board the *Alfred*, after which he was commissioned commander of the *Providence*. He quickly gained fame for his flamboyant and daring raids on the British fleets, notably capturing 16 prizes in a single cruise. He sailed to British waters raiding enemy ports. His knowledge of the coasts of northern English and Scottish waters made him an effective attacker of such ports as Whitehaven. The most famous attack came off the coast of Filey near Scarborough when he encountered the HMS *Serapis*. In a fierce battle, from which people watched from the beach, Jones's ship, the *Bonhomme Richard* was mortally hit. Instead of surrendering, Jones mounted a successful attack on the Serapis, capturing it while his own ship sank. Jones became the most famous naval seaman in American history and was dubbed the 'the father of the United States Navy.'

K

KEITH, GEORGE (1645–1715) was born in Scotland and educated at Marischal College, Aberdeen. Although his education was Presbyterian in 1662 he became a Quaker, for which he suffered persecution. He had considerable influence on the leading Scottish Quaker, Robert

Barclay. When Barclay's cousin Robert Gordon accused them of being Socinians Keith replied in *The Light of Truth triumphing* (1670) and *Universal Grace* (1671). In an attempt to impose a more formal orthodoxy on the Friends, Keith issued a 'Confession of Faith' to their yearly meeting in England in 1677. It was resisted by influential Quakers like George Fox, and never formally accepted. In the early 1680s Keith endured renewed persecution along with other Quakers, and in 1684 went to East Jersey as surveyor general. Although the colony was a Quaker haven, Keith took issue with many Friends who he felt were slack in doctrine. In 1689 he went to Philadelphia. There too his theological views, especially his reservations on the 'inner light' were disputed by many Friends after he presented them to the monthly meeting in Philadelphia in January 1692. The dispute split the Quaker community into two camps, with Keith forming his own society known as the Christian Quakers. The schism spread to England, where Keith returned in 1693 to attend the yearly meeting. The following year the meeting condemned his views and expelled him. He continued to defy his opponents, especially **William Penn** whom he accused of deism, before finally moving over to the Church of England in 1700. As an Anglican minister, Keith returned to the colonies in 1702 sponsored by the Society for the Propagation of the Gospel. He succeeded in converting approximately 700 Quakers. Most of these had already joined him under the Keithian group. He returned to England, in 1705 becoming rector at Edburton, Sussex where he died.

KING'S COLLEGE was founded in New York City in 1754. After the **War of American Independence** it became Columbia University.

KING GEORGE'S WAR is the title Americans give to the wars between 1739 and 1748 which in England are known as the War of Jenkins's Ear, fought against Spain, and the War of the Austrian Succession, fought against France. The Spanish war led to the taking of Porto Bello in 1739 and an abortive attack on Cartagena in 1740. The Austrian war began in 1740 when Prussia seized Silesia from Austria. **George II** sided with the Austrians, and fought in person at the battle of Dettingen in 1743, the last king of England to lead his troops into action. Further battles at Fontenoy in 1745 and Laufeldt in 1747 were won by the French, who declared war on Britain in 1744. In the colonies it resulted in the taking of Louisbourg on **Cape Breton Island**. This was handed back to the French at the treaty of Aix-la-Chapelle which ended the war in 1748.

KING PHILIP'S WAR (1675–1676) was fought between the colonists of New England and the Wampanoag Indians led by **Metacom**, whom the English called King Philip. Increasing numbers of settlers and decreasing numbers of natives created competition for lands and friction over competing jurisdictions. Metacom had persuaded almost all the Algonquin Indians to join with him in resisting the encroachment of the English. In 1675 he decided to make a stand when the colonists executed three of his followers for murdering a Christian Indian. Beginning in June he attacked and destroyed almost half the white settlements in New England over the summer. The colonists, fearing annihilation, hit back indiscriminately at all local Indians, including the Narragansetts of Rhode Island. Previously considered neutral, they threw in their lot with Metacom after 600 of their number were killed. The settlers sought allies elsewhere, particularly from the Mohawks of New York. This enabled them to defeat Metacom's advance. In August 1676, after the capture of his wife and son, he was shot dead by a man hired to assassinate him. This brought an end to the war. Metacom's head was displayed in Plymouth for the next 20 years. It reminded the colonists that he had nearly destroyed their settlements in New England.

KING WILLIAM'S WAR is the title Americans give to the war of 1688 to 1697 known in Europe as the Nine Years' War. North America was very much a sideshow to the conflict between France and the League of Augsburg, which England supported. **William III** had to fight for his throne against its former occupant **James II**, whom he defeated at the battle of the Boyne in 1690. A French naval victory off Beachy Head that year was offset by a crushing defeat at La Hogue in 1692. In Europe the war took the form of a series of sieges rather than of pitched battles. In America, following an attack by England's Indian allies on Lachine near Montreal in July 1689, **New France** counter-attacked against **New York** and **New England**. The attack on New York failed to take Albany but inflicted casualties on the colonists in Schenectady. The attacks on New England provoked **Sir William Phips** into sacking Port Royal in **Acadia** in 1690. A bold plan by Phips to follow this up by taking Quebec was abortive. Another attempt to take it in 1693 had to be called off. The French retaliated by taking Fort William Henry in Maine in 1696 and Port York in **Hudson's Bay** in 1697. The Treaty of Ryswick which concluded hostilities in 1697 ceded the Hudson's Bay acquisitions to France, which they held until the treaty of Utrecht which ended **Queen Anne's War**.

L

LEE, RICHARD HENRY (1733–1794) was born into a privileged gentry society in Westmoreland county, **Virginia**. Lee's father was a wealthy planter, who served on the governor's council. Lee was educated in England at the Wakefield Academy in Yorkshire and spent time in Europe. His first foray into politics was as a justice of the peace for Westmoreland county in 1757 after which he won a seat in the colonial assembly, the house of burgesses in 1758. From an early period, Lee was a strong proponent of the ban on slave importation. Taking the model of the northern colonies, he argued that slavery discouraged skilled labor immigrants. Lack of skilled artisans, he argued for instance, prevented improvements in agriculture and commerce.

In 1764 following reports of the **Stamp Act** to be imposed upon the colonies, Lee introduced the first motion to formally protest to the king and parliament. This was followed by a protest march led by Lee in Westmoreland county. The year following the Stamp Act, Lee organized the Westmoreland Association pledging resistance to the act. The association forced recalcitrant merchants to forswear the use of stamps, closed the Virginia courts in order to prevent them from using the stamps, and put pressure on British merchants to lobby for the repeal of the Act, notwithstanding Lee's initial application for the position of stamp collector.

Lee's brother, William, was a tobacco merchant and was active in London politics. His other brother, Arthur, also lived in London and had access to political information, which he shared with Richard. Lee was instrumental in organizing American resistance to British tax impositions. In 1774 he introduced a plan to close Virginia courts to all debt actions, and drafted a number of resolutions which ultimately resulted in the dissolution of the house of burgesses. His organization of a non-importation association widened to a national proposal when he was chosen to represent Virginia in the Continental Congress in 1774. Finally, he joined **John Adams** in urging a move for states to organize new government. Lee served in the Virginia house of delegates from 1777–1778 and 1780–1785. After the **American War of Independence**, Lee served in the United States congress until 1779 and again in 1784–1785. He served as one of Virginia's first senators in the United States congress and was elected president pro tempore in the senate in 1792.

LEISLER, JACOB (1640–1691) was born in Frankfurt am Main, Germany, the son of a Calvinist pastor. After his father's death in 1653 his mother moved to Hanau where he enlisted in a military academy. In 1660 he went to New Amsterdam as a soldier in the **Dutch** West India Company, where he married a wealthy Dutch widow in 1663. He set up in the fur, tobacco and wine trades. Leisler was a deacon in the Dutch Reformed church who sided with the strict Calvinists, objecting to the appointment of the Anglican Dominie Nicholas van

Rensselaer to his church. When the **Dominion of New England** collapsed, triggering the **Glorious Revolution**, Leisler became leader of the revolutionaries in **New York**. His refusal to obey Lieutenant Governor **Francis Nicholson** led the latter to leave for England. Meanwhile Leisler interpreted a letter from **William III** as giving him authority to act as lieutenant governor. The king, however, had no intention of recognizing him as such, and in January 1690 appointed Henry Sloughter to replace Nicholson. It took him until 19 March 1692 to reach New York. Meanwhile Major Richard Ingoldsby arrived there in January and proclaimed Sloughter as governor. When Leisler refused to recognize him an armed encounter took place between his supporters and those of Ingoldsby. Upon Sloughter's arrival Leisler accepted his commission as governor, but was nevertheless arrested and put on trial for treason. On 17 May 1691 he was executed.

LIVINGSTON, ROBERT (1654–1728) was born in Scotland, the son of a Presbyterian preacher who went with his family to Rotterdam in 1660. There he learned **Dutch** before going to America in 1673, where he settled in Albany, **New York**. His knowledge of Dutch proved useful there, helping him to acquire the posts of town clerk and secretary to the commissioners for Indian affairs. He acquired land from the Indians and through his marriage to the widow of Dominie Nicholas Rensselaer the wealthiest Dutch landowner in the colony. By 1686 Livingston was in possession of some 160,000 acres along the Hudson River valley. During the **Glorious Revolution**, he was an opponent of the regime of **Jacob Leisler** When the northern colonies became vulnerable to French attack in **King William's War**, and Schenectady was actually sacked by a raiding party in February 1690, Livingston went to New England to seek assistance. In his absence Albany came to terms with Leisler. Livingston survived as a commissioner for Indian affairs and returned to England from 1695 to 1696, when he obtained the post of secretary of Indian affairs for life. He was in England again from 1701 to 1705, protecting his position from the attacks of his enemies. Back in New York he became speaker of the assembly in 1708 and took its side against the governor. A previous governor, **Benjamin Fletcher**, observed of him that 'he has made a considerable fortune... his beginning being a little book keeper he has screwed himself into one of the most considerable estates in the province... he had rather be called knave Livingston than poor Livingston'.

LLOYD, DAVID (1656–1731) was born in Wales where he received legal training under the infamous Lord Chief Justice, George Jeffreys. Appointed by **William Penn** as Attorney General in 1686, Lloyd emigrated to **Pennsylvania** where his career became controversial. As a converted Quaker, Lloyd saw English interference in the colony's politics as a threat to the Quaker hegemony. Accordingly he opposed the continued union with the three lower counties, which were dominated by Anglicans. Among the many offices that he held were assemblyman, deputy-advocate of the vice-admiralty court, deputy master of the rolls, clerk of the Provincial Council, clerk of the Provincial Court, clerk of the assembly, register general, chief Justice of the Supreme Court in the colony, justice of Oyer and Terminer, clerk of the peace, and recorder and Justice of the Peace. He argued for the rights of the assembly when Pennsylvania was made a Crown Colony from 1692 to 1694. When Penn was restored to the proprietorship Lloyd became the leader of the anti-proprietary party.

LOGAN, JAMES (1674–1751) was born in Lurgan in Northern Ireland where his father, a Quaker, was a schoolmaster. When his father moved to Bristol to take over a school there he took his family with him. In 1697 James succeeded him as master of the Bristol school. Two years later he became secretary to the Quaker leader **William Penn**. Logan went with Penn to **Pennsylvania**, where he served from 1701 to 1717 as clerk of the Provincial Council, a body on which he sat from 1702 to 1747. When Penn returned to England in 1701 he also appointed him as commissioner of property and receiver general of his colony. This gave Logan tremendous influence on the distribution of lands in Pennsylvania. He defended the absentee proprietor against the opposition of **David Lloyd**. This created enemies in the colony who tried to impeach him in 1707, leading Logan to go to England to defend himself in 1709. He stayed until 1711, when the charges against him were dropped. Back in Pennsylvania he engaged profitably in the fur trade. After Penn's death in 1718 Logan handled the affairs of the proprietor's family in Pennsylvania, guarding them against the claims of the last governor appointed by Penn, Sir William Keith. He also looked after his own, becoming wealthy enough to establish himself on a substantial estate at Stenton near Germantown. From 1726 to 1739 he was active on the judiciary of the colony, becoming chief justice of the supreme court in 1739. He was a learned man, building up a library of 3,000 volumes which **Benjamin Franklin** persuaded him to give to the public. Initially called the Loganian Library the collection was later housed in the Library Company of Philadelphia, founded in 1731.

LORDS COMMISSIONERS FOR TRADE AND PLANTATIONS were established in 1675. A committee which partly evolved out of the King's privy council, it was made up initially of 21 men who were active in colonial affairs. It was a recognition of the growing importance of England's expanding empire and, along with it, its growing unwieldiness. With that, there was recognition of the necessity to gain control over colonial affairs in terms of its economy and jurisdiction. The committee was responsible for tightening up the **Navigation Acts**. It also acquired the power to hear judicial appeals from the colonies. By 1696, the committee was replaced by the **Board of Trade** and Plantations.

LOUDOUN, JOHN CAMPBELL, FOURTH EARL OF (1705–1782) was born in Scotland, where he pursued a military career, becoming governor of Stirling in 1741. He served as aide-de-camp to **George II** when the king took part in the European campaign of 1743 in **King George's War**. Loudoun played a major role defending the Hanoverian cause in the north of Scotland during the Jacobite rebellion of 1745. In 1755 he was promoted to the rank of major general. When the expedition of **Edward Braddock** to take **Fort Duquesne** ended in disaster and Braddock's death in 1755, Loudoun was chosen to succeed him and went to North America in 1756 as colonel of the Royal American Regiment. The campaign of 1757, however, was regarded as a setback for the British in the **French and Indian War**. Loudoun was recalled. He saw active service in Portugal in 1762, but retired from the army after the **Peace of Paris** ended the war in 1763.

LOYALISTS were those Americans who remained loyal to the Crown during the **War of American Independence**. How many they were is impossible to gauge precisely, and has aroused different conjectures. That there were many, perhaps as much as a third of all colonists, is now generally accepted. They were not evenly distributed throughout the colonies, being thin on the ground in New England but much more numerous in **New York** while the British were based in New York City. When they took Savannah and **Charles Town** loyalists in the south gravitated towards those ports too. They included many slaves responding to **Lord Dunmore**'s Proclamation offering them freedom if they joined the British army. After the defeat of the British at Yorktown the plight of the loyalists became a major issue in the negotiations leading to the **Peace of Paris** of 1783. The British tried to secure an indemnity from prosecution and even a restitution of their property, but the Americans resisted this. They were prepared to consider the cases of those who had not actually fought against them either in the regular army or in the regiments specially raised for them such as the green dragoons who fought under **Banastre Tarleton**. Congress however did little more than 'earnestly recommend' them to the consideration of the individual states, which few eventually did. Meanwhile between 60,000 and 80,000 left the USA. Half went to Quebec, **Nova Scotia** or the maritime provinces of Canada. About 7,000 followed in the footsteps of **Thomas Hutchinson** by going to England. Several thousand black loyalists also left the USA, mostly for Canada, about 1,000 of whom eventually settled in Sierra Leone.

M

MADISON, JAMES (1751–1836) was born in **Virginia**, the son of a planter. After private education he attended the College of **New Jersey** at Princeton where he was greatly influenced by its President, **John Witherspoon**, a Presbyterian and product of the Scottish Enlightenment. Madison graduated in 1769, one year earlier than the usual three years for commencement. Upon returning to Virginia, his decision on what career to pursue was overtaken by events. **The Coercive Acts** in 1774 had the effect of causing Madison to take a stand for civil and religious liberty. He joined the Committee of Safety and the Orange county militia, but his fragile health prevented him from full participation in military matters. Although Madison was brought up in the Anglican Church, his studies under Witherspoon's philosophy on religious liberty influenced him to the point that he denounced the persecution of Protestant dissenters in Virginia, and opposed the imprisonment of unlicensed preachers in Culpeper County. As a member of the Virginia Convention in 1776 he was able to influence the wording of the colonial constitution regarding religious freedom when the term 'toleration' of religion was changed to the 'free exercise'. In 1779 he was elected to Congress, and was instrumental in persuading Virginia to grant its claims to lands in the north west to the USA, which facilitated the ratification of the **Articles of Confederation**.

MARYLAND encompassing the upper Chesapeake Bay was granted by **Charles I** in 1632 to proprietor **George Calvert, first Lord Baltimore**. The colony was named after Queen Henrietta Maria, wife of Charles I. In the charter Baltimore was given powers such as those enjoyed by the Bishops of Durham. This clause gave the Calverts more personal authority than any other proprietors in the colonial period. They could collect dues and hold courts. The capital, originally located at St Mary's, was later moved to Annapolis. The founding of the colony was the result of socio-religious motives. The proprietor, a Roman Catholic, gave land to his fellow Catholics who were being oppressed in England. The first Jesuits to go to the colony arrived in 1634. However, other religious groups were also welcomed, including Anglicans, Puritans, and Quakers. Their presence led to the passage of a Toleration Act in 1649. The Act which gave toleration to all who professed belief in Jesus Christ, was promulgated by its Roman Catholic proprietor, **Cecilius Calvert, second Lord Baltimore** in an effort to safeguard his proprietorship from the new English Republic established during the **Interregnum**. However, Baltimore was removed as proprietor and not restored until 1656. **Charles II** confirmed Calvert's proprietorship following his own restoration in 1660. After the second Lord's death in 1675 **Charles Calvert, third Lord Baltimore** became proprietor. He was a focal point of the opposition of Protestant Marylanders in the **Glorious Revolution** which resulted in his being deprived of the proprietorship in 1691, though he was restored to it in 1715 following his conversion to Anglicanism. This revived the rivalry between the proprietors of Maryland and **Pennsylvania** which had begun when Charles II granted the latter to **William Penn**. Disputes over the boundary between the two colonies created friction which occasionally provoked violent confrontations. It culminated in expensive litigation between the Calverts and the Penns in the court of Chancery in London which was not resolved until they agreed to the running of the famous Mason–Dixon line, which began in 1763 and was completed in 1766. By then Maryland had become embroiled in the dispute over the **Stamp Act**, in which **Daniel Dulany** played a leading part.

MARY, QUEEN (1662–1694) was the oldest child and daughter of **James II**. She married William of Orange in 1677 and went to Holland, returning to England after the **Glorious Revolution**. Mary was declared joint monarch with **William III** in the Bill of Rights in 1689. She was a pious Anglican who welcomed the opportunity to promote Anglicanism in the colonies. One of the ways in which she did this was to grant a charter in 1693 for the establishment of the **William and Mary College**.

MASON, GEORGE (1725–1792) was born in Fairfax, **Virginia**, and educated at home by Scottish tutors. He was the son of a prominent tobacco planter and became a member of the Virginian elite which included **Washington** and the Lees. Possibly because of his grounding in the Scottish Enlightenment, Mason held strong views against government interference in civil and religious matters. He was among those in Virginia that led the resistance to the **Stamp Act** in 1765 and warned that if Parliament tried to pass another similar act, it would end in revolt. When Parliament passed the Boston Port Bill in 1773, Virginia voted money and supplies to help the Bostonians. Mason led the argument for armed resistance in Northern Virginian. He wrote the Fairfax Resolves and replaced Washington at the Virginia convention in 1776 where he dominated the drafting of the state constitution. His draft of the Virginia declaration of rights foreshadowed the sentiments expressed in the Declaration of Independence in terms of all men were due their right to life, liberty and the pursuit of happiness, and the United States Constitutional amendments on freedom of press, speech and religion.

Although Mason could have served on the Continental Congress, probably due to health reasons, he refused, instead concentrating his efforts in Virginia on the committee of safety throughout most of the war. After the war, he accepted a post on the Virginia delegation to the federal convention in 1787 where he opposed the ratification of the constitution primarily on the basis that it lacked a bill of rights. His pamphlet, *There is no Declaration of Rights* became a focus for like minded anti-federalists such as **Patrick Henry**. Among other points of disagreement on the document was his opposition to the continuation of the importation of slaves for another 20 years. He was also in favor of encouraging a plan for Native American Indians to become farmers rather than warriors, claiming that, if it came into effect, 'we shou'd probably hardly ever hear of another Indian War.'

MASON, JOHN (1586–1635) was born in England and educated at Oxford University. He became a seafarer, raising a fleet in 1610 to assist king **James I** to suppress a rebellion in Scotland. From 1615 to 1621 he was governor of Newfoundland. He surveyed the colony and published *A Brief Discourse of the New found land*. When he got back to England he became acquainted with **Sir Ferdinando Gorges**, treasurer for the Council of New England. The Council granted him a settlement in New England which included Cape Ann in what later became **Massachusetts**. Although he called it Mariana he never successfully settled it. In 1622 the Council granted to Gorges and Mason a huge area which was to become Maine and **New Hampshire**. In 1629 they divided it between them, Gorges claiming Maine and Mason New Hampshire. Mason joined the Council of New England in 1632, serving as its vice-president until its dissolution in 1635. Before it dissolved it confirmed and enlarged his grant of New Hampshire.

MASSACHUSETTS, located between the Merrimack River and the tip of Massachusetts Bay, was settled as a result of a charter granted by **Charles** I to the **Massachusetts Bay Company** in 1629. Since the charter did not specify the location of the Company's headquarters **John Winthrop**, whose motive was to found a religious society that would be an example to the world for its godly behavior, persuaded its principal investors to relocate it in Boston. The charter was used as the constitution not of a trading company but of a colony. Thus the General Court became the representative assembly while the freemen became the voters. Voting and holding office was open only to church members, or Puritans as they were known. The preeminence with which they placed their belief system upon the community meant that any competing beliefs or belief systems were not tolerated. This resulted in the expulsion of **Roger Williams**, the **Antinomian controversy** and the persecution of Quakers like **Mary Dyer**. Fears that the second generation was experiencing a declension – a decline in religious zeal – led to the **Half-way covenant**. They also contributed indirectly to the outbreak of witchcraft in Salem in 1692. The fears were an exaggerated response to the increasing prosperity and materialism of the colony. Although the land was hard to cultivate, there was an abundance of fish, furs, and timber. Trade in these commodities, especially with the West Indies, led Massachusetts to become more known for gain than godliness. After the **Glorious Revolution** this was reflected in the new charter of 1691 which changed the franchise from godliness to landholding. It also changed the method of selecting a governor. Where before governors had been elected by the General Court now they were to be appointed by the king, thus making Massachusetts a Crown colony. The Council, however, continued to be an elected body. This became an issue in the confrontation between the colony and the Crown in the 1760s and 1770s. Massachusetts seemed to the British government to be the nucleus of resistance to its policies, a perception strengthened by the experiences of **Thomas Hutchinson**, and the events in Boston culminating in the **Tea Party** of 1773. Among the **Coercive Acts** passed in 1774 to punish the perpetrators was the Massachusetts Government Act, which altered the arrangements made in 1691 for the election of the Council, providing for it to be nominated by the king instead.

MATHER, COTTON (1663–1728), the son of Increase Mather, attended **Harvard** where he studied theology and the sciences. In 1685 he obtained a living in North Church Boston, where he preached until his death. In 1689 he published *Memorable Providences Relating to Witchcraft and Possessions* in 1689, which contributed to the continued belief in witches culminating in the Salem trials of 1692. Mather's *Magnalia Christi Americana, or the ecclesiastical history of New England* (1702), chronicled the first 50 years in New England. Other writings by Mather are now obscure, including his contributions to the *Transactions of the Royal Society*, of which he became a Fellow in 1713. His interest in science and medicine led him to introduce inoculation against smallpox during an epidemic in Boston in 1721, when over 200 people were inoculated.

MATHER, INCREASE (1639–1723) was born in **Massachusetts** and educated at **Harvard** College and Trinity College Dublin. He returned to Massachusetts in 1661, where he became an outspoken critic of the **Half-Way Covenant**. He obtained a living in the North Church in Boston in 1664, and became President of Harvard in 1685. Mather led the resistance to the Crown's **quo warranto** proceedings against the colony in 1684. Having failed to prevent the resumption of the charter he went to England in 1688 and had three audiences with **James II** at which he asked for its reissue. When **William III** succeeded following the **Glorious Revolution** he sought to get the charter restored, but had to accept a new charter in 1691. On his return to Massachusetts he was directly involved in the Salem Witch Trials, but came to question the admissibility of spectral evidence. While his work *An Essay for the Recording of Illustrious Providence Defending the Existence of Witches*, acknowledged such evidence, another work, the *Case of Conscience Concerning Evil Spirits Personating Men* questioned its validity. Perhaps the rumor that his wife was next in line to be named as a witch gave him pause in his zeal to hunt out witchcraft. His involvement in the crisis led him to lose popularity, and his failure to stand up to the spread of liberal views in the colony led to him being dismissed as President of Harvard in 1701. Thereafter he devoted the rest of his life to writing.

MATHER, RICHARD (1596–1669) was born in Lowton, Lancashire, England, and became a minister in nearby Toxteth until 1633, when he was suspended for non-conformity. In 1635, he migrated to New England and became minister at Dorchester, **Massachusetts**. *The Whole Book of Psalms* which he published in 1640 was the first book to be printed in the English colonies in North America. Mather was a member of the Synod of 1648 and he drew up the **Cambridge Platform**. Later, realizing the growing threat to the church, he supported the **Half-Way Covenant**.

MAYFLOWER COMPACT was an agreement drawn up in a document of intent on 11 November 1620 which was signed by 41 of the passengers of the Mayflower while en route to North America. The document declared their intention to establish a colony in northern **Virginia** for the 'glory of God and the advancement of the Christian faith, and the honour of our King and country.' It proposed to establish laws through a created civil body for the better order of the new colony. However, the new colony was not established in northern Virginia but in New England at Plymouth.

MERCANTILISM, although an 18th-century term first coined by Adam Smith, was also used by historians to conceptualize the economic relationship between England and its colonial holdings. The mercantilist theory was based upon the assumption that a country's wealth was dependent upon its stock of silver and gold bullion. In order to have a favorable balance of trade, therefore, the country needed a strong export over import trade. To strengthen exports, importation of raw materials to be re-exported as finished products should be encouraged, while exportation of raw materials and the importation of manufactured goods should be discouraged. Tariffs would help regulate such movements of goods. England allegedly employed its mercantilist practice with its colonies through the mechanism of the **Navigation Acts**. Whether these represented a coherent economic philosophy rather than a series of ad hoc measures aimed at commercial rivals, e.g. in the Netherlands and Scotland, is however dubious.

METACOM, otherwise known as King Philip, was the younger brother of Wamsutta, who became the leader of the Wampanoag Indians in 1662. Wamsutta was known to the colonists as Alexander. Suspecting his intentions the authorities in Plymouth summoned him there to be interrogated about them. While in Plymouth he fell ill, and was allowed to return home on condition he left two sons as surety. Shortly afterward he died, and his subjects suspected he had been poisoned. Metacom, who succeeded him as leader, shared this suspicion and sought to build up a coalition of Algonquian-speaking Indians to challenge the colonists. His leadership signified an attempt by Native Americans on the eastern seaboard of the English colonies to stop the expansion of settlers. Metacom allied his peoples with the French while the Iroquois allied with the English government. Expansion in the New England area outpaced that of the rest of the colonies so much that it drew a response from the Algonquins between 1675 and 1676 in a series of devastating attacks led by Metacom in what became known as **King Philip's war**. The attacks ranged from the upper Connecticut Valley to Plymouth and Providence. Eventually, Metacom was defeated and killed.

METHODISTS were members of a religious movement which began in Oxford University, which its founders, John Wesley and **George Whitefield**, both attended. Wesley, a fellow of Lincoln College, Oxford, from 1726 to 1735, was instrumental in the formation of a Holy Club. This was established to stop students from slipping from devotion to Anglicanism by the secular distractions of the town by encouraging them to adhere strictly to the liturgy and ceremonies of the Church of England. It was this insistence on strictness which led them to be called 'methodists', initially a term of ridicule. Whitefield became a member of the club in 1735. That year **James Oglethorpe** invited Wesley to the newly established colony of **Georgia**. There he tried to implement the rigors of the Holy Club on the colonists, for example by not allowing them to take communion unless they had been baptized as Anglicans. Being a stickler for strict adherence to the rules made him unpopular when he refused to admit a woman to communion because she had not given prior notice of her intention to attend the service. On his return to England he was exposed to the influence of the **Moravian Brethren.** Their doctrines, particularly that of the 'new birth' made a significant contribution to his version of Methodism, which was to stress the need for regeneration. He himself experienced it at a service in London in May 1738. Wesley did not approve of other Moravian beliefs, however, such as their notion that good works were not necessary to salvation. This was because he was an Arminian, who believed that Christ died for all men. George Whitefield, on the other hand, was a Calvinist, who believed that only the elect would be saved. This disagreement led them to go separate ways in 1739. Wesley was much more influential in England, where his movement, which remained within the Church of England during his lifetime, vastly outnumbered Whitefield's. In the colonies, however, Whitefield had far more influence, being the moving spirit behind the **Great Awakening**.

MIDDLE COLONIES. A geographical expression used by some historians to distinguish between New England to the North and the Southern colonies. These 'middle' colonies included **New York**, **New Jersey**, **Pennsylvania** and **Delaware**. Whether they had anything more in common than geography, however, is debatable. Politically New York and New Jersey were Crown colonies, while Pennsylvania and Delaware were under the proprietorship of the Penn family. In religion, on the other hand, they were marked by diversity in comparison with the predominantly Congregational colonies to the north and Anglican colonies to the south. Prior to English settlement they had been claimed by Swedes and the Dutch, whose influence survived after their annexation by England. There were Quakers, particularly in New Jersey and Pennsylvania, Presbyterians, Anglicans, Moravians, Mennonites and Lutherans. This religious and ethnic diversity has been adduced in claims that the middle colonies were the first American 'melting pot'.

MOLASSES ACT. The Act was passed in 1733 to protect the interests of sugar producers in the British **West Indies** against French competition from Guadeloupe and Martinique. Colonial merchants on the American mainland, especially in New England, were obtaining the cheaper French molasses to distil into rum. The British planters protested against this practice, and used their political clout to exert pressure on the government to pass the Act which placed a prohibitive duty of sixpence per gallon on foreign sugars.

MORAVIANS were a religious sect founded in 1727 by Count Nicholas Zinzendorf in Herrnhut, Germany. The religion was a product of the Pietist revival which stressed the saving power of belief in Christ, and the necessity of a 'new birth'. Their beliefs and practices had a major impact on the early **Methodists**. In 1749 Parliament declared Moravian religion an 'Ancient Protestant Episcopal church', thus giving its imprimatur for the Moravians to settle in the English colonies. However, they had already begun emigrating in 1735 to **Georgia**. Their migration coincided with the religious revival on both sides of the Atlantic.

MORRIS, LEWIS (1671–1746) was born in New York City. Following the deaths of his parents he was raised by his uncle at Morrisania Manor, **New York**. Although his uncle was a Quaker Morris became an Anglican. From 1692 to 1698 he was a member of the Council set up by the proprietors of **New Jersey** to assist its deputy governor, **Andrew Hamilton**. In 1698 he was dismissed after objecting to the appointment of Jermiah Basse to succeed Hamilton on the grounds that not all of the proprietors had nominated him. He then became a leading proponent of the view that New Jersey should become a Crown colony, and went to England in 1702 when his objective was secured. He had hoped to become the first royal governor of New Jersey but was disappointed when Queen Anne appointed **Lord Cornbury** to the governorships of both New York and New Jersey. Morris was appointed to the Council of New Jersey, but his vigorous opposition to Cornbury led to his dismissal in 1707. He was then elected to the Assembly and continued to oppose the governor until Cornbury was removed in 1710. Once again Morris was passed over for the governorship of New Jersey, which along with that for New York was given to **Robert Hunter**. Morris's support for the new governor was rewarded in 1715 when he was appointed chief justice of New York, a post he held until 1733 when he was dismissed by governor **William Cosby** for his protests at the setting up of a court of chancery. Morris was elected to the assembly, from which he continued his protests against Cosby's rule, taking them to London in 1734. He finally realized his ambition for the governorship of New Jersey in 1738, when it was separated from that of New York. Ironically his term was marked by disputes with the assembly, which refused to pay his salary. Morris accused the lower house of claiming more powers than the House of Commons.

MORRIS, ROBERT (1735–1806) was born in England and emigrated to Maryland to join his father there in 1748. He was apprenticed to a merchant in Philadelphia who made him a partner when he had served his time. Morris took part in the demonstrations against the **Stamp Act**, serving in the non-importation committee until 1770. In 1775 he was chosen by the Pennsylvania assembly to represent them in the second continental congress. He was one of the signatories of the **Declaration of Independence**, and ratified the **Articles of Confederation** on behalf of Pennsylvania. In 1778 he ceased to be eligible to sit in congress and sat in the Pennsylvania legislature instead, where he was a conservative critic of the state's radical constitution. In 1781 he was appointed superintendent of finance by congress. Morris was instrumental in setting up the Bank of North America.

MORTON, THOMAS (d. 1646–1647) was born in England and studied law at Clifford's Inn in London. In the mid-1620s he went to New England, and helped to establish a settlement on the site of what later became Quincy, **Massachusetts**. In 1627 he named it Merrymount, notoriously celebrating the occasion by erecting a maypole, to the annoyance of the Pilgrims in Plymouth. They objected not only to his disrespect for Puritanism but also to his successful trading with the Indians. Relations with them were social as well as commercial, and Merrymount became notorious for its drunken orgies. To eliminate the challenge Morton posed to their own way of life the Pilgrims forcibly removed him from Merrymount, and sent him to England. They then had **John Endecott** cut down the offending maypole in 1628. The following year, however, Morton returned and again began to use Merrymount as a trading post with the Indians. By now he had to deal with the Puritans of Massachusetts as well as the pilgrims of Plymouth. Together they tried to impose a Puritan code on the settlement, but Morton refused to accept it. In 1631 he was brought before Governor **John Winthrop**, who punished him by seizing his goods, and sending him again to England. Morton stayed there until 1643, collaborating with **Sir Ferdinando Gorges** who also opposed the **Massachusetts Bay Company** because of its claim to his own grant of Maine. Morton wrote an account of his experiences in New England, *New English Canaan*. In it he attacked the settlers in Plymouth and Boston, claiming that their religious views inhibited the peaceful commerce with the Indians which was necessary to enable New England to prosper. When he returned there he was once more arraigned before the magistrates in Massachusetts, one of the charges against him being that he had criticized the colony in this work. He was imprisoned for a year. On his release in 1645 he moved to Maine, where he died.

MURRY, JUDITH SARGENT (1751–1820) was born in Gloucester, **Massachusetts** to a wealthy merchant family. She was educated at home, as was typical of education for girls at the time. By the Revolution, she turned her writing efforts from poetry to political essays. Her first essay, written in 1779, set the tone for her stand on women's status and rights of women. Looking forward to the new republic, she expressed the need for a new role for women to meet the new society. Her essay developed into a larger work published in 1784, entitled, *Desultory Thoughts upon the Utility of Encouraging a Degree of Self-Complacency, Especially in Female Bosoms.* She argued that women were the intellectual equal of men, and that there should be female academies to provide women with formal education in order to prepare women for their new role in the republic. Murray listed the attributes to be inculcated in the republican woman – that she be sensible and informed and if need be, economically independent. In later life, her successful publications supported Murray and her family.

N

NAVAL STORES ACT 1704. A statute encouraging colonial production of masts, hemp, pitch, and tar for the British navy. This act signaled the recognition of the colonies as a significant source of such stores over that of the unstable Baltic area.

NAVIGATION ACTS. A series of statutes was passed in England to regulate colonial trade with the intention of ensuring that it benefited the mother country. The first of these was enacted as an ordinance by the Rump Parliament in 1651. It laid down that no colonial produce could be exported to England other than in ships owned by Englishmen, Irishmen or colonists and manned by seamen at least three quarters of whom were English. European goods could only be carried to the colonies in ships belonging to the country where they originated or in English vessels. Because the Rump parliament consisted of the remnant of the House of Commons purged in 1648 to rig a majority in favor of executing king **Charles I** after the civil wars it was regarded as entirely illegitimate following the Restoration of the monarchy in 1660. Nevertheless the Navigation Act was held to be so vital that it was re-enacted that year, this time obtaining the assent of the Lords and **Charles II.** The opportunity was then taken to add certain colonial primary products, including sugar and tobacco, which could only be exported to England, where they would pay customs duties. To them were added other 'enumerated products' from time to time, such as naval stores and rice in 1705, and copper in 1722. Since the Navigation Act did not specify that they had to be shipped to England if they were taken from the colony where they were produced to another colony, this way of evading the duties was taken advantage of by the colonists. In 1673 this practice was prohibited by the **Plantation Duties Act**, which levied the duties in the colony from which they were exported if it was not the source of the commodities.

Meanwhile the **Staple Act of 1663** required European produce destined for the colonies to be taken there by way of England, with a small number of exceptions such as wine from Madeira and, since the legislation was meant to benefit England, servants from Ireland and Scotland. This last point, that the colonies were part of an English and not a British empire, was emphasized in an Act passed in 1696 'for preventing frauds and regulating abuses in the Plantation trade'.

This insisted that the ships engaged in the colonial carrying trade should not only be owned by residents of England or the colonies but should have been built there, a measure aimed chiefly at Scottish shipbuilders. The Act inaugurated administrative machinery to enforce the navigation system. Colonial governors were charged with overseeing their operation, paying a deposit of £1,000 to the **Board of Trade** on their appointment to ensure their compliance with this. Customs officials were empowered to search ships and warehouses and confiscate illegal cargoes. They could prosecute violators of the laws by issuing 'writs of assistance' summonsing them to appear in vice-admiralty courts which were introduced into the colonies in 1697.

NEWCASTLE, THOMAS PELHAM-HOLLES, DUKE OF (1693–1768) was educated at Cambridge University. He was made duke of Newcastle upon Tyne in 1715, and became one of the whig grandees of the early Hanoverian era, holding high office for almost the entire reigns of **George I** and **George II**. In 1717 he was appointed lord chamberlain, and 1724 to 1756 he was secretary of state. From 1757 until 1762 he was 1st lord of the Treasury. On the fall of **Sir Robert Walpole** in 1742 Newcastle and his brother **Henry Pelham** were embroiled in a struggle for power with other Whigs. In 1743 they overcame their rivals and formed a ministry which held power despite the initial misgivings of George II until Pelham's death in 1754. Then Newcastle exchanged the secretaryship for the first lordship of the Treasury. As secretary he enjoyed enormous influence over the colonies, taking over many of the functions previously exercised by the **Board of Trade**. For example, he appointed colonial governors. His appointments of governors such as **George Clinton**, **William Cosby** and **William Shirley** have been dismissed as disastrous for the colonies. Yet with the exception of Cosby, whose appointment no historian has commended, Newcastle's gubernatorial choices have been defended on the grounds that they were the fittest men available for the posts. He was ridiculed by some hostile contemporaries as being little better than a buffoon. Thus it was alleged that he was surprised to learn that Cape Breton was an island and did not know where Annapolis was. But this is belied by an examination of his efforts to put the colonies in a state of preparedness to defend themselves against French attack when the peace established by the treaty of Aix-la-Chapelle in 1748, which he realized was nothing more than a breathing space, was broken. He was responsible for advising George II to appoint **Lord Halifax** as President of the **Board of Trade**, who revived the authority of that body over the colonies. As prime minister from 1754 to 1756 Newcastle found himself opposed by **William Pitt**, whose opposition led Newcastle to resign. Pitt succeeded as premier, but his ministry was short lived, not least since it did not have the support of the king. In 1757 Pitt and Newcastle agreed to form a joint ministry, which successfully waged the Seven Years' War, known in America as the **French and Indian War**. When **George III** succeeded to the throne in 1760, however, he indicated that he would prefer his own choice of ministers. This brought about the resignation of Pitt in 1761 and of Newcastle in 1762. Newcastle was out of office until 1765 when he became Lord Privy Seal. He supported the repeal of the **Stamp Act** in 1766.

NEW ENGLAND is a geographical area encompassing the colonies of **Connecticut**, **Massachusetts**, **New Hampshire** and **Rhode Island**. The region was apparently first described as New England by **John Smith**, who published *A Description of New England* in 1616.

NEW FRANCE was a term sometimes applied to the whole of **Canada**, including **Acadia** and Newfoundland. More precisely, however, it is applied to the core settlements on the St Lawrence river now within the province of Quebec. Although the French were active in the area much earlier, notably with the explorations of Jacques Cartier in the early 16th century, Quebec itself was established in 1608. The governors of New France were appointed by the king, and reported to the minister of marine. They were especially charged with the defense of the colony, for which purpose troupes-de-la marine were established in 1683. Along with the militia they protected New France against the English to the south and their Indian allies in the **Covenant Chain**. The military preparations of the government spread beyond the borders of New France to defend French acquisitions along the Great Lakes and down the Mississippi to Louisiana. Thus forts were established at Detroit in 1701 and at Mobile in 1702. In the interval between the end of **King George's War** in 1748 and the start of the **French and Indian War** in 1754 the chain of forts was strengthened to deter British claims to the Ohio region, the main link being **Fort Duquesne**. In 1756 the last Governor of New France, General Louis Montcalm, took up his post. He was defeated in the attack on Quebec in 1759 by **James Wolfe**. Like Wolfe he died in the battle which sealed the fate of New France. It was ceded to Great Britain along with all other French claims in North America east of the Mississippi at the **Peace of Paris in 1763**.

NEW HAMPSHIRE. An area along the Merrimack and Piscataqua Rivers which was granted along with Maine to **Sir Ferdinando Gorges** and **John Mason** in 1622. In 1629 they divided it, Gorges claimed Maine while Mason claimed New Hampshire. Although some settlers went from England, the population was made up mainly of migrants from **Massachusetts**. That colony also laid claim to the territory. After Mason's death in 1635 his heirs maintained his claim to it against others. The conflicting claims were settled when it was made a Crown colony by **Charles II** in 1679. In 1687 New Hampshire was included in the **Dominion of New England** but regained its independence following the **Glorious Revolution**.

NEW HAVEN started out as a colony in its own right. It was founded by **John Davenport** and **Theophilus Eaton** who initially migrated to Boston. They arrived at the height of the **Antinomian controversy** during the mid-1630s, and proceeded to migrate south to an Indian inlet of Long Island and later further west to Quinnipiac. From the Quinnipiac Indians they purchased a plot in 1638 which later became the town of New Haven. This gave its name to the colony, which by 1643 included the towns of Branford, Guildford, Milford, Southwold and Stamford. The settlement was not merged with **Connecticut** until 1665.

NEW JERSEY was originally part of the duke of York's province of **New York**. It was subsequently sectioned off and granted by the duke to **George Carteret** and **John Berkeley**, long time colonial investors. The initial government provisions followed the Carolina model with the usual liberty of conscience, freedom of trade and an elected assembly. The cost of an acre for prospective buyers was a penny. As with other Restoration colonies, it was hoped that settlers from other colonies would help to fill this one as well as from England. Berkeley's debts forced him to sell his half of the investment. In 1674 John Fenwick, a Cromwellian Quaker, purchased this portion on behalf of another Quaker, Edward Byllinge. This arrangement caused disputes between the two Quakers which were only resolved by the setting up of a Quaker trusteeship. The trusteeship, headed by **William Penn**, Gawren Lawrie, and Nicholas Lucas, took responsibility for the settlement. At this point the Quaker interests were separated from the Carteret holdings. The result was the division between East New Jersey and West New Jersey. Upon the death of Carteret, the Quakers purchased the remaining half thereby making the two halves whole. In 1688 **James II** incorporated New Jersey into the **Dominion of New England**. New Jersey remained under proprietary rule until 1702 when it became a royal colony. The colony's political infrastructure was similar to most of the other colonies consisting of a governor, council, and assembly. Although the governor was considered the 'first gentleman of the colony,' he was nevertheless answerable ultimately to the Crown.

NEW MEDITERRANEAN SEA COMPANY was formed in 1686 as a corporation by former members of the **Free Society of Traders** and the old Mediterranean Sea company, the Levant Company. Organized by Dr Daniel Coxe, a London physician and titular governor of **New Jersey**, the membership was a transatlantic one which included English government members such as William and Henry Ashurst. The company was launched to exploit the fur trade in the northern part of **Pennsylvania** and beyond. By 1691, the company was defunct mainly due to internal disputes and the consequences of **the Glorious Revolution** in England.

NEW PENNSYLVANIA COMPANY was formed in 1693 by **William Penn**, who knew the London merchants who bought shares in the company. The company was created out of the failure of the **Free Society of Traders** and the **Susquehanna Company**. The main motive for its creation was for Penn to show his loyalty to the English government in order to regain control of his colony. Thus the company committed itself to making and delivering to the English government pitch, hemp, timber, and flax for the use of the Royal Navy.

NEW YORK was originally a Dutch trading outpost, known as New Netherland. The colony fell under English auspices, first in 1664, after the Second Anglo-Dutch war and finally after the Third Anglo-Dutch war and the 1674 Treaty of Westminster. It was renamed New York for its royal proprietor, James, duke of York. After the English take over, the Dutch culture was blended with English settlers and some French Huguenots, and German Palatines. The multicultural makeup gave rise to a certain amount of religious plurality ranging from Dutch Reformed to Anglican faiths. As a proprietary colony, its political structure was under the control of its owner. However, the political climate in England after 1680 pressured the duke of York to grant an assembly in 1683. When the duke succeeded as **James II** in 1685, however, the assembly was made redundant when the king subsumed the colony under the wider **Dominion of New England**. At the **Glorious Revolution** in 1688 and the overthrow of James II, New York proclaimed its loyalty to the new regime of **William** and **Mary**. Consequently, the colony's leading families revolted against the incumbent governor **Francis Nicholson**. The rebellion was led by **Jacob Leisler**, a German merchant. Ultimately, upon the assumption of the new king and queen, Leisler was imprisoned and executed under a new governor appointed by the Crown. The politics of the colony were affected by the aftermath of the rebellion for decades, when political parties representing Leislerians and anti-Leislerians made New York one of the most faction ridden of the colonies. Economically, New York's primary trade was fur. After the end of the 17th century, other exports such as timber, food stuffs and livestock grew. Trade was mainly with the West Indies.

NEW YORK CHARTER OF LIBERTIES AND PRIVILEGES 1683 was a document drawn up by the freemen of New York, to insure their liberties as Englishmen (although many of the signers of the document were Dutch), property rights, and political inclusion. It called for a representative assembly which under the duke of York, it had been lacking. Another significant item in the frame of government pertained to religion. New York had a religious plurality that had to be safeguarded particularly regarding the suspicions over its proprietor's Roman Catholicism. While religious toleration was guaranteed for Christian believers, the frame decentralized control to local areas for contributing support of the majority church in each area. Although the duke acquiesced to the charter in so far as granting an assembly, upon his ascending the English throne as **James II**, he dissolved the assembly.

NEW YORK CITY was first called New Amsterdam after it was settled by the **Dutch** in 1626. It was named New York after its acquisition in 1663 by the English, whose king, **Charles II**, made his brother James duke of York proprietor. Hence it was renamed after James's duchy. It reverted to New Amsterdam in 1673 following the reconquest by the Dutch during the third Anglo–Dutch war, and was finally established as New York at the treaty of Westminster in 1674 which ended the war. During the **Glorious Revolution** it was the scene of the rebellion by **Jacob Leisler**. At that time it had approximately 3,000 residents. By 1700 there were 5,000 and in 1760 18,000.

NICOLLS, RICHARD (1624–1672) was born in England, and pursued a military career, commanding a troop of horses in the English civil war, in which he took the royalist side. He went into exile with **Charles II** and his brother James, duke of York, serving in the latter's household. After the Restoration he returned to England as the duke's groom of the bedchamber. When Charles II granted the Dutch claims in North America to his brother, Nicolls commanded the expedition sent out to acquire them. When he arrived off New Amsterdam in August 1664 the governor surrendered it to him. He then became Deputy governor of **New York**, as the colony was renamed, under the proprietor, James, duke of York. Nicolls greatest challenge as governor was to successfully assert his authority over an already established population. He treated the Dutch, who had settled mainly up the Hudson River valley, and the English, who had established themselves in Long Island even before the conquest, as separate communities. He largely left the Dutch officials in charge of their own affairs, while he extended a code of laws known as the Duke's Laws to the English and introduced assize courts modeled on those which were held in counties in England. Long Island was even named Yorkshire and divided into three Ridings for this purpose. In 1667 Nicolls returned to England where he died fighting in the third Anglo–Dutch war at the battle of Sole Bay.

NICHOLSON, FRANCIS (1655–1728) was born in Yorkshire where he was brought up in the household of the duke of Bolton, who might have been his father. Nicholson entered the army, serving at Tangier from 1680 to 1684. When **Sir Edmund Andros** went to North America to head the **Dominion of New England** in 1686 Nicholson accompanied him as captain of a company of foot. He went to **Connecticut** to demand the surrender of its charter. In 1688 the Dominion was extended to include **New York** and **New Jersey,** and Nicholson became lieutenant governor of the Dominion under Andros. While Andros chose to stay in **Boston** Nicholson took up his post in New York. When the **Glorious Revolution** broke out his authority was challenged by **Jacob Leisler**. Nicholson decided to go to England, where in 1690 his decision was vindicated when **William III** made him lieutenant governor of **Virginia** under the absentee governor Lord Howard of Effingham. Nicholson was a keen supporter of the establishment of the **College of William and Mary**. In 1692 he was replaced as lieutenant governor by Andros, but became governor of **Maryland** in 1694. He presided over the transference of the colonial capital from St Mary's to Annapolis. In 1698 he was again appointed lieutenant governor of Virginia and oversaw the move of its capital from Jamestown to Williamsburg. He was quarrelsome and hot-tempered, however, and this made him enemies. Among them was **James Blair** president of the College of William and Mary, who was instrumental in having Nicholson recalled in 1705. Back in England he was elected Fellow of the Royal Society in 1706. When the northern colonies planned an attack on Canada in 1709, Nicholson offered to lead an expedition from Albany to Quebec. To publicize the project he sent four Indian sachems to England. Their public appearances in London and elsewhere proved to be very popular.

The government however failed to provide sufficient resources for the descent on Quebec and instead Nicholson took part in the attack on Port Royal, **Nova Scotia** which was taken and renamed Annapolis Royal in honor of the Queen. In 1711 the Canadian plan at last seemed to be possible, and Nicholson took part in an expedition to Quebec, which had to be aborted when the naval arm of the two-pronged attack ran into dense fog in the St Lawrence River and foundered. Nicholson was appointed governor of Nova Scotia in 1712, holding the post until 1715, when he retired to England. He was brought out of retirement in 1720 to become the first royal governor of **South Carolina**. He roused the opposition of merchants there through his support for the issue of paper money and was recalled in 1725. Nicholson's tenure of the governorships of New York, Virginia (twice), Maryland, Nova Scotia and South Carolina was unique in the history of colonial America.

NORTH, FREDERICK, LORD (1732–1792) began his political career in 1754 as Member of Parliament for Banbury, a borough controlled by his father, Francis, first earl of Guildford. North remained in the Commons until he became second earl of Guildford on his father's death in 1788. He was made a lord of the treasury in 1759, a post he held until the formation of the first **Rockingham** administration in 1765. On the death of **Charles Townshend** in 1767 he replaced him as chancellor of the exchequer. After the fall of the **Grafton** ministry in 1770 he became prime minister, a position he held until 1782. **George III** gave him his entire support, demonstrating that he did so by making him a Knight of the Garter in 1772. In 1777 the king cleared North's debts. The prime minister repealed all the **Townshend duties** except those on tea, securing for the British a 'period of quiet' in their dealings with the American colonies which lasted until 1773. It was his policy towards India which brought this period to a close. North's attempt to help the East India Company overcome acute financial difficulties by shipping tea directly to the colonies led to the **Boston Tea Party**. The passage of the **Coercive Acts** in reaction to this could be seen as an overreaction. They ensured that the resistance in the colonies to his measures would not be confined to **New England** but would unite the eastern seaboard against him. North was overwhelmed by the enormity of the problems which the ensuing conflict posed for him. He frequently offered his resignation, admitting in 1779 'I am not equal in abilities to the station which I ought to hold'. The following year saw him even more beleaguered. Irish patriots took a leaf out of the colonists' book by demanding more legislative independence from Britain, while the Protestant Association led by Lord George Gordon provoked the most serious riot of the 18th century in London, and there were attacks on the influence of the Crown in the House of Commons. Although North rode out these storms he could not survive the defeat of British arms at Yorktown. When North heard the news he exclaimed 'Oh God it is all over'. In March 1782 he resigned. Although he was resigned to recognizing American independence he disliked the peace terms negotiated by the **earl of Shelburne**, claiming that they betrayed the **loyalists**. He therefore combined with **Charles James Fox** to defeat them in the Commons in February 1783, thereby bringing an end to Shelburne's ministry. In the ensuing jockeying for office he startled many contemporaries by joining with his former opponent **Charles James Fox** to force the king to appoint them. Although the new prime minister was officially the duke of Portland, with North serving as home secretary and Fox as foreign secretary, it has ever since been known as the Fox–North coalition. It was this ministry which brought the **Peace of Paris** of 1783 to a successful conclusion. George III was determined to bring the ministry down at the first opportunity, which presented itself in December 1783 when it brought forward arrangements for the government of India which slighted his authority. The influence of the Crown was used to full effect to reduce the coalition's majority in both Houses until George felt confident in dismissing Fox and North and replacing them with William Pitt the Younger. Pitt became prime minister for the next 21 years. North spent the rest of his political career in opposition.

NORTH CAROLINA. When **Charles II** issued a charter for Carolina in 1662 no distinction was made between north and south. The colony, however, did diverge geographically from the start, with settlements around Albermarle Sound in the north and Charles Town in the south. In 1691 the north received a deputy governor under the governor who resided in Charles Town. In 1712 a separate government was instituted in each colony. In 1718 **George I** insisted on approving the proprietor's choice of governor for North Carolina, making it essentially a crown colony. It was not until 1729 that the proprietors sold their rights to the crown.

NOVA SCOTIA, although claimed by **King James I** of England (1603–1625), who was also James VI of Scotland (hence its name, New Scotland), was first effectively settled by the French, who established themselves at Port Royal in 1605. It then formed part of **Acadia**. The settlement was small, numbering maybe 2,000 colonists who struggled to eke out a living from farming and fishing. During **Queen Anne's War** the British captured Port Royal, renaming it Annapolis Royal in honor of the Queen. Nova Scotia was ceded to Great Britain by France in the Treaty of Utrecht of 1713. By the middle of the 18th century Halifax had been established as the main naval base for the Royal Navy in the Americas. The 13,000 French settlers were regarded as a potential fifth column when war broke out again between the British and the French in the middle of the 18th century. In 1755 over half of them were forced to move from the colony to other parts of North America in a process completed in 1758 which would now be regarded as 'ethnic cleansing'. Many of them found their way to Louisiana where they became known as Cajuns, a corruption of Acadians. By 1776 there were approximately 20,000 white inhabitants in Nova Scotia, about half of them New Englanders who had migrated there since 1760. Where initially they were welcomed as being potentially more loyal to Britain than the French settlers who had been eliminated, ironically in the **War of American Independence** these 'Yankees' were regarded as potential rebels. In fact they remained loyal, many swayed by the religious fervor of Henry Alline, one of their number who had gone to Nova Scotia from Rhode Island in 1760. He led a religious revival which has been compared with the **Great Awakening**.

O

OGLETHORPE, JAMES EDWARD (1696–1785) was educated at Eton school and Oxford University. In 1707 he went into the army and fought in **Queen Anne's War**. After that ended with the Treaty of Utrecht he went to France and then enlisted with the imperial army under Prince Eugene of Savoy against the Turks. He betrayed his Jacobite leanings by attending the court of the exiled Stuart James Edward in St Germain and Italy before returning to England in 1719. In 1722 he was returned to parliament as member for Haslemere, Surrey, a seat he held until 1754. As an opposition Tory his contributions were marked by the advocacy of naval rather than military strategy, or 'blue water' policy. He was also known for his philanthropy, publishing a pamphlet against impressment for the navy in 1728 and contributing to an investigation of debtors' prisons between 1729 and 1730. This led him to conclude that many were languishing uselessly in them when they could be usefully employed if arrangements could be made with their creditors. He determined to launch such a scheme by setting up a colony in North America where insolvent debtors could be given a fresh start. As a result of his efforts and those of others, notably the earl of Egmont, a trust was established which obtained a charter for the colony of **Georgia**. Oglethorpe made three visits to Georgia in the 1730s, where he took charge of the colony's defense against Spain. This was very necessary after the outbreak of war with Spain in 1739. In 1740 he led an abortive attack on St Augustine in Florida. Two years later he repelled a Spanish attack on Georgia at the battle of Bloody Marsh. In 1743 he returned to England, and was active in the Jacobite rebellion of 1745 on the Hanoverian side, though as a former Jacobite himself he came under suspicion. He was even court martialled, albeit he was acquitted. In later life he became a prominent figure on the London literary scene, known to such leading authors as James Boswell, Oliver Goldsmith and Dr Samuel Johnson.

OHIO COMPANY. In 1749 **George II** granted 500,000 acres in the Ohio River valley to the Ohio Company on condition that at least 100 families would settle there, and a fort would be constructed. This was meant to be a buffer against French claims to the region. The area was explored between 1749 and 1754 by Christopher Gist. The outbreak of the **French and Indian War** thwarted further progress, and after it ended the **Proclamation of 1763** banning colonial expansion west of the Appalachians prohibited official settlement.

OTIS, JAMES (1725–1783) was born in Barnstaple **Massachusetts** and educated at **Harvard**. He then set up as a lawyer, becoming a justice of the peace in 1756 and deputy advocate – general of the colony's vice-admiralty court in 1757. He resigned from the latter post in 1761 to take up the cause of merchants who challenged the right of Charles Paxton, the commissioner of customs, to issue writs of assistance, warrants which gave him unlimited powers to search for contraband goods. Otis challenged their legality in the superior court so powerfully that **John Adams** was later to claim that 'American independence was then and there born'. Otis's argument that the writs were unconstitutional, however, apparently foundered on their having been authorized by an act of parliament, though in 1766 the attorney general in Britain was to rule that the statute in question did not extend to the colonies. Otis became a leading opponent of parliament's claims to tax America, publishing *The Rights of the British Colonies asserted and proved in 1764 and A Vindication of the British Colonies* in 1765. Towards the end of the decade, however, his mental abilities were severely affected by alcohol, and he was regarded as insane. His insanity was aggravated in 1769 when a customs official beat him severely. For the rest of his life his family had to take care of him.

P

PAINE, THOMAS (1737–1809) was born in Thetford, England. He left school at the age of 12 to become an apprentice to his Quaker father, a stay maker. Although his apprenticeship was disrupted by a spell in the navy he apparently completed it, as he worked for stay makers in London and Dover before setting up his own business in Sandwich. He married in 1759 but his wife died the following year. Paine then entered the excise service. His employment was disrupted following his dismissal in 1765, upon which he became a schoolmaster. When he was re-employed as an exciseman in 1768 he settled down in Lewes, Sussex. There he became a member of a debating club in which he earned a reputation as a pugnacious debater, especially when speaking in support of his whig principles. In 1771 he married Elizabeth Ollive and also became her partner in the running of her family's business, a grocery and tobacconist shop. He still continued as an exciseman, but found the post so poorly paid that in 1772 he published a pamphlet, *The Case of the Officers of the Excise*, stating their case for more pay. His campaign did not endear him to the government, and this may have influenced the decision to dismiss him from the service in 1774. That year also saw the breakup of his marriage and the bankruptcy of his business.

Since his old world had fallen apart Paine sought a new one by leaving England for America. Before he left he obtained a letter of introduction from **Benjamin Franklin**. This enabled him, after his arrival in Philadelphia on 30 November, to obtain employment as editor of a new journal, the *Pennsylvania Magazine: or American Monthly Museum*. Since Robert Aitken, proprietor of the magazine, was anxious not to get involved in polemical disputes, Paine published an attack on chattel slavery in *The Pennsylvania Journal*, a weekly paper. This brought him to the notice of **Benjamin Rush**, who entertained similar views. After the battle of Lexington, however, Paine no longer exercised any restraint about publishing articles critical of British attitudes towards the colonies in the *Pennsylvania Magazine*. Aitken took umbrage at this and refused to offer Paine a contract. Although he continued to contribute copy to the journal he spent the fall of 1775 working on a pamphlet urging American independence, which he showed to Franklin and Rush. They approved the contents, the only change being suggested by Rush, who persuaded Paine to alter the title from *Plain Truth* to *Common Sense*. The tract appeared on 10 January 1776. Much of it is devoted to political theory, in which Paine sought to demonstrate that government was a necessary evil, and that hereditary monarchy was an absurdity. For all its vivid writing it is hard to see how these passages had such an impact on public opinion. But when he came to posit the choice between reconciliation and independence Paine really did seem to stand for common sense. 'No man was a warmer wisher for a reconciliation than myself before the fatal nineteenth of April 1775 [the confrontation at Lexington], but the moment the event of that day was made known, I rejected the hardened sullen-tempered Pharaoh of England for ever'. He articulated sentiments which many shared, but had not expressed so clearly. The pamphlet was a prodigious best seller, and prepared Americans to encourage and support the **Declaration of Independence** in July 1776.

That summer Paine enrolled in the armed forces, becoming aide-de-camp to General Nathanael Greene. Initial military setbacks led him to write *The American Crisis* to bolster the morale of the continental army in the winter of 1776–1777. In March he became secretary to the Congressional committee on foreign affairs, a post he had to resign the following year when he accused Silas Deane, one of the American representatives in Paris, of corrupt dealings with the French. In 1779 he obtained a less exalted public post as clerk to the Pennsylvania Assembly. Paine entered the debate about the future of western territories claimed by some states, especially **Virginia**. In *Public Good* published in 1780 he argued that they should be handed over to Congress, a solution eventually adopted in the North West Ordinance. The following year he again found employment with Congress, which sent him to France to try to obtain more financial support from the French. On his return Congress paid him to publish the case for the states to raise more in taxes to finance the common cause. His final published contribution to that cause was his *Letter to the Abbe Raynal on the affairs of North America*.

In 1787 he went to England to try to raise money for a pet scheme to build an iron bridge. Back in Europe he became involved in the political controversies created by the French Revolution, advocating the *Rights of Man* in a treatise with that title published in two parts in 1791 and 1792. These were regarded as so seditious that Paine had to flee prosecution for seditious libel and fled to France. There he was returned to the Convention for Calais and took part in the framing of the constitution of 1793. He fell foul of the Jacobins who imprisoned him and he might have been executed had he not claimed American citizenship and appealed to the ambassador James Monroe to obtain his release. After that Paine's reputation suffered from his public criticism of **George Washington** whom he accused of failing to help him, and even more from his attack upon revealed religion in *The Age of Reason*. On his return to the United States in 1802 he was shunned as an atheist. He died in 1809 in New Rochelle, New York.

PARIS PEACE OF 1763 concluded the **French and Indian Wars** in North America and the Seven Years' War in Europe. The French ceded their possessions on the American continent east of the Mississippi to Britain. They also compensated Spain, which lost **Florida** to the British, by granting them Louisiana. In the **West Indies** Britain acquired from France the **ceded**

islands, though she handed back Martinique and Guadeloupe. Spain also regained Cuba in exchange for Florida.

PARIS PEACE OF 1783 is sometimes styled the peace of Versailles. Yet though Britain negotiated treaties with France and Spain at Versailles, the definitive treaty with the United States of America was signed in Paris on 3 September 1783. The French treaty returned Tobago to France and gave Florida back to Spain. The **earl of Rockingham** had opened negotiations with the USA on taking office in February 1782, but preliminary articles were not agreed to until 30 November, by which time Rockingham was dead and **Shelburne** was prime minister. He was anxious to retain close commercial ties between Britain and her former colonies, and therefore offered them several concessions. Thus he agreed to cede the territories between the Ohio and Mississippi rivers, annexed to Canada in the Quebec Act of 1774, to the USA. At the same time he tried unsuccessfully to persuade the Americans to compensate loyalists. Shelburne's concessions to the USA and failure to get a deal for loyalists led to his peace preliminaries being rejected by the House of Commons, and his own resignation, in February 1783. The Fox–North coalition which succeeded the Shelburne ministry, however, was no more successful in getting help for loyalists, and accepted similar terms including the recognition of the independence of the United States.

PARSONS' CASE arose following a slump in tobacco prices in the mid-1750s, when the Assembly in **Virginia** passed Acts in 1755 and 1758 commuting payments from tobacco to specie. They were called the Twopenny Acts as they fixed the price at 2d a pound. Ministers of the **Anglican Church** led by John Cannon, Professor of divinity at the **College of William and Mary** objected that their salaries were significantly reduced by this measure. Cannon went to London to protest and persuaded the Privy Council to veto the Acts. The Parsons' Case became a cause celebre in the colony, in which **Patrick Henry** first emerged as a public figure.

PELHAM, HENRY (1695–1754) was the younger brother of Thomas Pelham-Holles, first duke of **Newcastle**. He was elected to the House of Commons in 1717 and as a supporter of **Sir Robert Walpole** became a lord of the Treasury in 1721, secretary at war in 1724 and paymaster general in 1730. After the fall of Walpole in 1742 Pelham jockeyed for power with other whigs, and eventually won, becoming prime minister in 1743. Although at first **George II** disliked Pelham, he came to trust him, especially for his prudent management of the nation's finances. When he died the king said 'now I shall have no more peace.'

PENN, THOMAS (1702–1775). Born in Bristol, the second son of **William Penn** by his second wife Hannah Callowhill. After William's death he and his brothers John and Richard eventually inherited the proprietorship of **Pennsylvania**. Like his brothers Thomas left the Society of Friends to become an Anglican. He went to Pennsylvania in 1732 staying until 1774. While there he was involved in the so-called '**Walking Purchase**'.

PENN, WILLIAM (1644–1718) was born in London, the first son of Lord Admiral William Penn. He was converted to Quakerism sometime between 1667 and 1668, becoming a leading spokesman for the sect if not its most influential proponent for religious toleration. Penn wrote both religious and political tracts which dealt with issues from religious freedom to electioneering propaganda such as his controversial polemic, *Sandy Foundation Shaken*, and *England's Great Interest in the Choice of this New Parliament*. Penn was involved in the development of the colonies, particularly **New Jersey**, to some extent **Virginia**, and primarily in the formation of **Pennsylvania**. In 1681, he was granted the proprietorship of what was to become Pennsylvania. He set about promoting the colony for its commercial possibilities as well as for its religious toleration through a number of tracts such as, *Some Account of the Province of Pennsylvania*, and *Some Proposals for a Second Settlement of Pennsylvania*. Although Penn concentrated on the development of his new holdings, he remained involved in English and European affairs to the extent that he reached high political influence during the reign of **James II** from 1685 to 1688. With the overthrow of James II in 1688, Penn's political star fell to the point that he was suspected of treasonous activities resulting in the loss of the government of Pennsylvania. By 1694, he was able to clear his name and regain the proprietorship of the colony. Throughout his proprietorship, Penn was in constant conflict with neighboring colonies over boundaries and subsequent trade disputes. He also came into conflict with his own colonists over issues such as the paying of rents. Although in the long run, the colony's commercial ventures paid off, in the beginning they were less than successful. A number of companies were created such as the **Free Society of Traders**, the **New Mediterranean Sea Company**, and the **Susquehanna Company** but proved too fragile to be profitable. Although Penn visited the colony twice in his life, he never intended to settle there. He viewed it as a commercial enterprise, one that he intended to sell, and in 1703 he began negotiations with the Crown on its sale. Penn ran into financial trouble and in 1708 he was imprisoned only to be released after the duchess of Marlborough and some Quaker friends paid off the debt. In 1712, Penn suffered a stroke and gradually became incapacitated. He died in 1718.

PENNSYLVANIA was established in 1681 upon a grant from the Crown to **William Penn**. The grant, which included the **Delaware** area, was the largest tract of land to be given by the English Crown in the 17th century. Geographically, Pennsylvania filled the gap in the English colonies by linking **New York** and **Maryland** thereby consolidating what can be loosely called, **the middle colonies**. It became the cultural prototype for the United States because of its religious and ethnic pluriformity. Besides Quakers, Pennsylvania was made up of Anglicans, Baptists, Dutch Reformed, Presbyterians and other sects. Penn's intention for Pennsylvania as a 'holy experiment' can be seen in the colony's charter which has no religious restrictions other than that there should be an Anglican minister, if a petition for one with 20 signatures were to be submitted. In 1701, with a new Frame of Government, Delaware was separated from Pennsylvania with its own assembly.

PEPPERELL, SIR WILLIAM (1696–1759) was born in Maine, where he joined the militia in 1712, rising to the rank of colonel over the following decade and in 1726 becoming commander. Pepperell served on the **Massachusetts** Council from 1727 to 1759. In 1730 he became a chief justice of the colony. He was involved in the attack on Cape Breton in 1745 when he was made a colonel. The following year his involvement was recognized when he was made a baronet, the first colonial to be so honored. He raised a regiment in the **French and Indian War**, being promoted to the rank of lieutenant general in 1759. On his death that year he was one of the wealthiest men in Massachusetts.

PEQUOT WAR (1637–1638) arose as a result of the expansion of the settlements in **Plymouth** and **Massachusetts** along the northern shore of Long Island Sound to **New Haven**, and up the Connecticut River valley to Hartford. This alarmed the Indians who inhabited these areas. Among them were the Pequots, who felt threatened by the establishment of the town of Saybrook at the mouth of the Connecticut River. In 1637 their fears led them to wage war on the English settlers. The latter, however, led by John Mason, were able to exploit divisions between the local Indians. Mason was able to recruit Mohegans and Narragansetts, who aligned themselves with the English in order to attack the Pequot base at Mystic. The fort there was set on fire, leading to the deaths not only of the garrison but of 700 men, women and children. Mason wrote a history of the war, though it was not published until 1736, in which he attributed the victory of the colonists to the intervention of Providence. In the end, the Pequots accepted the Treaty of Hartford in which the name of Pequot was outlawed.

PHILADELPHIA was the first American city to be laid out on a grid pattern, chosen by its proprietor **William Penn**, who probably based it on his first hand acquaintance with Turin, the new capital of Savoy. Penn chose the site for the chief city of **Pennsylvania** when he went there in 1681. The name, meaning the 'city of brotherly love' was taken from one of the cities in the Levant mentioned in the New Testament. Several merchants whom Penn attracted to trade with his colony would be familiar with the original from their membership of the English Levant company. Located between the Delaware and Schuylkill Rivers, the new Philadelphia at first fronted the Delaware, where Front Street and Society Hill, named after the **Free Society of Traders**, whose merchants lived there, still bear the mark of their colonial origins. The city grew rapidly, from a handful of Swedish settlers who were located there when Penn obtained his charter to 5,000 by 1700, 10,000 by 1720, 13,000 by 1740 and 20,000 by 1760. It is sometimes claimed that the total reached 40,000 by 1775, making it the second city in the British empire in size after London, but this is an exaggerated figure. Nevertheless it was the largest in North America, becoming the major entrepot for the Atlantic trade. From it were exported flour ground from the wheat grown in Pennsylvania, the 'bread basket' of the colonies, to ports along the eastern seaboard and even the **West Indies**. In 1774 Philadelphia became the seat of the **Continental Congress** and after the **Declaration of Independence** the first capital of the United States of America, except when it was occupied by British troops between 1777 and 1778 during the **War of American Independence**.

PHIPS, SIR WILLIAM (1651–1695) was born in Maine, where he was apprenticed to a ship's carpenter. After serving his apprenticeship he set up his own business in **Boston**. He was knighted in 1687 for his discovery of a sunken treasure ship off Hispaniola (Haiti). During the **Dominion of New England** he was provost marshal of Boston under **Sir Edmund Andros**. Phips went to England in 1688 where he liaised with **Increase Mather** in abortive negotiations for the reissue of the Massachusetts charter. He was back in Boston during the **Glorious Revolution** and became involved in the campaigns of **King William's War**, taking a conspicuous part in the attack on Port Royal. He again went to England to become the first royal governor of Massachusetts under the colony's new charter of 1691. On his return to Boston he found the colony embroiled in the controversy surrounding the **Salem Witch Trials**. Phips was instrumental in bringing them to an end. As governor he earned a reputation for arbitrariness, particularly in cases involving breaches of the **Navigation Acts**. He was very lax in enforcing them, siding with violators. Thus he publicly caned a captain of the Royal navy and physically stopped a customs officer from seizing a ship. In 1694 he was ordered to go to England to face charges of negligence in his duties, and died suddenly after arriving there.

PITT, WILLIAM (1708–1778) entered parliament in 1735 and quickly made his mark in the opposition to **Sir Robert Walpole**. He continued in opposition to Walpole's successor **Henry Pelham** until he was brought into the ministry as paymaster general. Pelham, who had held the post himself, and knew its potential to enrich its occupant, thought he had literally bought Pitt off. But Pitt ostentatiously refused the opportunities the post offered for enrichment, earning a reputation for integrity. After the duke of **Newcastle** succeeded as prime minister on Pelham's death in 1754 Pitt felt overlooked for high office and opposed the new ministry. The disastrous opening of the Seven Years' War in 1756 gave him an opportunity to claim that he knew he could save the country and that nobody else could. **George II** felt obliged to ask him to form a ministry in December 1756, which he did in conjunction with the duke of Devonshire. This only lasted until April 1757, however, when Pitt was dismissed. There ensued several months of wrangling which ended with the formation of a joint ministry by Newcastle, who became first lord of the Treasury, and Pitt, who was made secretary of state. The Pitt–Newcastle ministry presided over the successes of the Seven Years' or **French and Indian War**. Although Pitt was once given almost sole credit for them it is now generally accepted that they were the responsibility of a united Cabinet and that Newcastle deserved some of the credit too. The accession of **George III** in 1760 brought about a change in ministerial fortunes, as the new king was suspicious of the politicians he inherited from **George II**, and wished to promote others, especially the earl of **Bute**. Pitt resigned in 1761 when the Cabinet refused to declare war on Spain. In opposition he spoke against the terms of the peace treaty, which in his view threw away the advantages of the great victories he had presided over. When the policies of **George Grenville** provoked an outcry in the American colonies Pitt declared his dislike of them. In the debate on the repeal of the **Stamp Act** he even claimed that the British parliament had no right to tax the colonies, drawing a distinction between legislation and taxation. Thus he supported the **Declaratory Act** which asserted that parliament could pass legislation which bound the colonies in all cases whatsoever, insisting that this did not include taxation. When the ministry of the marquis of **Rockingham** fell in 1766 Pitt, now ennobled as Lord Chatham, succeeded him as prime minister. While denying that parliament could tax the colonies directly, Pitt conceded that indirect taxes were legal. Thus when he succumbed to manic depression in 1767 his chancellor of the exchequer, **Charles Townshend**, drew on this to introduce colonial import duties. The colonists were not prepared to accept any taxes, direct or indirect, imposed by a parliament in which they were not represented, and these too raised a storm of opposition in the colonies. On recovering from his illness in 1768 Chatham was so appalled by what had been done in his name that he resigned. Thereafter he made several theatrical appearances in the House of Lords. These showed that he did not support American independence, but still hoped for reconciliation between Britain and the colonies. He collapsed during a debate in the Lords in April 1778, and died in May.

PLANTATION DUTIES ACT 1673 was one of the **Navigation Acts** which placed a tax on all enumerated articles that were shipped between the colonies without bond first being posted in England. The duty initially aimed at those colonies where the enumerated articles originated. In this case, the legislation aimed at the southern region, particularly the West Indies and Virginia. The tax on articles included one penny per pound of tobacco and five shillings per hundredweight of sugar. Later the northern colonies were added. There was disagreement over the interpretation of the Act and objection to the Act itself, particularly by London merchants who argued, for instance, sugar was shipped to New England on its way to England. The West Indian islands received in return from New England timber and other necessities. To force a tax would upset the colonial trade balance. There was also the argument that the people that were being taxed did not have a voice in Parliament to argue their case against it. This is one of the first attempts to argue for no taxation without representation, albeit the argument was not widespread.

PLYMOUTH COLONY. In 1619, a patent was issued by the **Virginia Company** to a group of separatists from the established Church of England who would become known as the Pilgrims. They sailed in 'The Mayflower' to the Cape Cod region in 1620, originally settling near present day Provincetown, then moving across the Bay to settle Plymouth. The colony's constitution was based upon **the Mayflower Compact** which stressed God's covenant with man. Apart from being briefly incorporated in the **Dominion of New England** Plymouth retained its separate identity until 1691 when it was absorbed into Massachusetts.

POCAHONTAS (c. 1596–1617) was the favorite daughter of the chief of **the Powhatan Confederacy** who was instrumental in maintaining stable relations between the settlers of Jamestown, **Virginia** and the Indian tribes in that area. In 1607 she interceded with her father Powhatan to save the life of John Smith. In 1613 she herself was taken prisoner by **Samuel Argall**, who used her as a hostage to bargain with Powhatan to end hostilities with the colonists. Pocahontas became converted to Christianity by the colonists in 1614, assuming the name of Rebecca and marrying **John Rolfe**. Her affinity with the English settlers and her favored standing with her powerful father made her a valuable asset to the peaceful co-existence of the two cultures. In 1616 Rolfe took her to England, where she was feted by the Court and the elite. However her health deteriorated so much that Rolfe decided to take her back to Virginia. She was too ill to make the journey, and went ashore at Gravesend, where she died in March 1617.

PONTIAC'S WAR is sometimes called a rebellion, though Pontiac himself, as leader of the Ottawa Indians, could not be a rebel as he was not a British subject. In an effort to maintain their independence from the British after the defeat of the French in 1673, Pontiac and his allies attacked British forts in the Great Lakes region, capturing all but two. They then moved south to Fort Pitt where they besieged the fort but unsuccessfully. They were finally driven back and defeated, thus ensuring British control.

POPULATION. Before the first official census conducted by the USA in 1790 population estimates can only be informed guesses. Demographic historians have established a series of decennial totals, starting in 1630 which show a growth in the total populations of the 13 colonies which were to become the USA, from 50,000 or so in 1650 to around 250,000 in 1700 to over 2,000,000 in 1770. At this rate of increase, as **Benjamin Franklin** observed, the population was doubling every 25 years. There has been speculation as to how this rate of increase occurred. At first of course it was overwhelmingly due to migration. It has been estimated that 90,000 whites went from Europe to North America between 1650 and 1700, mainly from Britain, and 370,000 migrated between 1700 and 1780. During the colonial period some 300,000 blacks were imported as **slaves** into the colonies, mostly after 1680. These figures, however, cannot account for the rise in overall numbers. This could only be explained by natural increase, due either to a low death rate or a high birth rate. These rates varied regionally. Mortality rates in the disease environment of the **Chesapeake Bay** were horrendous in the early years of the settlements in **Virginia** and **Maryland**, and their populations could only be sustained in the 17th century by immigrants. By contrast **New England** was relatively healthier, and life expectancy among migrants from England was higher than that in the mother country. At the same time there was an increase in the birth rate, as the gender balance in New England was similar to that in England, while the age of marriage was lower in the 17th century. Again by contrast most migrants to the Chesapeake in the early years were single young men who went as indentured servants. This led to an imbalance between the sexes which impeded natural growth, a condition which was not rectified until the end of the century. By the 18th century the growth of the black population was also due to an increase in the birth rate as well as an influx of slaves. The increase in the slave population was unique in the European colonies in America. Even the British West Indies experienced a greater ratio of deaths to births so that the growth in the numbers of blacks was due to a constant supply of slaves from Africa.

POWHATAN CONFEDERACY was the name given by European settlers to a North American Indian group located in the tidewater area of **Virginia** between the Potomac River and the Great Dismal Swamp. Its beginnings can be traced from the late 16th century and lasted until the middle of the 17th century. Its relations with the settlers in Virginia were volatile with its most stable period occurring during the rule of its founder, Chief Powhatan. Powhatan may have considered the settlers as a pawn in the ongoing game of territorial disputes with other Indians. However, during his life and the life of his daughter, **Pocahontas**, some semblance of stability occurred between the two cultures.

POYNINGS LAW. In 1495 Sir Edward Poynings, Henry VII's representative in the Irish Parliament, got it to pass a law whereby all legislation dealt with by it had previously to be approved by the English privy council. This precedent was used in some of the colonies to require the same conditions of colonial legislation. Thus in 1675 Poynings law was applied to **Virginia**. In most cases, however, colonial legislation had to be approved by the Privy council after and not before it had been passed by the assemblies.

PRESBYTERIANS were theologically Calvinist, and therefore had much in common with the **Congregationalists** of **New England**, the Dutch Reformed Church in New York, and the **Huguenots** who went from France to settle in North America, most of them in **South Carolina**. What distinguished them from other sects based on Calvinism was their system of church government, which operated by representative assemblies called presbyteries, which themselves were represented in synods. This model of church government was adopted by the Presbyterians who emerged in Scotland after the Reformation. A distinctive feature of Presbyterianism, therefore, was its opposition to the episcopal system of government, administered by bishops, which was retained by the established Church in England. It also opposed Congregationalism, which had no such formal apparatus, though Congregationalists summoned ad hoc synods, such as that which condemned **Anne Hutchinson** in 1637 and adopted the **Cambridge Platform** in 1648. The standard confessional of the colonial Presbyterians was the *Westminster Confession of Faith and Catechisms* of 1646. This was the attempt of English Presbyterians who had risen to power after the first civil war to settle the religious issues generated by it on Presbyterian lines. It was accompanied by a *Directory of Public Worship* issued by Presbyterian divines in England, who differed from their Scottish brethren who wanted to establish one Presbyterian church in both nations. The attempt failed, and after the Restoration Presbyterianism in England again found itself on the defensive against a triumphant Anglicanism. A Presbyterian form of church government was finally established in Scotland at the Revolution Settlement, when bishoprics introduced by the Stuarts were abolished. In England Presbyterians were covered by the Toleration Act of 1689. Their influence, however, was severely weakened in 1719 when a Synod in London divided Unitarians among them from Trinitarians. Many of the latter eventually seceded and went over to the Church of England. In America, by contrast, Presbyterianism became a dominant force in the middle colonies during the **Great Awakening**.

PRICE, RICHARD (1723–1791) was born in Wales, the son of a dissenting minister. After attending Welsh dissenting schools he went to an academy in Moorfields, London in 1740. There he acquired expertise in mathematics and physics and an interest in radicalism. On leaving the academy he became a dissenting minister. In 1765 Price became a Fellow of the Royal Society, his application for the fellowship being sponsored by **Benjamin Franklin**. Like Franklin he also became a member of the Club of Honest Whigs. His mathematical skills enabled him to write *Observations on Reversionary Payments* published in 1771. That year the **earl of Shelburne** became his patron, introducing him to a circle which included Isaac Barre and **Joseph Priestley**. Price became a prominent defender of the American colonists, publishing *Observations on the Nature of Civil Liberty*, in 1776, *Additional Observations* in 1777 and *Observations on the importance of the American Revolution* in 1784. He achieved notoriety in 1789 with his *Discourse on the Love of our country*, which compared the Glorious Revolution of 1688 unfavorably with the French Revolution. It provoked **Edmund Burke** to riposte with *Reflections on the Revolution in France*.

PRIESTLEY, JOSEPH (1733–1804) was the son of a dissenting cloth worker in the West Riding of Yorkshire. After his mother's death in 1739 he was brought up by his aunt and uncle, Sarah and John Keighley of Heckmondwike. When John died in 1745 Sarah, his father's sister, saw that Priestley received an education which would prepare him to be a dissenting minister. At Batley grammar school and in a dissenting school in Heckmondwike he showed a prodigious ability to acquire languages, among them Latin, Hebrew, French and German. In 1750 he entered the new dissenting academy at Daventry where his studies also took in ancient history, the bible, mathematics, medicine and Newtonian physics. His decision to adopt Arianism separated him from his evangelical family and estranged him from his congregation in his first living at Needham Market. In 1750 he moved to Nantwich to become a minister and schoolmaster there. He earned such a reputation as a teacher that the acclaimed Warrington academy, which had previously declined to appoint him, offered him a tutorship in languages and belles lettres.

At Warrington he devised a syllabus more appropriate for pupils who were destined more for commerce than for the profession. This laid greater stress on history than on languages, leading him to draw up a Chart of Biography in 1765 and a New Chart of History in 1769. The first led to his election as Fellow of the Royal Society, in which he was supported by **Benjamin Franklin**, with whom he had become acquainted through their mutual interest in electricity. Priestley published *The History and present state of electricity* in 1767. That same year he was invited to become minister at Mill Hill Chapel in Leeds. By then he had become a complete convert to Unitarianism, which he expounded in a number of publications, including *An appeal to the serious and candid professor of Christianity*. He also became involved in political controversy, defending dissenters in *Remarks on some paragraphs in ... Blackstone's commentaries*, and Americans in his anonymous *Present state of Liberty in Great Britain and her colonies*, both published in 1769. His scientific interests were not neglected, 'Observations on different kinds of air' earning him the Royal Society's Copley medal in 1773. In June that year he moved to Calne in Wiltshire to be near Bowood, the country seat of **the earl of Shelburne** who had invited him to join his circle of savants and scientists. Priestley kept up his radical political stance, notably in his *Address to Protestant Dissenters on the approaching elections* of 1774. When the **War of American Independence** broke out, however, he felt it prudent not to engage in polemics in public, though in private he supported the independence of the colonies. It was while he was at Bowood that he made his most famous scientific discovery, that of oxygen. In 1780 he left Shelburne's service to become a minister in Birmingham. He found another group to make up for leaving Shelburne's circle in the Lunar Society there. Priestley supported the dissenters in their campaign in the late 1780s to have penal laws against them repealed, and welcomed the outbreak of the French Revolution. This provoked an attack on his property when 'church and king' riots broke out in Birmingham in 1791, during which his house and laboratory were destroyed. He fled from that city to London, then in 1794 emigrated to the USA, settling in Northumberland in the forks of the Susquehanna in Pennsylvania, where he died.

PRINCETON UNIVERSITY was originally the College of **New Jersey** established at Elizabethtown, New Jersey in 1746. It moved to Princeton in 1756 and was later renamed Princeton. The college was formed out of the **Great Awakening** under the guidance of the new light **Presbyterians**. The intention was to train ministers, but as educational needs for higher learning increased, the college expanded its mission.

PROCLAMATION OF 1763 drew a boundary line to restrict expansion past the watershed of the Appalachian mountains. This was to try to appease the Indian population, whose uneasiness following the expulsion of the French from North America, left them vulnerable to further inroads from the colonies. Their unease found expression in **Pontiac's War**. The Proclamation also created new colonies out of the territories taken from France and Spain in Quebec, Florida, and Grenada in the West Indies.

PROMOTIONAL LITERATURE. Pamphlets, tracts and other publications flowed from the presses to encourage colonization. Before the first successful settlement at Jamestown promotional literature took the form of promoting voyages of discovery and settlement in general. Among the most celebrated of these publications was **Richard Hakluyt's** *Discourse concerning western planting* (1584). It advocated the establishment of colonies for a variety of reasons, including checking the expansion of England's rival Spain, obtaining naval stores for building the fleet, and thereby employing the poor. Among a host of strategic and economic considerations it also mentioned the spread of Protestantism in the New World. Following the establishment of **Virginia** promoters of settlement tended to stress the advantages of a particular colony over that of alternative sites. They praised the soil, climate, flora and fauna of the Chesapeake Bay, or of New England, or of the Carolinas. Thus Alexander Whitaker wrote from Jamestown shortly after its foundation to assure the **Virginia Company** that their settlement 'would flowe with milke and honey', Francis Higginson sang the praises of **Massachusetts** in *New England's Plantation* (1630), while the proprietors of **Carolina** sang those of their grant in *A Brief Description of the Province of Carolina* (1666). One of the most enterprising promoters of a specific colony was **William Penn** who extolled the virtues of his own grant of **Pennsylvania** over those of any other colony in *Some Account of the Province of Pennsilvania* (1681). 'I shall say little in its praise. To excite desires in any, whatever I could truly write as to the soil, air and water' he modestly asserted 'this shall satisfy me, that by the blessing of God, and the honesty and industry of man, it may be a good and fruitful land'. The launching of **Georgia**, England's last colony in North America, was accompanied by a tract written by its principal promoter, **James Oglethorpe**, *Some Account of the Designs of the Trustees for establishing the colony of Georgia* (1733). It followed the now time honored practice of claiming that it stood a better chance of flourishing than other colonies such as Virginia and Pennsylvania had done when they were first launched.

PROPRIETARY COLONIES is a term used to distinguish those colonies which were granted by the Crown to proprietors from those whose governors were appointed directly by the monarch or were elected by the freemen, which are known as **Charter Colonies**. **Maryland** was the first such colony, being granted to **Lord Baltimore**. **New York** and **New Jersey** were originally proprietary colonies, being granted to James duke of York by his brother **Charles II**. New York became a Crown colony, however, when the duke succeeded his brother as **James II**. Since he had granted New Jersey to proprietors, however, it remained a proprietary colony until 1702, when it too became a Crown colony. **The Carolinas** were also granted to a number of proprietors by Charles II, but were subjected to the Crown by **George II**. **Pennsylvania** was a proprietary colony, the first proprietor being **William Penn**. After his death his sons John, Richard and **Thomas** succeeded him as proprietors. Proprietorships were contingent upon their laws not being contrary to those of England.

PROVIDENCE ISLAND is an island off the coast of Nicaragua. It was claimed by a company set up by English **Puritans** who used **Bermuda** as a launching pad for an expedition claiming Providence in 1631. Its use as a base to harass Spanish possessions on the isthmus of Panama led to reprisals by Spain who took the island in 1641.

PURITANS. 'Puritan' was originally used as a term of abuse for people who refused to accept the Elizabethan Settlement of the Church of England. As such it could be applied to various objectors, from those who objected to such practices as bowing at the name of Jesus, exchanging rings in marriage, and crossing an infant's head in baptism to those who condemned the retention of bishops to govern the Church. The common ground they shared was their assertion that these 'relics of popery' as they called them were not sanctioned by Scripture. Only mention in the Bible legitimated any religious belief or practice to the puritan mind. Under Elizabeth and **James I** Puritanism was largely contained within the Church of England, most Puritans being content with the settlement made by the Queen to wait for an opportunity for a more 'thorough godly reformation'. A few, however, did secede and become separatists, the most notable being those who went with **William Bradford** to Holland and subsequently sailed as Pilgrims in 'The Mayflower' to found **Plymouth**. Under **Charles I**, however, Puritans became alarmed at what they perceived to be the rise of Arminianism in the Church of England. Many left in the Puritan migration to **Massachusetts**. Those who remained formed the core of the king's opponents who fought him in the civil wars between 1642 and 1648. During the wars the Puritan movement split into several rival sects, including Presbyterians, Congregationalists, Baptists and Quakers. There was no way of containing all their rival beliefs and practices in a single national church. Attempts to create an exclusive established church failed during the **Interregnum** and the reign of **Charles II**. In the Revolution Settlement of 1689 its impracticality was realized with the passing of the Toleration Act. This upheld the Church of England as the established church, but allowed other Protestant sects to worship separately.

Q

QUAKERS are otherwise known as the Society of Friends. Their beliefs were based on the inner light and the possibility of universal salvation. Their spiritual leader, George Fox, claimed that they restored Christianity to its original purpose. They gained a semblance of toleration under the Protectorate during the 1650s and began to establish themselves in North America as early as 1656 when some went to **New England**. Their biggest inroads were made in the Quaker proprietorships of **New Jersey** and **Pennsylvania** where they were able to influence the political and cultural makeup of the colonies. Their main supporters in colonial development included **William Penn**, Quaker proprietor of Pennsylvania. A thorn in his flesh and that of other Quakers was **George Keith**.

QUARTERING ACT, or properly the American Mutiny Act, of 1765 was passed in response to a request from General **Thomas Gage** for help with the problem of quartering troops under his command. There was insufficient accommodation in barracks, and the British Mutiny Act, permitting the army to requisition alternative lodgings, did not apply to the colonies. The Act was therefore passed enabling them to be billeted in uninhabited buildings, though not in private houses. It also required colonies where troops were stationed to provide them, at the public expense, with basic necessities such as heat and light, bedding and beer. The **New York** assembly objected to this, claiming it was tantamount to a tax, and when in December Gage asked them for provisions according to the Act the members refused. In June 1766 it voted some of the provisions, though not all, and protested that the requirement was unfair since it fell only on colonies where troops were maintained. Faced with this defiance the British government ordered the governor of New York to ensure that the assembly obeyed the law. When it responded by refusing to vote any supplies, the British government passed the Restraining Act suspending the proceedings of the assembly until it complied. It decided to do so and voted the supplies required. When the governor took this to be compliance the British government did not implement the Restraining Act.

QUEEN ANNE'S WAR is the title given by American historians to the war fought between 1702 and 1713 which is known in England as the War of the Spanish Succession. As the English title suggests, it was fought between rival claimants to the throne of Spain and its possessions in Europe and the New World. These were the French duke of Anjou, who styled himself Philip V, and the Austrian archduke Charles, who was known by the British, who backed his claim, as Charles III. The main actions were fought by the duke of Marlborough, who won famous victories at the battles of Blenheim (1704), Ramillies (1706) Oudenarde (1708) and Malplaquet (1709). The Spanish possessions in the Americas recognized Philip from the outset, and this added a dimension to the conflict in the colonies lacking in the previous **King William's War**. It put the southern and West Indian colonies in the front line, whereas previously the main theater had been in the northern colonies. This led to the dispatch of a fleet under Admiral John Benbow in 1702 to the Caribbean which took St Kitts. **South Carolina** also became involved, with a descent on St Augustine in **Florida** being launched in 1702 from **Charles Town**. France used Louisiana as a base to attack Nevis in 1706, while the British harassed the fledgling French colony with an attack on Mobile in 1709. The north was not spared hostilities, the French inflicting a particularly demoralizing defeat on the frontier of **Massachusetts** with a raid in 1704 on **Deerfield**. There were two abortive attempts by **New England** colonists in 1707 to take Port Royal in **Nova Scotia**. These were redeemed in 1710 when Port Royal was finally taken and renamed Annapolis. An ambitious attempt to take Quebec in 1711 had to be abandoned when the fleet which made up the naval arm of a joint venture by the army and navy foundered in thick fog in the St Lawrence River. In 1713 the war was concluded with the Treaty of Utrecht, when Britain recognized Philip V as king of Spain and its American territories in exchange for Gibraltar and Minorca in Europe and Newfoundland, **Nova Scotia** and St Kitts in America.

QUEBEC ACT was passed in 1774 in the same session as the **Coercive Acts** with which it is often associated. In fact it was not intended as a response to the **Boston Tea Party** but as a measure necessary for the government of the French Roman Catholics who had become British subjects following the conquest of **Canada**. The **Proclamation of 1763** had envisaged the convening of an assembly in Quebec, but not enough Protestants had migrated there to form an electorate. The Act therefore set up a council to be appointed by the governor. At the same time it established the Catholic church and recognized civil law. The establishment of Catholicism and the acceptance of a judicial system which did not involve trial by jury antagonized many American colonists. Perhaps more galling to them was the fact that the Act incorporated the area north of the Ohio River, where many had hoped to move, into the province of Quebec.

QUO WARRANTO is a Latin phrase meaning, 'By what warrant?' It was a medieval procedure by which a royal writ was issued demanding to know by what authority claims of privileges were made. It was revived under the later Stuarts who employed the writ to investigate the autonomy claimed by boroughs and colonies. This was particularly true after the Exclusion crisis of 1679–1681 when **Charles II** used it to undermine the urban power bases of the whigs. Many boroughs, including London, had to surrender their charters. The king then issued new ones which gave the crown control over the corporations. The procedure was also employed against colonies which were deemed to be opposed to royal rule. Thus **Massachusetts** was obliged to surrender its charter in 1684. **James II** instigated similar proceedings against **Maryland** and **Pennsylvania**. After the **Glorious Revolution** the Crown never again employed the procedure as a weapon against its political opponents.

R

RANDOLPH, EDWARD (1632–1703) was born in Canterbury and educated at Cambridge University. He married Jane Gibbon, a relative of Robert Mason, a proprietor of **New Hampshire**, who sent him to **New England** in 1676 to assert his proprietary claims. Randolph took the opportunity to investigate colonial attempts to evade the **Navigation Acts**. His reports led to his appointment as collector of customs in New England in 1678. This led him to advocate making **Massachusetts** a Crown colony, which was to come about in 1684 when he was able to get a **quo warranto** against the colony challenging its charter. As a result the colony was made a royal colony. Randolph played a key role in the **Dominion of New England**. He was seized by the ringleaders of the **Glorious Revolution** in Boston in 1689, who sent him to England. There, however, he was exonerated, and in 1691 was appointed surveyor general of the customs in America. Between 1692 and 1695 he investigated almost every creek and inlet from **North Carolina** to Maine. The results of his investigations were instrumental in the drawing up of one of the most stringent of the **Navigation Acts** in 1696. From 1697 to 1700 he was again in the colonies. His arrogance and irascibility made him so unpopular that he spent nine months in prison in Bermuda. Back in England he encouraged the **Board of Trade** to pursue its policy of reducing proprietary to Crown colonies. He returned to the colonies in 1702, characteristically impounding the ship that carried him there. The following year he died in Virginia.

REGULATORS were active in the Carolinas in the 1760s. In **South Carolina** they were frontiersmen who protested that they were not being protected by the agents of the government in **Charles Town**, who represented the interests of the settled areas of the tidewater rather than the settlers in the backcountry. Thus the regulators accused them of appeasing **Indians** rather than protecting their homesteads from attack. In **North Carolina**, though the regulators also resided in the backcountry, they criticized the authorities in the east for interfering too much rather than too little in their affairs, raising exorbitant taxes and charging excessive fees. The regulation in North Carolina was a much more serious affair, culminating in a confrontation between Governor Tryon and the regulators at the battle of Alamance in May 1771, which resulted in a decisive victory for the government.

RHODE ISLAND was established as the result of the banishment from **Massachusetts** of several religious dissidents exiled by the Puritan authorities in the late 1630s. These included **Roger Williams, William Coddington, Anne Hutchinson** and **Samuel Gorton**. At first they settled in various locations, Williams in Providence, Coddington and Hutchinson in Portsmouth until they quarreled when Coddington moved to Newport, while Gorton established himself at what became Warwick. In 1644 Williams obtained a patent from the English parliament for their incorporation as Providence Plantations. They came together in a federation in 1647 but political struggles between them, especially between Coddington and Williams, led to its disintegration. Coddington went to England to get his claims recognized in 1651, only to have them successfully challenged by Williams the following year. It was not until 1665 that the colony received a charter. Boundary disputes with Massachusetts were not settled until 1747.

ROANOKE ISLAND was the first English settlement in North America, located between the outer banks of what became North Carolina. In 1584, Sir Walter Raleigh sent 100 soldiers, craftsmen, and scholars to establish a settlement. However, the lateness in the season when they arrived and their antipathy with the local **Indians** did not ensure the colony's initial success. When Raleigh arrived at the island in 1586, the settlers left with him. Later another seafarer under the direction of Raleigh left 15 men to keep the fort. Additionally, Raleigh was able to recruit 115 men, women, and children for the venture in 1587. The war between Spain and England prevented any supplies and reinforcements to get to the island until 1590, by which time the settlers had disappeared leaving a deserted colony. Limited funds, poor organization, and war were the main contributing factors to the failure of the colony. The most lasting contribution of the settlement to colonial history were the depictions of the island and its inhabitants by the painter John White.

ROCKINGHAM, CHARLES WATSON-WENTWORTH, SECOND MARQUESS OF (1730–1782) succeeded his father, the first marquess, in 1750. By becoming a peer at the age of 20, he never stood for election to the House of Commons. As a member of the House of Lords he was unique as the only one with the rank of a marquisate, and was generally known as 'the Marquess'. He was also one of the richest men in the British Isles, with estates in Northamptonshire, Ireland and Yorkshire, where his seat of Wentworth Woodhouse was situated not far from Sheffield. His father had been a prominent court whig, and Rockingham enlisted under their banner, supporting the **duke of Newcastle**. This connection obtained for him the post of lord of the bedchamber to **George II** in 1751, which he retained following the accession of **George III** in 1760. When Newcastle was dismissed in 1762 Rockingham resigned the post in the royal bedchamber. This was the only office he had held at the center of power when in 1765 he was asked to form a ministry and became prime minister, replacing **George Grenville**. The first Rockingham administration was primarily remembered for its repeal of the **Stamp Act**. Rockingham's attitude was marked more by pragmatism than principle. He never denied the right of parliament to tax the colonies, a position he upheld in the **Declaratory Act**. But he was concerned about the impact of the American non-importation of British goods on the economy. Although he was a landowner he was not ignorant of commercial activity. On the contrary, he was so interested in the Yorkshire woolen industry that a pamphlet on the subject was dedicated to him as early as 1752. In that year he married Mary Bright, who added £60,000 to his fortune from her family estates in Hallamshire near Sheffield, where the local iron industry was located which also suffered from the colonial embargo on British manufactures. Rockingham was dismissed from the premiership in 1766 by the king over a disagreement on the government of Canada. Rockingham then went into opposition, where he became the focus of a group which evolved into what became known as the Rockingham whigs. After the general election of 1768 they numbered about 60 in the Commons and 30 in the Lords. Their chief spokesman was **Edmund Burke**, who had become Rockingham's private secretary. He enunciated their principles, which despite Rockingham's own background of court whiggery were much closer to the views of the country whigs who had opposed **Sir Robert Walpole**. Thus they suspected a design on the part of the Court to increase the influence of the Crown, and sought to offset this trend by advocating a reduction in the ability of the king to use his patronage to reward his parliamentary followers, a measure known as economical reform. Although Rockingham condemned the **Boston Tea Party** – he was a proprietor of the East India Company whose property was thrown into the harbor – he also opposed the **Coercive Acts**. He thus became known as a 'friend of America' though his objections to coercion continued to be pragmatic rather than principled. By 1778, however, he had reluctantly come to the conclusion that American independence was inevitable, and castigated the policy of suppressing the colonists as 'repugnant to the principles of Christianity'. When **Lord North** resigned in 1782 Rockingham formed his second administration. This brief ministry succeeded in passing a measure of economical reform and in granting independence from the privy council to Ireland. Negotiations with the Americans which were to conclude with the **Peace of Paris** of 1783 were still in train when Rockingham suddenly died in July 1782.

ROGERS, ROBERT (1731–1795) was born in New Hampshire, and became a soldier there. His Rangers acquired fame as a troop of independent regulars which fought in the **French and Indian War**. In 1759 they took part in a controversial raid on the Indian village of St Francis near Crown Point, in which they earned the reputation of 'white devils' after killing the inhabitants. Rogers' Rangers took Detroit from the French in 1760. The following year Rogers served in South Carolina against the Cherokees, then returned north to take part in **Pontiac's War**. After the suppression of the Indians he went to England, where in 1765 he published a *Concise History of North America* and his *Journals*. These were brought to the attention of **George III** who appointed Rogers to the command of a fort in the territories acquired from France in the Great Lakes region by the **Treaty of Paris of 1763**. He was court martialled for intriguing with the French, and though he was acquitted left active service to return to England from 1769 to 1775. The outbreak of the **War of American Independence** saw him back in North America in command of the Queen's American Rangers. Once again his loyalty to the Crown was called into question and he returned to England in 1780 under a cloud. He died there in 1795, never having again visited his homeland.

ROLFE, JOHN (1585–1622) was commissioned by the **Virginia Company** in 1609 to take settlers to the colony. He arrived in Jamestown in 1610 after first landing in **Bermuda**. In 1612 he crossed the West Indian nicotiana tobacum, which was a mild tobacco, with the Virginia tobacco nicotiana rusticum to produce a hardy and more palatable product. The result was Virginia's first and most profitable export item. During his stay in the colony, he met and married Chief Powhatan's favorite daughter, **Pocahontas**. The marriage helped to stabilize relations between the **Powhatan confederacy** and the settlers. Rolfe and his wife went to England in 1616. While there he defended Virginia against its detractors in *A True Relation of the State of Virginia*. In 1617 Pocahontas died as they were returning to America. Rolfe settled in Virginia, remarrying and becoming a councilor as well as a member in the House of Burgesses.

ROMAN CATHOLICS were suspected of owing allegiance more to the Pope than to the Crown in Protestant England. Catholic plots against Queen Elizabeth and **James I**, especially the Gunpowder Plot of 1605, seemed to confirm this view. They were therefore subject to severe penal laws and persecution. **Charles I**'s French Queen, Henrietta Maria, a Catholic herself, persuaded him to grant them a colonial haven in **Maryland**, named after her. The establishment of the colony was viewed with suspicion by neighboring Anglican **Virginia**. Suspicions of Henrietta Maria's influence on her husband also informed the opposition to the king which culminated in the civil wars in England. The triumph of the militantly Protestant parliament led to the removal of the Catholic Lord **Baltimore** from the proprietorship of Maryland. Although he was restored to it before the Restoration the domination of the colony by Catholics, despite their being a minority in Maryland, was a major cause of the **Glorious Revolution** in the colony. Parallels were drawn between Baltimore's policies and those of **James II**, whose avowed Catholicism was a crucial factor in the Glorious Revolution in England. Fears of Catholic influence, most of it pure paranoia, even informed the Revolutions in Massachusetts and New York. During the wars against France between 1689 and 1763 the fact that the French in Canada were Roman Catholics strengthened the colonial resolve to win, especially during the **Great Awakening** when Catholicism was viewed as Anti-Christ by the reformers. This sentiment lay behind the inclusion of the Quebec Act among the **Coercive Acts** passed in 1774, even though it was a mere coincidence that it was enacted at the same time as the others.

RUSH, BENJAMIN (1746–1813) was born 12 miles north of **Philadelphia** and to a long line of dissenters of whom the first to emigrate to North America was his great-great-grandfather, John, known as 'the Old Trooper,' since he had commanded a troop of horses on the parliamentary side during the English Civil Wars. Benjamin was instructed in the Episcopal Church until his father's death. His mother, a Presbyterian, then put her son under the tutelage of the Reverend Gilbert Tennent at the Second Presbyterian Church in **Philadelphia**. At the age of 13 Rush was admitted as a junior at the **College of New Jersey** (later renamed Princeton) where he was greatly influenced by the college's president, Samuel Davies. Davies taught Rush the 'art of inquiry,' thus instilling objective discipline in the investigative process. This was reinforced and developed further under Dr William Cullen at Edinburgh University. Initially, Rush considered the ministry, then law, and finally went into medicine. He attributed the decision to the influence of his Uncle Finley. Rush was introduced to Edinburgh society with letters of introduction by **Benjamin Franklin**. Through Franklin, Rush was able to make the right connections with Sir Alexander Dick and William Cullen. He made enough of an impression during his stay that a year later, he was nominated to the Medical Society, later renamed the Royal Medical Society of Edinburgh. While in Edinburgh, he claimed to have exercised his reason on the subject of government for the first time when he saw the absurdity of hereditary government. These thoughts were influenced by Rush's readings of Algernon Sidney and Rush's antimonarchical friend, John Bostock. Rush's political outlook was further enhanced when he visited **John Wilkes** and Catherine Macaulay.

He made his political mark in the years leading to the American Revolution and the creation of the United States Constitution. He was instrumental in Thomas Paine's *Common Sense* by contributing many of the ideas found in the work and by supplying the title. He was a signer of the Declaration of Independence and attributed his love of liberty to his family's Cromwellian background. **John Adams** wrote that he knew of 'no Character living or dead, who has done more real good in America.'

S

SALEM WITCH TRIALS were held in a special court presided over by **William Stoughton** between February and August 1692. Forty three people, most of them women, were accused of being witches. Nineteen were found guilty and hanged. The accusations arose out of implications made by several young girls, who claimed they had been possessed by the devil after dabbling in a seance with a West Indian slave called Tituba. It spiraled out of control when she confessed to being in league with the devil and implicated several others. The alleged victims claimed that they had been visited by their tormentors in the shape of specters. While their corporeal bodies were in one place the devil took on their appearance in a spectral body. Stoughton accepted such evidence and continued to believe it even when others began to entertain doubts about it. Among the latter was **Increase Mather**. Another was **Sir William Phips** who arrived as the governor of Massachusetts in May. He closed the court at Salem when spectral evidence was successfully challenged and the cases collapsed.

SALUTARY NEGLECT was an expression used by **Edmund Burke** in a speech he made in the House of Commons in 1775 referring to the policy he claimed had been adopted towards the American colonies before the passage of the **Stamp Act** in 1765. Reflecting on their remarkable economic growth he observed 'the colonies in general owe little or nothing to any care of ours ... but ... through a wise and salutary neglect, a generous nature has been suffered to take her way to perfection'. How far this was a valid verdict on colonial policy before the 1760s is debatable. It did not fit the period 1651 to 1696 which saw the passage of the **Navigation Acts**. Nor could the colonies be neglected in times of war which characterized the period 1688 to 1713 which saw **King William's and Queen Anne's Wars**, or the years 1739 to 1748, which saw **King George's War** and above all 1754 to 1763 which witnessed the **French and Indian War**. Insofar as a period of neglect can be detected it is the relatively peaceful interval between 1713 and 1739, though even this included the transformation of **North and South Carolina** from proprietary to crown colonies, the launching of **Georgia** and the passage of the **Molasses Act**. The main influence on colonial policy during those years was exercised by the **duke of Newcastle**. Newcastle's attitude towards the colonies has been criticized as being marked more by negligence than neglect. Thus he took no legislative initiatives involving them, and used them more as a source of patronage for his own political interests.

SCOTCH-IRISH is a term used in America of immigrants from Ulster in Northern Ireland who were for the most part **Presbyterians**. They were prominent in the settlement of **New Jersey**, **Pennsylvania** and the back country of the **Carolinas**.

SEVEN YEARS WAR see FRENCH AND INDIAN WAR

SHELBURNE, WILLIAM PETTY, SECOND EARL OF (1737–1805) was born in Ireland and went to Oxford University before joining the army. In 1760 he became aide-de-camp to **George III**. The following year on the death of his father he succeeded to the earldom of Shelburne. He was made President of the **Board of Trade** in George Grenville's ministry, a post he held for only four months, during which he was involved in the publication of the **Proclamation of 1763**. His resignation was partly due to his support of **John Wilkes** but also to his prickly personality which made him an almost impossible colleague. **George III** called him 'a worthless man' and dismissed him from being his aide-de-camp. He declined the offer of a post in the first **Rockingham** ministry, having become attached to **William Pitt**. He voted for the repeal of the **Stamp Act** and against the passing of the **Declaratory Act**, one of five peers to do so in the House of Lords, who were outvoted by 125. When Pitt as earl of Chatham became prime minister in 1766 Shelburne was appointed secretary of state for the southern department. During Chatham's absence from the cabinet Shelburne found himself opposed to **Charles Townshend** and the duties he placed on American imports. His own influence in colonial affairs was drastically reduced when the southern secretary's responsibility for them was transferred to the newly created secretaryship for the colonies in 1768. His marginalization led him to resign in 1769. In opposition to **Lord North** Shelburne followed the line laid down by Chatham, being against coercion of the colonies but also opposed to their becoming independent. On the fall of North's ministry in 1782 George III asked Shelburne to form a government, but he accepted that Rockingham had a better claim, and acted as intermediary between them during the formation of the marquis's second administration. Rockingham redistributed the responsibilities of the two secretaries, one becoming responsible for home affairs and the other for foreign affairs. Shelburne got the home office, which dealt with the colonies too, while his rival **Charles James Fox** became foreign secretary. Thus both were involved with the powers which had fought in the **War of American Independence**. Shelburne still hankered after some kind of federal scheme which would keep the Americans in the empire, while Fox was prepared to recognize them as independent. Consequently both sent agents to the conference in Paris which was convened to thrash out the settlement. When Rockingham died suddenly in the summer of 1782 Shelburne succeeded him as prime minister. Although this gave him sole charge of the negotiations he was obliged to recognize the independence of the United States of America. When he presented the terms he had negotiated to the House of Commons in February 1783 they were defeated, largely because the majority of members were convinced that they did not give sufficient consideration to **loyalists**. The defeat caused the downfall of Shelburne's ministry.

SHIRLEY, WILLIAM (1694–1771) was born in England and educated at Cambridge University. He was called to the bar in 1720 and practiced law in London. In 1731 he went to **Boston** with a letter of recommendation from the **duke of Newcastle** to Governor Belcher of **Massachusetts**. This opened the way for him to be the colony's advocate general in 1733 and to succeed Belcher as governor in 1741. Shirley directed the attack on Louisbourg in 1745, the highlight of the colonial campaigns in **King George's War**. In 1748 he obtained a grant from the British government of £183,649, which enabled him to phase out the paper money which had been a bone of contention between previous governors of the colony and merchants in Boston. From 1749 to 1753 he was in Paris at the negotiations to fix the boundary between **New England** and **Canada**. He was commissioned as major general in 1755, and was one of the five governors who met at Alexandria to concert strategy with General **Edward Braddock**. Shirley was charged with the taking of Niagara, but retreated to Boston after reaching Oswego where he found the French to be too powerfully entrenched. In 1756 he was ordered to go to England by **Lord Loudoun**, and the following year he was replaced as governor of Massachusetts. In 1761 he was appointed governor of the **Bahamas**.

SLAVERY involving perpetual involuntary labor, was widespread in the New World long before the first English settlements were established. The first Africans were brought to **Virginia** in 1619. Whether they were sold as slaves is not altogether clear, for there were free blacks on the colony's eastern shore in the first decades of settlement. Some of them came to own slaves themselves. By the late 17th century, however, they were overwhelmingly outnumbered by slaves. The use of slavery in the Chesapeake colonies was primarily due to the expanding tobacco farming, and the decrease in voluntary labor by **indentured servants**. In **South Carolina** the staple crop of rice was largely farmed by slaves from the outset. By the 1660s slavery became institutionalized through legislation in various colonies. Along with its institution slavery was distinguished from indentured servitude by color. In 1672, free blacks were prohibited from purchasing white labor. The laws pertaining to blacks in 1691 restricted social interaction such as interracial marriages. Finally, in 1705, the slave laws disallowed blacks from testifying in court and from holding public office. Though the early years of colonial development did not see great numbers of slaves, by 1763 the slave population constituted approximately a fifth of the total number with most of the slave population concentrated in the south. In Virginia and **Georgia**, slaves numbered half of the population. **North Carolina** and **Maryland** held about one-third of its numbers in slavery. Two-thirds of South Carolina's population were slaves. There was moral opposition to slavery mainly from the north and particularly in **Pennsylvania** among the **Quakers**. There was a hierarchical system and gender differences among slaves. Some could aspire to be house servants, which were held to be superior to field hands. African-American women were constrained in two ways. Before, the slave laws, women had some freedom, but like their white counterpart, they could not directly participate politically. Unlike their counterparts, they were 'titheables' as early as 1643.

Slaves became involved in the **War of American Independence** when Lord Dunmore, the last governor of **Virginia**, issued a Proclamation announcing that they would obtain their freedom if they joined the king's forces. Many chose to do so, and after the **Peace of Paris** of 1783 they were among the **loyalists** for whose fate Britain took responsibility.

SLAVE TRADE. The first slaves to arrive in the English mainland colonies did so as early as 1619. But they were not required in substantial numbers until towards the end of the 17th century, when the declining intake of indentured servants, and an increase in European demand for tobacco, created a labor shortage in the **Chesapeake Bay**, which was solved by importing slaves directly from West Africa. Meanwhile the rice producing region of **South Carolina** had begun to be exploited, requiring an intensive labor force which again was supplied from Africa. It is estimated that between 1700 and 1760 165,000 slaves were shipped to North America, 155,000 to the staple producing colonies of the **Chesapeake Bay** and **Lower South**. These totals are eclipsed by the numbers who went to the sugar islands in the British **West Indies**, which came to nearly one million between 1700 and 1780. Such figures are really the roughest of estimates, and no statistics can do justice to the horrors of the 'middle passage' in which Africans, many of whom had never seen the sea, were chained in close confinement, and where disease killed between 10 and 20 per cent of the cargoes of slave ships. There were very few voices raised against the iniquity of the slave trade during the colonial period. A notable exception to the general acquiescence in the traffic were the objections of the **Quakers**, though many of them owned slaves themselves.

SMITH, JOHN (1580–1631) was a highly successful soldier at an early age, serving in the Low Countries and against the Turks. He became one of the first councilors of **Virginia** after leading the first group of settlers to Jamestown in 1607. He was instrumental in saving the fledgling colony from extinction by imposing strict order among the settlers. He was taken captive by the **Powhatan confederacy,** but his life was spared by the special pleading of **Pocahontas**, the chief's daughter. Smith surveyed and mapped the **Chesapeake Bay** area for the **Virginia Company** investors. In 1608 he became president of the council in Virginia. The colony was on the verge of extinction because its inhabitants were not equipped with the farming skills to survive. By the autumn of 1608, out of 105 settlers, only 35 survived. Smith took control of the colony's government and was able to organize the survivors into a productive community which ensured its survival. As a soldier he held the civilians who settled in the colony in contempt, regarding them as the wrong social types to create a viable economy. By harsh discipline he contrived to remedy their shortcomings. Although he was successful, his style of management was extremely unpopular. By 1609, after many arguments and challenges to his authority, Smith left the colony. He returned to England and became a critic of the Virginia Company. Smith went to **New England** in 1614 where he mapped the Penobscot Bay to Cape Cod. He sailed back to England never to return to Virginia. Much of the rest of his life was spent producing **Promotional Literature** for colonial ventures. His *General Historie of Virginia, New England and the Summer Isles* was published in 1624.

SOCIETY FOR THE PROMOTION OF CHRISTIAN KNOWLEDGE (SPCK) is an Anglican organization founded in 1699 by Thomas Bray, rector of Sheldon in Warwickshire, to combat atheism and deism. Bray created a cooperative between local associations in order to distribute bibles and Christian information among their congregations. Also, charity schools were established with the encouragement of the SPCK.

SOCIETY FOR THE PROPAGATION OF THE GOSPEL IN FOREIGN PARTS (SPG) was formed in 1698 by the established Church of England and granted its charter in 1701. Its primary aim was to promote Christianity and guidance in the English colonies to those colonists who had left the Anglican Church. Up until the formation of the SPG there was no concerted effort to establish the Church's influence. Due to the individual characteristics of colonial grants which, for the most part, did not mention an established religion, the Anglican Church's influence was mostly felt in the Chesapeake and **West Indies**. Although there was no mention of Indians and Blacks in its charter, nevertheless, the society later expanded its missionary work in those directions.

SOUTH CAROLINA until 1719 was the southern part of the **Carolinas**. The governor appointed by the proprietors resided in **Charles Town**, though after 1691 they nominated a deputy for the northern part of the colony along the Albermarle Sound. In 1719 proprietary rule was thrown off and the assembly asked the crown to take over. **Francis Nicholson** became the first royal governor of South Carolina in 1720. The proprietors objected and it was not until 1729 that agreement was reached between them and the **Board of Trade** whereby they were compensated financially for the loss of their proprietary rights. An Act of parliament then ratified the colony's change in status.

SPOTSWOOD, ALEXANDER (1676–1740) was born in Tangier where his father was physician to the garrison. He pursued a military career, obtaining an ensign's commission in 1693. From 1702 to 1710 he served under the duke of Marlborough as quartermaster general of the forces in the Netherlands in **Queen Anne's War**. In 1710 he was made lieutenant governor of **Virginia**, and acted for the nominal governor, the earl of Orkney. Spotswood incurred the opposition of leading Virginia planters such as **William Byrd II** in 1713 when he passed an act to inspect tobacco to be exported or used as legal tender. The act was subsequently vetoed by the Privy Council. He further provoked the gentry by proposing a court of oyer and terminer which they claimed should be confined to members of the Council, but which he insisted he could appoint others to. **James Blair** President of the **College of William and Mary** also found fault with him. The political tension in the colony led to his being removed from the governorship in 1722. By then he had acquired an estate of 85,000 acres in Spotsylvania county and a settlement on the frontier which he named Germania, after the Germans he had persuaded to settle there as a buffer against the Indians. Spotswood spent the years from 1724 to 1730 in Scotland as quartermaster general of the forces there, returning to America on being appointed to the post of deputy postmaster for the American colonies. When war broke out with Spain in 1739 he raised a regiment and became its colonel. He was on his way to a conference with other colonial governors in 1740 when he became ill in Maryland and retired to Annapolis where he died.

STAMP ACT 1765 was a measure proposed by prime minister **George Grenville** in 1764, though he waited a year to enact it. It is sometimes still claimed that he gave the colonies time to come up with alternative revenues which their assemblies could raise. This was never the case. Instead Grenville waited to give the colonial assemblies time to assent to it or recommend a parliamentary alternative. When none did he went ahead and imposed a stamp duty on a wide range of colonial documents, including legal transactions like contracts, conveyances and wills, and publications like newspapers and pamphlets. To enforce the duties vice-admiralty courts were established at **Boston**, **Philadelphia** and **Charles Town**. Although there was little objection in parliament the American MP Isaac Barre did warn about its impact on the colonists, whom he memorably called 'sons of liberty'. Many did raise objections, especially journalists and lawyers most affected by the Act. The Lower House of the **Virginia** assembly passed the so-called **Virginia Resolves** which denounced taxation without representation. In Boston Andrew Oliver, alleged to be selected as a distributor of Stamps, was attacked by a mob which burned his house and when he fled hanged him in effigy. Another target of mob violence was the lieutenant governor of **Massachusetts**, **Thomas Hutchinson**, whose house was also destroyed. In October nine colonies sent delegates to the **Stamp Act Congress** in New York. The outcome was the adoption of non-importation agreements by colonial merchants who boycotted British goods. This had adverse economic consequences on manufacturers in Britain who put pressure on the British government to repeal the Act. By then Grenville had been replaced as prime minister by

Lord Rockingham, whose ministry repealed the Act in 1766. He felt it necessary, however, to pass the **Declaratory Act**, upholding the right of the British parliament to pass laws for the American colonies.

STAMP ACT CONGRESS met in New York in October 1765. Only nine colonies were represented at it, as **Georgia**, **North Carolina** and **Virginia** were prevented from sending delegates by their governors declining to convene their assemblies while **New Hampshire** decided not to send any. Those who attended, after declaring their loyalty to the Crown and parliament, passed 14 resolutions denying the legality of taxation without representation, ending with an address to the King and parliament to repeal the Stamp Act.

STAPLE ACT 1663 was one of the **Navigation Acts**. It required goods being shipped to the colonies from countries other than England and Wales to go through English ports en route. The only exceptions were servants and horses from Ireland and Scotland, salt destined for curing fish in **New England** and Newfoundland, and wine from the Azores or Madeira.

STONO REBELLION was a slave uprising in **South Carolina** which occurred in 1739. With war brewing between Spain and England over the establishment of **Georgia**, the Spanish authorities in **Florida** offered to give sanctuary at St Augustine for any slave who went there from the British colonies. At first only 15 slaves were involved, but after they had seized firearms they were joined by others. Although they numbered less than 100 all told, whites were so paranoid about an insurrection in the only mainland colony which had a black majority, that they exaggerated its scope into a major rebellion. They mustered the militia which easily suppressed it. The rebels were executed with exemplary savagery.

STOUGHTON, WILLIAM (1631–1701) went with his family to **Massachusetts** in 1632, where he was educated at **Harvard College** in 1650. He then returned to England where he obtained an MA at Oxford University and became a Fellow of New College. In 1659 he also obtained a living in Sussex. After the Restoration of **Charles II**, however, he was deprived of both. He went back to Massachusetts where he obtained the ministry at Dorchester. He returned to England as the colony's agent from 1677 to 1679, defending it against the charges of **Edward Randolph**. Stoughton served as deputy governor of the **Dominion of New England** until the arrival of the governor **Edmund Andros**. Yet when the Dominion collapsed in the **Glorious Revolution** he was one of those who led the uprising against Andros. Stoughton became lieutenant governor of Massachusetts under its new charter of 1691. The following year, as chief justice, he presided over the court at Salem which tried those accused of witchcraft. The governor **Sir William Phips** brought an end to the court's proceedings in October 1692. Stoughton, however, was appointed as chief justice of a new supreme court in 1693, and renewed the trials. When Phips reprieved those he condemned to death he refused to attend the court. Stoughton got his revenge on Phips, being involved in the governor's recall to England in 1694, following which he acted as governor. He never repented his proceedings against those he considered to be witches, continuing to believe in spectral evidence even after others, like **Increase Mather** lost faith in it.

SUGAR ACT of 1764 replaced the **Molasses Act** of 1733. It lowered the duties from sixpence to three pence a gallon. However, where previously colonists had managed to evade the duty, now there was to be a serious effort to impose it, with the creation of a court of vice-admiralty in Halifax Nova Scotia to deal with offenders. Moreover the intention was no longer merely to prohibit the trade in French sugars but avowedly to raise revenue in the colonies 'for defraying the expenses of defending, protecting and securing the same'. It was this shift of emphasis, from regulating commerce to raising taxes, which caused objections to the Act in the continental colonies.

SUSQUEHANNA COMPANY. There were two companies with this name in the colonial period. The first was formed by **William Penn** to develop **Pennsylvania**'s economy by extending the fur trade west and northward. To this end Penn planned to allow other than English nationals such as Scottish investors into the scheme. The company was stillborn because the **Navigation Act** of 1696 prohibited non-English investors. This was backed up by the institution of the Admiralty courts in the colony, the result of which meant direct and swift action could be taken against any abuse of power by proprietors and chartered companies. The second Company was launched in 1753 to acquire land, its projectors soliciting the **Connecticut** General Assembly to grant what was thought to be their territory in the Wyoming Valley of **Pennsylvania**. This claim led to political and sometimes physical clashes between the two colonies. In 1763, the dispute was settled in England in favor of Pennsylvania's claims.

T

TARLETON, BANASTRE (1754–1833) was the son of a Liverpool trader in sugar and slaves. He was educated at the Middle Temple and University College Oxford. On his father's death in 1773 he was left a legacy of £5,000 which he squandered on gambling. By 1775, when he bought a commission in the dragoons, there was little of it left. Tarleton went to take part in the **War of American Independence**, seeing action in **South Carolina** and the middle states before becoming involved in the southern strategy of the years 1780 to 1781. By then he commanded the British Legion, a company of American Loyalists known from their uniforms as the green dragoons, though they included infantrymen in their ranks too. They played a significant role in the capture of **Charles Town**. In the fighting immediately afterwards he defeated forces sent from **Virginia** to relieve the port, but his conduct earned him a reputation for brutality which he never subsequently lost. A run of victories in 1780, including Camden, came to an abrupt end at Cowpens in January 1781, where most of Tarleton's men were killed or captured. He himself was wounded at Guilford Court House, and surrendered with **Cornwallis** at Yorktown. Tarleton himself got over the York River into Gloucester County, and hoped Cornwallis would join him to escape north and fight another day. But a storm made his gesture futile. Despite his reputation as a butcher in America Tarleton was regarded as a hero on his return to England. Then in 1786 criticism of his conduct in America appeared in the British press. He responded with a *History of the Campaigns of 1780 and 1781 in the southern provinces of North America*. This sought to redeem his reputation by besmirching that of Cornwallis, but did not succeed.

TENNENT, GILBERT (1703–1764), the eldest of four sons of **William Tennent**, was born in Armagh in Northern Ireland, emigrating to North America in 1718. He obtained the degree of M A from **Yale College** in 1725, and was admitted to the Philadelphia Presbytery. After a brief tenure of a living in New Castle, **Delaware,** which he left under a cloud, he went to New Brunswick, **New Jersey**, where he was ordained. He teamed up with **Theodore Frelinghuysen** to preach to joint congregations, Tennent in English, his partner in Dutch. In 1739 they were visited by **George Whitefield**. His message was undiluted Calvinism, telling his hearers, according to a hostile witness, that 'they were all damned, damned, damned! This charmed them, and in the dreadfullest winter I ever saw, people wallowed in the snow night and day for the benefit of his beastly braying.' Tennent attacked any sign of Arminianism, for instance in a sermon he preached at Nottingham **Pennsylvania** in 1740 on *The Danger of an Unconverted Ministry*. The following year he returned from a tour of the northern colonies to attend a synod in Philadelphia which brought to a head the conflict between the Old and New Sides in the **Great Awakening**. This resulted in a split which led Tennent to withdraw in a schism which lasted until 1758. He settled a new side Presbyterian church in Philadelphia in 1743, where he criticized the pacifism of the **Quakers** in Pennsylvania during **King George's War**. After becoming a trustee of the College of New Jersey (**Princeton**) he went to England in 1753 to raise funds for it.

TENNENT, WILLIAM (1673–1745) was born in Ireland and educated in Scotland, graduating from Edinburgh University in 1695. He was ordained as deacon in the Anglican Church of Ireland in 1704 and minister in 1706. After emigrating to **Philadelphia**, however, he converted to Presbyterianism in 1718. He became pastor at Neshaminay **Pennsylvania** in 1726, a living he held until his death. In 1736 he built 'Log College' on some land he had acquired between Philadelphia and New York for the training of clergy who like him took the 'new side' in the **Great Awakening**. In 1738 the 'old side' Presbyterian Synod decreed that all ordinands should have diplomas from Old World Universities or from **Harvard** or **Yale**, or otherwise should be specially approved. This was aimed specifically at Log College, which was closed down after Tennent's death, though it experienced a rebirth with the College of New Jersey (**Princeton**), thanks in part to the efforts of his son, **Gilbert Tennent**.

TOWNSHEND, CHARLES (1725–1767) was elected as MP for Great Yarmouth in 1747. The following year he became a member of the **Board of Trade** when **Lord Halifax** became President of it. This gave him direct knowledge of the state of the American colonies. After a brief spell at the Admiralty from 1754 to 1755 he went into opposition, attaching himself to **William Pitt**. He returned to office as treasurer of the chamber when Pitt became prime minister, and remained in the ministry when Pitt resigned in 1761, taking the post of secretary at war. In 1762 he became President of the Board of Trade and the following year paymaster general, a post he held until 1766. When Pitt, now Lord Chatham, became prime minister again that year he made Townshend his chancellor of the exchequer. Chatham's increasing absence from business led Townshend to take the lead in fiscal policy. One of his initiatives was the **Townshend duties** in 1767. He justified them on the grounds that the defeat of a measure to levy the land tax at four shillings in the pound, and its lowering to three shillings, required revenues to be raised urgently to make up the short fall. He was also implementing policies devised when Halifax had been President of the Board of Trade, on which he had served as a member, but which could not be introduced at the time because of the Seven Years' War. Townshend did not live to face their consequences, dying shortly after their introduction.

TOWNSHEND DUTIES were levied on goods such as glass, lead, painter's colours, paper and tea by **Charles Townshend** in 1767. As a follower of **William Pitt** he accepted his mentor's distinction between direct taxes on the colonies, which he considered unconstitutional, and indirect taxes, which were not only legal but in his view acceptable to the colonists. If that distinction had once been valid, it was no longer the case in the colonies, where any attempt by the British government to raise revenue by statute was bound to incur resistance. When the duties did run into opposition Townshend's successor as chancellor of the exchequer, **Lord North** undertook to repeal all but that on tea. When he became prime minister North implemented this decision, and took much of the tension out of relations between Britain and the American colonies.

TREATY OF UTRECHT ended the War of the Spanish Succession or **Queen Anne's War** in 1713. Louis XIV recognized the Protestant Succession in the house of Hanover and therefore the eventual accession to the British throne of **George I**. In North America France gave up territorial claims to Hudson's Bay, Newfoundland and **Nova Scotia**. Also involving the colonies indirectly was the grant by Spain to Britain, along with Gibraltar and Minorca, of the Asiento, or right to engage in the **Slave Trade** to Spanish possessions in the New World.

TREATY OF WESTMINSTER 1674 brought an end to the third Anglo–Dutch war. The Dutch finally recognized England's sovereignty over their former colony of New Amsterdam which was thereafter called **New York.**

TWO PENNY ACT CONTROVERSY. Two Acts so-called were passed in Virginia, one in 1752 the other in 1758. The first aroused little protest, since it was temporary, lasting only ten months. The second, meant to be permanent, caused bitter controversy. It allowed colonists to commute payments in tobacco into cash at the rate of 2d per pound of tobacco. The Anglican clergy objected that this rate of exchange was too low, and would decrease their incomes substantially. The British Privy Council disallowed the Act. **Patrick Henry** declared that in disallowing the Act **George III** 'from being the father of his people had degenerated into a tyrant, and had forfeited all right to his subjects' obedience'.

V

VANE, HENRY SIR (1613–1662) the younger, was the eldest son of Sir Henry Vane the elder, a substantial landowner in England. He was educated at Oxford University and then visited leading Protestant centers in Europe. After a diplomatic mission to Vienna he was denied further favors from **Charles I**, probably because of his increasing criticism of what he perceived as Arminian tendencies in the Church of England. In 1635 his radical religious views led him to go to **New England**. He settled in **Boston,** where his social standing quickly obtained him advancement in the affairs of **Massachusetts**. By 1636 he was Governor of the colony, and consequently presided over its affairs during the **Pequot War** and the **Antinomian controversy**. Vane secured the alliance of the Narragansett Indians against the Pequots, and purchased **Rhode Island** from them. He supported **Anne Hutchinson** in her dispute with **John Winthrop**. However, in 1637, Vane lost the election to the Governorship to Winthrop, and returned to England. This left a power vacuum in Massachusetts and Winthrop was able to regain support. Consequently, Hutchinson was banished from the settlement. Vane remained in England throughout the period of the Commonwealth, becoming a prominent opponent of the king, and later of Oliver Cromwell. When **Charles II** was restored in 1660, Vane was charged with treason. He was found guilty and was beheaded.

VICE ADMIRALTY COURTS were set up in the colonies following the last of the **Navigation Acts** in 1696, which authorized them. They tried breaches of the laws by merchants. Colonists particularly objected to them because they were presided over by judges and did not have juries. Their jurisdiction was therefore decried as arbitrary, especially as they had first been introduced by **James II**, without statutory authority, in the **Dominion of New England**.

VIRGINIA, located between 35 and 40 degrees parallel, was the first area for a permanent English settlement in North America. In 1607 Jamestown was established on the north bank of the James River by the **Virginia Company of London**. The climate and location were not conducive to a flourishing population with its high humidity and swampy ground. For this reason, the investors soon realized that 'seasoning' the settlers was important to the healthy growth of the colony. The fortunes of the colony fluctuated. Within a year of its establishment, the population was decimated by starvation and disease. The appointment of Captain **John Smith** as Governor went some way toward stabilizing the settlement. In 1611, another attempt was made to save the colony when **Sir Thomas Dale** imposed what amounted to martial law in order get control of the situation. Although these measures proved effective they were resented by the colonists whose complaints reached England and threatened to undermine the efforts of the Virginia Company to make emigration to the colony attractive. To counter this adverse publicity the Company agreed to set up a representative assembly at Jamestown in 1619. This was the first such assembly in North America, and went some way towards stabilizing the colony. Nevertheless the Indian rebellion of 1622 threatened to annihilate the colonists. It was a blow from which the Virginia Company never recovered. In 1623 **James I** intervened in its affairs and the following year Virginia became a Crown colony. The survival of the colony was finally assured with the blending, growing and export of tobacco. The success of tobacco caused an increased demand for laborers. At first it was supplied by indentured servants. By the late

17th century, however, **indentured servitude** was declining, to be replaced with increased numbers of **slaves**. It has been suggested that the changeover was accelerated by the participation of indentured servants in **Bacon's Rebellion** against Governor **Sir William Berkeley**. It was more likely due to the increase in the standard of living back in England, which made indentured servitude less attractive. Virginia became more stable after the suppression of Bacon's rebellion, not experiencing any disturbance in the **Glorious Revolution**. In the 1690s the **College of William and Mary** was built, and the capital moved from Jamestown to the college's location in Williamsburg. By contrast with the starvation and vicissitudes of the early 17th century Virginia settled down in the 18th century to become one of the more stable and prosperous colonies. Its tobacco culture, to be sure, was vulnerable to fluctuating prices caused by over production and elastic demand. But the planter aristocracy of such families as the Byrds, Carters, Lees and Washingtons presided over a society which seemed impervious to revolutionary upheaval. Even the **Great Awakening**, though the **Baptists** made some inroads into the Anglican establishment, did not disturb the Old Dominion as much as it did other colonies to the north and south. Yet in the run up to the **War of American Independence** the Virginian gentry took the lead in many of the disputes with Britain and were conspicuous in the hostilities when they broke out. Virginia provided the draftsman of the **Declaration of Independence, Thomas Jefferson** and the commander of the continental army, **George Washington**. A cynical view of their anti-British stance would dwell on the indebtedness of many of the tobacco planters to merchants in London and the Proclamation of Lord Dunmore, the last royal governor of Virginia, which offered freedom to any slaves who left their masters and signed up for service under the Crown. Yet there was far more to their resistance to British measures than mere self-interest. There was a code of honor among the Virginia gentry which was deeply offended by the arrogant claims of an imperial authority which assumed a superiority to which it was not obviously entitled. On the contrary, **Patrick Henry**, Thomas Jefferson, **James Madison** and George Washington yielded to none of the ministers of **George III** in learning or political sophistication.

VIRGINIA COMPANY was chartered in 1606 as a joint stock company to launch the colony of **Virginia**, sending out three ships which anchored in the James River in 1607 and established Jamestown. The Company obtained two other charters from the Crown in 1609 and 1612. Difficulties faced by the infant colony which threatened its very survival created factions on the board of the company led by Robert Rich, earl of Warwick, and Sir Edwin Sandys. Warwick supported the martial law imposed on the colony by **Lord de la Warr, Sir Thomas Dale, Sir Thomas Gates** and **Sir Samuel Argall**. Sandys was concerned that these were alienating colonists and deterring new settlers. In 1617 he was made assistant to its treasurer, Sir Thomas Smyth, and in 1619 he replaced Smyth as treasurer of the company in what was seen as a coup against arbitrary rule in the colony. It was followed by the recall of the governor **Argall**, whose successor, **Yeardley**, ended the era of draconian rule in Virginia and instituted the colony's assembly. When Sandys' treasurership came up for renewal in 1620 **James I**, who regarded him as a thorn in his flesh, intervened in the company's election protesting that any other candidate, even the devil, would be preferable to him. The Spanish ambassador, Gondomar, was also putting pressure on the king to resist Sandys, claiming that the settlement at Virginia infringed the rights of Spain in America. Encouraged by the king Warwick accused Sandys of corruption in his handling of its finances, and he was imprisoned in 1621. His imprisonment was regarded as political by his supporters, and when his opponents failed to make good their charges he was released. Fresh accusations in 1623 led to his house arrest. Meanwhile the massacre of settlers in Virginia by Indians in 1622 caused a collapse of confidence in the company's ability to make it prosper, giving James an opportunity to wind it up and take the colony into the care of the Crown. When the company was dissolved in 1624 George Sandys, Edwin's brother, was appointed to the council of Virginia, now a crown colony, by the king. He remained on the council until 1627 when his opponents on it got him removed. He returned to England, where he became an agent for the Virginia assembly in 1638. In 1642 he petitioned parliament to revive the old Virginia company, provoking a protest from the colonial assembly to the king who assured it that he would not restore the company.

VIRGINIA RESOLVES were proposed by **Patrick Henry** to the assembly in Williamsburg on 30 May 1765. Henry put forward seven proposals, five of which were adopted by the assembly. The fifth maintained that the assembly had 'the only exclusive right and power to levy taxes and impositions on the inhabitants of this colony, and that any attempt to vest such a power in any person or persons other than the general assembly is illegal, unconstitutional and unjust and also a manifest tendency to destroy British as well as American freedom'. The two which were not passed maintained that the colonists were not obliged to obey any law imposing taxation on them by parliament, and that anybody maintaining that parliament had the right to tax the colonies should be deemed an enemy to Virginia. Notwithstanding the failure to adopt the last two all seven were widely published in the colonial press implying that they had all been passed.

W

WALKING PURCHASE was the name given to a notorious scheme in **Pennsylvania** undertaken in 1735 by **James Logan** and **Thomas Penn**. Penn claimed that his father **William Penn** had made a treaty with the Delaware **Indians** whereby they conveyed to the proprietor of Pennsylvania an area which could be walked across in one and a half days. Since this had not been taken up it was now implemented. Thomas Penn and Logan arranged for relays of walkers to mark out the area, who walked 66.5 miles in the allotted time, thereby maximizing the territory acquired. The Delaware Indians claimed that they had been cheated. They were relocated from the land they had to abandon by the Iroquois, who had them move west of the Susquehanna River.

WALPOLE, SIR ROBERT (1676–1745) was a Whig Member of Parliament from 1701 to 1742, when he was made first earl of Orford. Following his appointment to the posts of chancellor of the exchequer and first lord of the Treasury in 1721 he became known as prime minister, and is generally regarded as the first to hold that position. He held it until 1742, a length of tenure which has never been equaled let alone surpassed. His policy towards the colonies is usually characterized, in **Edmund Burke**'s term, as one of 'salutary neglect'. He did, however, preside over the transformation of **North** and **South Carolina** into Crown colonies in 1729, the establishment of **Georgia** and the passing of the Hat Act in 1732 and the Molasses Act in 1733, all of which demonstrated government interference in colonial affairs. Had his Excise scheme come into operation in 1733 it would have affected the tobacco trade from the colonies, as it provided for the storage of tobacco into Britain in bonded warehouses. In the event Walpole had to withdraw the scheme. This was the biggest blow to his authority before his resignation in 1742.

WAR OF AMERICAN INDEPENDENCE started with skirmishes at Lexington and Concord in April 1775. Learning that minutemen – so called because they claimed they could be ready for action in a minute – had stored weapons at Concord. General **Thomas Gage** sent troops commanded by Colonel Francis Smith to seize them. Warned of their advance the minutemen intercepted them at Lexington. Who fired the 'shot that rang round the world' is unknown, though it was probably a minuteman. Smith's men retaliated and killed eight Americans. The British then advanced to Concord but found themselves crossing hostile ground and Smith gave them the order to retreat to Boston, during which seventy five of them lost their lives. Boston was then besieged by Americans who retreated after the battle of Bunker's Hill, only to return under **Washington**'s command. In March 1776 the British left Boston for **Nova Scotia**.

General **William Howe**, sent to replace Gage, arrived in **New York City** with 32,000 men at the end of June. On 27 August Howe defeated Washington at the battle of Brooklyn Heights and chased him across **New Jersey** into **Pennsylvania**. On 25 December, however, Washington crossed the Delaware and took Trenton and Princeton. The campaign of 1777 in this area culminated in Howe's defeat of Washington at Brandywine creek on 11 September and his entry into Philadelphia while his opponent retreated to Valley Forge to spend a miserable winter. Further north, however, an American army led by Horatio Gates defeated General **Burgoyne** at Saratoga on 17 October. This persuaded France to offer the USA an alliance in February 1778. **Sir Henry Clinton** replaced Howe as commander of the British forces. He moved them from Philadelphia to New York City. Washington pursued them across New Jersey, engaging them at Monmouth court house on 28 June.

The main theater now became the southern states. In December the British captured Savannah. The French fleet besieged the port from April to October 1779 but then withdrew after heavy losses. The British then advanced into **South Carolina**, taking **Charles Town** in May 1780. Clinton returned to New York, leaving **General Cornwallis** in command of British troops in the south. They defeated Horatio Gates at Camden in August and then advanced into **North Carolina**, but had to return to South Carolina when Nathanael Greene defeated loyalists at King's Mountain in October. When American troops under Daniel Morgan posed a threat to him Cornwallis sent loyalists led by Banastre Tarleton to intercept him. Morgan defeated Tarleton at the battle of Cowpens in January, and then moved to North Carolina to join up again with Greene. Cornwallis met up with them at Guilford court house in March 1781, which proved to be a pyrrhic victory for the British. They then advanced to Yorktown in the **Chesapeake Bay**, where they found themselves cut off on a peninsula between an army led by Washington and the Comte de Rochambeau and the French fleet blockading the Bay. Since escape was impossible Cornwallis surrendered to Washington on 17 October 1781. This defeat led to the downfall of **Lord North**'s ministry and paved the way for the **Peace of Paris** in 1783.

However, although war on mainland America was virtually over after Yorktown, naval warfare continued. The defense of the West Indies against French attack was the particular concern of Admiral Rodney, who won a signal victory over de Grasse at the battle of the Saintes on 12 April 1782. The French had taken Monserrat, Nevis and St Kitts, and threatened Jamaica. With Rodney's victory British colonies in the West Indies were recovered.

WAR OF JENKINS' EAR broke out in 1739 as a result of attacks by Spain on British merchant sailors. In this instance, in an effort by Spain to enforce its navigation laws, particularly in the Caribbean, British boats were seized and their crews were detained. While in captivity one Captain Jenkins was mutilated by having his ear cut off. Word of this treatment helped the opposition in England to force **Sir Robert Walpole** to declare war on Spain.

WAR OF THE AUSTRIAN SUCCESSION 1740–1748. see **King George's War**.

WAR OF THE LEAGUE OF AUGSBURG 1688–1697. see **King William's War**.

WAR OF THE SPANISH SUCCESSION 1702–1713. see **Queen Anne's War.**

WASHINGTON, GEORGE (1732–1799) was born in Virginia, and became surveyor for Fairfax and Culpeper counties in 1748–1749. Upon the death of his half-brother, Lawrence, Washington acquired and settled in Mount Vernon on the Potomac river in 1752. He also obtained a post in the adjutancy corps making the rank of Lieutenant colonel. Thus, from 1752 to 1758 he was district adjutant for the northern neck, between the Potomac and the Rappahannock. In 1753 he was sent to protest against French building of forts in the Ohio region. Although his mission failed, Washington published an account of his trip to the region entitled, *The Journal of Major George Washington*. First published in the colonies and then in Britain, this first-hand account of the wilderness foreshadowed Lewis and Clark's description of their expedition 50 years later. Washington's account also illustrates his awareness of the imperial tensions between Britain and France and the importance of the Iroquois Confederacy in that delicate imperial balance. The journal helped to bolster Washington's reputation internationally. When the protest was ignored he led a contingent of the Virginia militia in 1754 towards **Fort Duquesne**. Finding the French entrenched there he built Fort Necessity, but was unable to defend it when attacked by the French to whom he surrendered. Washington lost his command, but his fortunes were revived the following year when he joined the expedition commanded by General **Edward Braddock.** After Braddock's defeat he was made commander in chief of the Virginia militia. He was on the campaign which succeeded in taking Fort Duquesne from the French in 1758. From 1759 to 1774 Washington was a burgess in the Virginia assembly.

Washington's rise to prominence was rooted in his place in the Virginian aristocracy which had its transatlantic links. He was related by way of his elder step-brother with the Fairfax family who amassed 5 million acres in Virginia including its northern neck. The Fairfax patronage, along with the death of Lawrence, enabled Washington to rise in social, military, and political influence. When Washington petitioned for the post in the Virginia militia, Fairfax used his connection with Virginia's governor, Dinwiddie. Dinwiddie, in turn, took Washington under his wing. By 1757, however, the relationship became strained over the conduct of the war. At the same time, Washington's hopes to succeed Braddock as commander of His Majesty's American forces were dashed when John Campbell, **the Earl of Loudoun** was appointed. Nevertheless, Washington knew the importance of deference and subsequently congratulated his lordship on his appointment. His awareness of the importance of deference and patronage sometimes ran counter to his personal beliefs when it came to promotion within his Virginia regiment. Washington's advocacy of promotion based on merit was sometimes thwarted. When he wrote Loudoun, in deferential terms, requesting a regular commission, Loudoun's response was to ignore the request and disband the Virginia regiment. At the end of 1758, Washington resigned his commission and returned to domestic life. He was elected to the House of Burgesses and began courting Martha Custis, the wealthiest widow in Virginia. With the marriage, he acquired the Custis estate of three plantations along the York River and a sizable tobacco plantation enough to merit transatlantic trade using the services of the London mercantile house of Cary & Company. His relationship with Cary & Company was strained at best and further deteriorated when Washington received news that he was fast falling into debt. Tobacco prices were dropping due to cheaper imported tobacco from Europe, lavish spending of the colonial society, and increasing charges by the mercantile houses. These troubles were compounded by the 1765 **Stamp Act**. To reduce his dependence upon Britain, Washington switched his main production from tobacco to wheat, fishing, and manufacturing. Though not in political rebellion at this point, Washington was in personal revolt against the British. His comment upon the Stamp Act that such measures were likely to have the ironic but salutary effect of reducing American dependence on British import, was expression for economic independence and not necessarily political. By 1776, the two became merged with the threat of military action. Washington became the logical choice to lead the American forces. The Continental Congress appointed him commander of the continental army in 1775, which he led to victory against the British at Yorktown in 1781. He laid down his command and retired to Mount Vernon, returning to public life to preside over the constitutional convention in **Philadelphia** in 1787. Following the ratification of the constitution he became the first President of the United States.

WEISER, CONRAD (1696–1760) was born in Germany, and went with his family to **New York** in 1710 in the scheme to settle Palatines in the Mohawk river valley. There he learned the Mohawk language after spending the winter of 1713–1714 with the Indians. In 1729 he moved to **Pennsylvania** acquiring a farm in Tulpohocken. He arranged conferences with the Iroquois in Philadelphia in 1731 and 1736, winning them over to the proprietary interest. In 1744 at the treaty of Lancaster he negotiated the transfer of lands in the Ohio territory from the **Indians** to the colonies of Maryland, Pennsylvania and Virginia. Thereafter he was eclipsed as a negotiator with the Indians by **Sir William Johnson.**

WEST INDIES. During the course of the 17th century the English acquired a number of islands in the Caribbean. St Christopher, or St Kitts as it was called, in the Leeward Islands was the first, in 1622. Its acquisition was quickly followed by that of Barbados (1625), Nevis (1628), and Antigua and Montserrat (1632). Subsequent disruption of colonizing activity caused by the civil wars led to a lull in the West Indies until in 1655 an expedition sent out by Oliver Cromwell took **Jamaica** from Spain. This marked the final acquisition of settlements in the area until Dominica, Grenada, St Vincent and Tobago were ceded to the British by the French at the **Peace of Paris** in 1763. Initially the islands cultivated a variety of crops, including coffee, indigo, ginger and tobacco. Tobacco indeed became the principal crop until the introduction of sugar in the middle of the 17th century, which came to dominate the economy of the Caribbean colonies. Exports of sugar rose from 22,017 tons in 1700 to 41,425 tons in 1748, and rum from 207 gallons to around 2,000,000 during the same period. The overall share of the islands in Britain's overseas trade increased to 20 per cent at the end of the colonial period, principally due to sugar and its by-products. This made the West Indies far more important economically to the British government than the mainland colonies, even those which produced cash crops such as tobacco and rice.

The cultivation of sugar had profound social as well as economic consequences. Processing it from the raw cane to the final refined product involved backbreaking work which a free labor force proved reluctant to perform. Recourse was therefore had increasingly to **slave** labor. The result was a growing imbalance between the white and black populations on the islands. By 1750 the ratio between them was estimated at 1:9. This was much greater than on any mainland colony, even **South Carolina**, the only one with a black majority, which reached 1 in 6. Moreover where in the tobacco producing colonies of the Chesapeake Bay and the rice regions of South Carolina and Georgia the slave populations increased naturally, in the harsher sugar economies of the islands they had to be constantly imported from Africa to sustain the labor force.

The islands did not rebel against British rule in the **War of American Independence** despite objecting to the **Stamp Act** and other impositions. This was largely due to the fact that they felt they benefited more than they lost from being in the British Empire. The alternative was not independence but French occupation. Thus Monserrat, Nevis and St Kitts were taken by the French in 1782 and Jamaica too was threatened before Admiral Rodney's victory over de Grasse at the battle of the Saintes in April 1782. This ensured that the British regained their Caribbean possession in the treaty of Versailles with France in 1783.

WEST, THOMAS, BARON DE LA WARR (1577–1618) was educated at Queen's College Oxford, but left without taking a degree. He fought in Ireland under the earl of Essex in 1599, and was implicated in the Essex' rebellion in 1601. Elizabeth nevertheless admitted him to her privy council in 1602, the year he succeeded his father as Baron de la Warr. In 1606 he became a member of the council of the **Virginia Company**, which sent him to the colony in 1609 as governor and captain general. He arrived just in time to prevent the evacuation of Jamestown following the 'starving time'. As governor he implemented a draconian regime which probably saved Virginia from extinction. In 1611 he returned unexpectedly to England leaving **Thomas Dale** in charge of the colony. On his way back to it in 1618 he was shipwrecked and drowned. His name was given to the river, bay and subsequent colony of **Delaware**.

WESTERN DESIGN. In 1655, Oliver Cromwell launched an expedition against the Spanish West Indies. The Admiral in charge of the expedition was Admiral William Penn, father of **William Penn**. It was intended to capture Hispaniola, but the attempt was unsuccessful. It did, however, succeed in capturing Jamaica.

WHEATELY, PHILLIS (1754–1784) was a black slave who gained international recognition as a poet and a focal point for the anti-slavery movement. Brought to America as a slave for a Boston family, the Wheatelys, she was educated with their children. She was soon recognized as gifted and was encourage in her literary talents. Subsequently, the family was able to arrange for her works to be published in a collection entitled, *Poems on Various Subjects, Religious and Moral*. Her works, rather than advocating freedom for blacks, expressed gratitude for being brought out of the darkness of Africa into the Christian light of North America. Nevertheless, **Benjamin Rush** used her poetic works as proof to his argument that Africans were not intellectually inferior to the white European. Not all of his peers agreed including **Thomas Jefferson** who responded that her work was below the 'dignity of criticism.'

WHITEFIELD, GEORGE (1714–1770) was born in the Bell Inn Gloucester, where his father was the landlord. Whitefield was educated at Oxford University where he became a member of the 'Holy Club', whose members included John Wesley and other early Methodists. In 1735 he experienced a 'new birth' and was ordained deacon in the Church of England in 1736. He toured through England for two years, giving sermons, the most celebrated being *The Nature and Necessity of our new birth in Jesus Christ in order to salvation* (1737). His first visit to the colonies took place in 1738 when he went to **Georgia**, returning to England the following year to be ordained as a minister. His experience in America seems to have confirmed his Calvinism, for he began to stress the doctrine of predestination. This led to a breach with John Wesley, who preached free will. The two then went their separate ways, though both remained within the Church of England. Wesley's Methodist movement had much more impact in the British Isles than Whitefield's, which eventually became an elite connection patronized by the countess of Huntingdon. By contrast, whereas Wesley's influence in North America was negligible, Whitefield's was vast. Whitefield was back in America before the end of 1739, visiting almost all the colonies along the eastern seaboard preaching in the open air and raising funds for an orphanage in Georgia. While on his tour he met **Jonathan Edwards** and **Gilbert Tennent**. Whitefield went back and forth between the colonies and England on five further occasions, becoming the leading light in the **Great Awakening**. On his second visit, from 1744 to 1748, he encountered opposition, especially in **New England** and **the middle colonies**, even from some who had welcomed him on his first. One of those, George Gillespie, a Presbyterian minister in **Pennsylvania,** published *Remarks upon Mr George Whitefield, proving him a man under delusion*. Whitefield found the south much more congenial to his views, especially when these espoused a defense of slavery. Some supporters in South Carolina gave him a Providence Plantation which employed slaves to provide funds for his orphanage in Georgia. He extended his slave holdings on his third visit to America between 1751 and 1752. In 1754 he returned with children for the orphanage. Although he visited northern colonies, he spent most of the ten months covered by this visit in the south. His next visit, from 1763 to 1765, however, was spent mainly in Boston, New York and Philadelphia. On his final visit, from 1669 to 1670, he was taken ill and died in Newburyport, **Massachusetts**. Whitefield had an incalculable impact on the colonies, breaking down boundaries and making them aware of a common cause. For this he has been regarded as the first American.

WILKES, JOHN (1725–1797) was born in London where his father was a distiller. His mother was a Presbyterian, and Wilkes was brought up as a dissenter, attending Leiden University. In 1747 he married Mary Mead, who brought as her dowry the manor of Aylesbury where he lived as a country gentleman even after the marriage broke down and the couple separated. In 1757 he entered the House of Commons as MP for Aylesbury. When **William Pitt** resigned as prime minister in 1761 in protest at the failure to declare war on Spain Wilkes made his maiden speech in support of him. He also opposed the **Peace of Paris** of 1763 as a betrayal of the victories achieved under Pitt in the **French and Indian War**. His criticism of the treaty was most outspoken in his weekly paper *The North Briton*, the forty-fifth issue of which attacked the king's speech to parliament commending its terms. Wilkes was prosecuted for seditious libel. The warrant for his arrest, however, did not name him but was issued against the authors, printers and publishers of *The North Britain* number 45. Wilkes protested that such general warrants were illegal. His membership of parliament gave him immunity from legal proceedings unless they involved treason, felony or breach of the peace. Seditious libel had previously been outside these categories but in November the House of Commons resolved that it amounted to a breach of the peace, and consequently Wilkes was not protected by parliamentary privilege. Fearing that the authorities were bent on crushing him he fled to France. In his absence the court of king's bench found him guilty of publishing a seditious libel, *The North Briton*, adding for good measure an obscene libel, *An Essay on Woman*, in which Wilkes had parodied Alexander Pope's *Essay on Man*. General warrants, however, were declared unlawful.

Wilkes stayed abroad until 1768, when he returned to England to stand in the general election, hoping to acquire immunity from arrest as an MP. When a friend urged him to be prudent he allegedly retorted 'What the devil have I to do with prudence? ... I must raise a dust or starve in a gaol'. He stood first in London, where he came bottom of the poll. Then he stood in Middlesex, where he topped it. He then surrendered himself to the law and was sentenced to two years in prison for libel. In February 1769 the House of Commons resolved that he was disqualified from being a member as a convicted libeler and a writ was issued for a by-election in Middlesex. Wilkes announced his candidature and was returned unopposed. Again he was declared unqualified to take his seat and another writ was issued, with the same result. On the third occasion a rival candidate stood, and although Wilkes outpolled him comfortably he was declared duly elected by the House of Commons. The decision caused an outcry. That a populous county electorate had its will thwarted by a parliamentary majority mostly chosen by small and venal boroughs was regarded as an affront to the freeholders of Middlesex. Wilkes became a symbol of radical agitation for a more representative House of Commons. The Society of Supporters of the Bill of Rights was launched to agitate for reform. Its first task, however, was to raise money to pay off debts estimated at £14,000 to save Wilkes from arrest by his creditors. The fact that they had been incurred by an extravagant, not to say debauched, lifestyle was a cross Wilkites found hard to bear. Some refused and founded a rival Constitutional Society. Thwarted in his attempt to enter the Commons Wilkes built up a power base in the City of London, where he was elected as an alderman. He exploited the City's privileges to claim that it alone had the right to arrest within its borders. When the House of Commons sought to arrest journalists who had reported its debates they were offered sanctuary in the City. The confrontation led the ministry of **Lord North** to back down, and the reporting of parliamentary debates was acknowledged as a right of a free press. Wilkes culminated his career in the City by becoming mayor of London in 1774.

The general election of that year saw him returned to parliament as MP for Middlesex. He had already earned himself the reputation of being a 'friend of America'. In 1769 the Lower House of Assembly in **South Carolina** had voted him £1,500. The British government had instructed the governor not to allow this, whereupon the Assembly insisted on its right to vote money without the assent of the governor or council. The Wilkes Fund controversy was still rumbling in the colony when the **War of American Independence** broke out. Wilkes criticized the use of arms to enforce British policies on the colonists in a speech he made in the Commons on 6 February 1775 when he declared that 'men are not converted Sir by the force of the bayonet at the breast'. In November 1778 he advocated that American independence should be recognized, since ' a series of four years' disgraces and defeats are surely sufficient to convince us of the absolute impossibility of conquering America by force, and I fear the gentle means of persuasion have equally failed.'

WILLIAM AND MARY COLLEGE was established at Williamsburg in Virginia in 1693 by royal charter issued by King **William III** and **Queen Mary**. The charter owed much to the activities of **James Blair**, who became the first Principal of the College.

WILLIAM III (1650–1702) was born in Holland, the posthumous son of the head of the house of Orange. Orangists were proscribed from holding office by the de Witts who governed the

Dutch Republic after his father's death. In 1672, however, the de Witts fell when the French invaded the Netherlands. William was called to head the resistance to the French attack, and saved the Republic from the invasion. He spent the rest of his life fighting the aggression of Louis XIV. It was to get England out of the orbit of France and aligned with the League of Augsburg that he landed in Devon in November 1688 precipitating the **Glorious Revolution**. William was crowned king jointly with his wife **Mary II**. His ambition of involving England in a war with France was realized when the English fought in **King William's War** from 1689 to 1697. William's policy of maintaining effective authority in North America is demonstrated with his gubernatorial appointments of men like **Benjamin Fletcher** and **Lord Bellamont** and his support of the **Board of Trade**.

WILLIAMS, JOHN (1664–1729) was born in **Massachusetts** and educated at **Harvard College**. Williams became the first pastor of **Deerfield** in the Connecticut River valley. When it was taken in a French and Indian raid in 1704 he was captured and taken to **New France**. Williams was released from captivity in 1706 following the intercession of Governor **Joseph Dudley**. After his return to New England he published *The Redeemed Captive returning to Zion* (1707). He was reinstated in Deerfield, helping to rebuild the devastated town. He served as chaplain on the expedition to Port Royal in 1711 during **Queen Anne's War**. When the war ended in 1713 Williams went to **Canada** to arrange for the return of prisoners.

WILLIAMS, ROGER (c. 1606–1683) was born in England and became known to the great jurist Sir Edward Coke, who employed him as a clerk, and sent him to be educated at Pembroke college, Cambridge. There he was exposed to radical religious beliefs which he espoused. In 1629 he became chaplain to the Puritan Sir William Masham. He also became acquainted with **John Cotton, Thomas Hooker** and **John Winthrop**. In 1631 he decided to follow them to Massachusetts, but refused to accept a living in Boston because the church members still claimed to be part of the Anglican community. He preferred the separatists of **Plymouth** colony, where he went only to disagree with them too. The dispute was probably over the rights of **Indians**, especially over land which he thought had not been respected by the colonists. He returned to Salem where he also asserted the claims of Indians to the land, denying that the king had the right to grant them by charter to Englishmen. When in 1635 he urged the Salem church to separate from the Church of England he was condemned by the General Court, which ordered him to return home. Instead he fled to what became **Rhode Island**, purchasing land from the Narragansett Indians. There he established the town of Providence. His dealings with the Narragansetts were instrumental in obtaining their alliance with the colonists against the Pequots in the **Pequot War**. In 1639 Williams became a Baptist and founded the first Baptist church in the colonies at Providence. Characteristically he left the Baptists shortly afterwards. He never stayed long in a single denomination, being what he himself called a seeker. In 1643 Williams returned to England to get a charter for 'the Providence Plantations of Narragansett Bay.' The charter included the Newport and Portsmouth areas, which later became Rhode Island. While in England he published *The Bloudy Tenent of Persecution* which recounted his own treatment at the hands of the Puritans and called for toleration of divergent views. On his return to Providence in 1644 he served a term of three years as its governor. He made another trip back to England in 1651 to get the charter confirmed by the new Republic. When he returned to Providence in 1654 he again became president of the plantation, serving until 1657. At the Restoration of the monarchy in 1660 Williams obtained a charter from **Charles II** for Rhode Island. It included a guarantee of religious toleration. Ironically Williams was to object to Quakers proselytizing in the colony. Another irony was that his efforts to maintain peaceful relations with the Indians, which had led him to publish a *Key into the Languages of America* in 1643, failed to prevent the Narragansetts joining **Metacom** in what the colonists called **King Philip's War**. During the conflict Providence was sacked. Williams spent his last years as a rather disillusioned man, looking back nostalgically at his early life.

WINTHROP, JOHN (1588–1649) was born in England and was educated at Trinity College, Cambridge. He also studied law at Gray's Inn, and his legal training helped to secure the post of attorney in the Court of Wards in 1627. Increasing disillusion with the religious state of England, however, led him to resign the post in 1629. He became Governor of the Massachusetts Bay company and persuaded other supporters to take its charter to America thus effectively removing its headquarters and power base from English shores. In April 1630 he sailed on the 'Arbella', one of four ships, to New England. On the voyage he preached a lay sermon 'The model of Christian charity' which set out his vision for the new colony. Winthrop was the driving force in setting up the 'city upon a hill' as an example to the rest of the world and particularly to those who longed for a godly reformation back in England. He stressed that they were not separating from the Church of England but hoped to reform the Anglican religion by emphasizing the idea of the Covenant with God. By keeping the faith and living a godly life, salvation was assured. Since God already knew who would be saved and who would not, knowing who these saints were was problematic. Winthrop became one of the elect who would decide who would become one of the saved. This led Winthrop and his visible saints to ensure purity in the colony. The general court passed legislation that prohibited all but the visible saints from participating in the political arena. Winthrop served as Governor of Massachusetts from 1629 to 1649 with only one significant break, from 1634 to 1637, the crucial years of the **Antinomian Controversy**.

WITHERSPOON, JONATHAN (1723–1794) migrated from his native Scotland in 1768 to become one of the founding fathers of the American Revolution. A product of the Scottish Enlightenment, he was educated at the University of Edinburgh. He arrived in colonial North America at the invitation of **Benjamin Rush, George Whitefield**, and the trustees of Princeton University to take the university position of President. Almost immediately after his arrival in the colonies, he was active in provincial politics. By the end of **the American War of Independence**, Witherspoon had been active on virtually every major committee that substantially influenced the creation of the United States. Starting with the committee of correspondence for Somerset County in New Jersey, he was an outspoken advocate for independence becoming the first person in New Jersey to publicly state the need for such a measure. As the war drew to a close, Witherspoon was instrumental in drawing up the instructions for the American Peace Commission in France in 1781. Throughout the war, Witherspoon's sermons were printed and distributed in America and Britain, the most political of which was, *The Dominion of Providence Over the Passions of Men* (1776). He also helped to influence American political philosophy with his own which was grounded in the Scottish Enlightenment. Witherspoon passed enlightened tenets on to his students of whom **James Madison** was one. The writings of Witherspoon influenced Jeffersonian thoughts and writings particularly as seen in the Declaration of Independence. Witherspoon's early lectures on moral philosophy parallel that of the Declaration in terms of tyrannical governments and what justifies their overthrow. For this, Witherspoon hearkens back to the English Civil Wars and the overthrow of the 'tyrant' King **Charles I**. Also the term 'Providence' as used in the Declaration dovetails with Witherspoon's view of God's role in the world. Witherspoon's advocacy of independence led him to be the first man in New Jersey to call for independence. He was the only clergyman to sign the Declaration.

WOLCOTT, ROGER (1709–1767) was born in **Connecticut** of which he became deputy governor 1741–50 and governor 1751–54. Wolcott published *Poetical Meditations* in 1725.

WOLFE, JAMES (1727–1759) was the son of a general, and pursued a military career. He became a lieutenant in 1743 following his participation in the battle of Dettingen in **King George's War**. In 1745 he took part in the suppression of the Jacobite rebellion, and fought in the decisive battle of Culloden which ended in April 1746. Following his return to the European theater he was wounded at the battle of Laffeldt in 1747. After the outbreak of the **French and Indian War** he was made brigadier general in North America, and took part in the siege of Louisbourg. In 1759 he was appointed major general and put in charge of the forces sent to take Quebec. On 18 September he took the city, dying in the moment of victory.

WOMEN. Although women in the colonial period were relegated to the domestic sphere, receiving little education, and virtually no political power, by the end of the colonial period, access to these areas began to open up. Nevertheless, conditions in the colonies speeded up opportunities for women. During the 17th century, when the sex ratio was uneven with men out-numbering women, particularly in the southern colonies, and the mortality rate of children was high, women were necessarily in positions of power. They could negotiate for better lives. Also, because women tended to outlive the men, women became the trustees for the son's estate until they reached adulthood. Nevertheless, there were shared gender attitudes transatlantically. Once the gender ratio was more balanced in the colonies, women retreated back into their domestic roles. By the 18th century, women were being educated but with the aim to prepare them as better wives and helpmates. In the area of religion, women were able to exercise their influence in the public sphere. After 1680, women constituted approximately 55 to 70 per cent of congregations. There were limits to how much influence they had as in the case of **Anne Hutchinson** in **New England.** But in the southern and, particularly, in the middle colonies, the more liberal atmosphere of the Quakers and Baptists allowed for broader participation in such things as voting in church affairs. Outside of the religious sphere, there was much less oppor-tunity for formal participation. However the opportunities varied throughout the colonies. Multi-culturalism and urbanization contributed to opening up of gender equality. While New England and the southern colonies were more restrictive in gender equality, the middle colonies were not. This was largely due to the multi-cultural makeup and the influence of previous settle-ments such as in the case of the Dutch in New York where women were not as materially dependent upon men. Urbanization created an environment for women to become commer-cially active and with commercial clout came political clout. By the revolution, though, the gender ratio evened out and women's roles became more traditional, like those women in the mother country. Within the domestic sphere, the women assumed the role of, not only child-bearers, but helpmates and partners to their husbands. Significantly, these roles gave women the authority over the household while their spouses were away. Although the American Revolution opened up possibilities of greater freedom for white males, it did little to improve the lot of females. **Abigail Adams'** plea to her husband to 'remember the ladies' fell on deaf ears.

WYATT, SIR FRANCIS (c. 1575–1644) was born in England and educated at Oxford University. He received his knighthood in 1618, when he also married Margaret Sandys, the niece of Sir Edwin Sandys, one of the most powerful men in the **Virginia Company**. Wyatt replaced **Sir George Yeardley** as Governor of **Virginia** and went to Jamestown in 1621. His appointment was well received as he seemed to bring an end to the discord which had marked the colony's politics since its establishment. His governorship was, however, marred by the massacre of colonists by the Indians in 1622 which precipitated the dissolution of the Virginia Company. Wyatt was nevertheless kept on as governor by the king when Virginia became a crown colony. He asked to be replaced on hearing of his father's death in 1626 and was succeeded by Yeardley. In 1639, however, he returned once again to the colony as its governor, but his second stint was less popular than the first and he was replaced by **Sir William Berkeley** in 1640.

Y

YALE COLLEGE was established at Saybrook in Connecticut in 1701 to train ministers for the Independent churches of New England. **Harvard College** had been founded for this purpose too, but by the end of the 17th century many strict Calvinists felt that the Harvard trained ministers were being exposed to Arminian teachings and were therefore not orthodox in their Calvinism. In 1718 a gift from Elihu Yale led to its adopting his name. Yale moved to New Haven in 1745.

YEARDLEY, SIR GEORGE (1588–1627) was a soldier who, like **Sir Thomas Gates**, had served in the Netherlands. He set out with him in 1609 to go to **Virginia** and was shipwrecked on **Bermuda**. He did not reach Virginia until 1610. When **Sir Thomas Dale** left the colony in 1610 he left Yeardley in charge as deputy governor. He relaxed the severe regime implemented by **Lord de la Warr** and Dale. In 1617 he was replaced by Samuel Argall, and returned to England the following year, where he was appointed as governor of Virginia by the Virginia Company and knighted by the king. Acting upon the advice of the company he convened the first assembly in the colony when he went back in 1619. **Sir Francis Wyatt** replaced him as governor from 1621 to 1626, when Yeardley again became governor until his death.

Z

ZENGER, JOHN PETER (1697–1746) was born in Germany and went to **New York** in 1710 as one of the 'poor palatines' sent out under a scheme organized for their relief. He was apprenticed to the printer **William Bradford**. He moved to Maryland and became as printer of laws for the colony, which conferred naturalization on him. By 1722 he was back in New York and three years later went into partnership with Bradford. In 1726 he set up on his own, and launched the *New York Weekly Journal* in 1733 as a rival to Bradford's *New York Gazette*. Where Bradford defended the actions of Governor **William Cosby** Zenger criticized them. In 1734 he was arrested for libel, and when he failed to raise the enormous bail of £600 was imprisoned. During his ten months in prison the *New York Weekly Journal* continued publication thanks to his wife who collected the copy from his cell.

In 1735 he was tried on a charge of criminal libel. **Alexander Hamilton**, the eminent Pennsylvania lawyer who defended him, persuaded the jury to find him not guilty. In doing so he argued that they should not only consider whether or not he was the publisher of the journal, which was all that the prosecution claimed they had to establish, but that his intent was seditious. Previously juries in libel cases had not been allowed to base their verdict on the intentions of the accused, and the Zenger case set an important precedent in the law concerning seditious libel. Zenger himself benefited from his ordeal by becoming public printer in 1737 for the colony of New York, to which New Jersey was added the following year.

Selected Bibliography

There are several editions of original sources dealing with the colonies. Particularly useful are *Settlements to Society 1607–1763: A Documentary History of Colonial America* edited by Jack P. Greene (New York, 1975); *Colonies to Nation: A Documentary History of the American Revolution* edited by Jack P. Greene (New York, 1975); and *English Historical Documents: American Colonial Documents to 1776* edited by Merrill Jensen (1955). Biographies of many individuals are available in the *Oxford Dictionary of National Biography* edited by H. G. C. Matthew and B. Harrison, 60 vols (Oxford, 2004). The editors made the decision to include people born in the American colonies before 1776, making the *ODNB* an invaluable work of reference for Atlantic historians. It can be consulted online at oxforddnb.com. The following selections from an enormous historiography were all published in London unless otherwise indicated.

GENERAL SURVEYS

American History

Bailyn, Bernard, Davis, David Brion, Donald, David Herbert, Thomas, John J., Wiebe, Robert H. and Wood, Gordon S. *The Great Republic: A History of the American Republic* volume one, 4th edition (Lexington, Massachusetts, 1992).

Butler, Jon *Becoming America: The Revolution before 1776* (Cambridge, Massachusetts, 2001).

The Cambridge Economic History of the United States, volume one, The Colonial Era edited by Stanley L. Engerman and Robert E. Gallman (Cambridge, 1996).

Greene, Jack P. *Pursuits of Happiness: The social development of early modern British colonies and the formation of American culture* (Chapel Hill, North Carolina, 1988).

Hofstadter, Richard *America at 1750: a social portrait* (New York, 1971).

McFarlane, Anthony *The British in the Americas 1480–1815* (1992).

Meinig, D. W. *The Shaping of America: a geographical perspective on 500 years of history: volume one; Atlantic America 1492–1800* (1986).

Middleton, Richard *Colonial America: A History 1607–1776* 3rd edition (Oxford, 2002).

Simmons, R. C. *The American Colonies from Settlement to Independence* (1976).

Speck, W. A. and Geiter, Mary K. *Colonial America from Jamestown to Yorktown* (2003).

Taylor, Alan *American Colonies: The settlement of North America to 1800* (2001).

A Companion to Colonial America edited by Daniel Vickers (Oxford, 2003).

British History

Brewer, John *The Sinews of Power: War and the English State 1688–1783* (1989).

Clark, J. C. D. *English Society 1660–1832: Religion, Ideology, and Politics during the Ancien Regime* (second edition, 2000).

Colley, Linda *Britons: Forging the Nation 1707–1837* (1996).

Coward, Barry *The Stuart Age: England 1603–1714* (2003).

Harris, Tim *Politics under the Later Stuarts: Party Conflict in a Divided Society, 1660–1715* (1993).

Harris, Tim *Restoration: Charles II and his Kingdoms 1660–1685* (2005).

Harris, Tim *Revolution: The great crisis of the British Monarchy 1685–1720* (2006).

Hirst, Derek *England in Conflict 1603–1660: Kingdom, Community, Commonwealth* (1999).

Holmes, G. *The Making of a Great Power: Late Stuart and early Georgian Britain 1660–1722* (1993).

Holmes, G. and Szechi D. *The Age of Oligarchy: Pre-Industrial Britain 1722–1783* (1993).

Hoppit, J. *A Land of Liberty: England 1689–1727* (Oxford, 2000).

Kishlansky, Mark *A Monarchy Transformed: Britain 1603–1714* (1997).

Langford, Paul *A Polite and Commercial People: England 1727–1783* (Oxford, 1989).

O'Gorman, Frank *The Long Eighteenth Century: British Political and Social History 1688–1832* (1997).

Prest, Wilfred *Albion Ascendant: English History 1660–1815* (Oxford, 1998).

Smith, David L. *A History of the Modern British Isles 1603–1707: The Double Crown* (1998).

Smith, Hannah *Georgian Monarchy: Politics and Culture 1714–1760* (Cambridge, 2006).

Wilson, Kathleen *The Sense of the People: Politics, Culture and Imperialism in England 1715–1785* (1995).

ATLANTIC ASPECTS

Anderson, Fred *Crucible of War: The Seven Years' War and the fate of Empire in British North America 1754–1763* (New York, 2000).

Armitage, David *The Ideological Origins of the British Empire* (Cambridge, 2000).

The British Atlantic World 1500–1800 edited by David Armitage and M. J. Braddick (New York, 2002).

Bailyn, Bernard *The Ideological Origins of the American Revolution* (Cambridge, Massachusetts, 1967).

Bailyn, Bernard *The Origins of American Politics* (New York, 1968).

Strangers within the Realm: Cultural margins of the first British Empire edited by Bernard Bailyn and Philip D. Morgan (Chapel Hill, North Carolina, 1986).

Bliss, Robert *Revolution and Empire: English Politics and the American Colonies in the seventeenth century* (Manchester, 1990).

Breen T. H. and Hall, Timothy D. *Colonial America in an Atlantic World* (2003).

Brumwell, Stephen, *Redcoats: The British Soldier and the War in the Americas 1755–1763* (Cambridge, 2002).

Canny, Nicholas *The Elizabethan Conquest of Ireland: A Pattern Established 1565–1576* (New York, 1976).

The Oxford History of the British Empire volume one: Origins of Empire: British Overseas Enterprise to the Close of the Seventeenth Century edited by Nicholas Canny (Oxford, 1998).

Elliott, Sir John *Empires of the Atlantic World: Britain and Spain in America 1492–1830* (2006).

Fischer, David Hackett *Albion's Seed: Four British Folkways in America* (Oxford, 1989).

Greene, Jack P. *Peripheries and Center: Constitutional Developments in the Extended Polities of the British Empire and the United States 1607–1788* (Athens, Georgia, 1986).

Griffin, Patrick *The People with no name: Ireland's Ulster Scots, America's Scots Irish and the creation of the British Atlantic World 1689–1764* (Princeton, New Jersey, 2001).

Haggerty, Sheryllynne *The British-Atlantic Trading Community: Men, Women and the distribution of goods* (2006).

Hall, Michael Garibaldi *Edward Randolph and the American Colonies 1676–1703* (New York, 1969).

Henretta, James A. *'Salutary Neglect' Colonial Administration under the Duke of Newcastle* (Princeton, New Jersey, 1972).

Katz, Stanley N. *Newcastle's New York: Anglo–American Politics 1732–1753* (Cambridge, Massachusetts, 1968).

Kulikoff, Allan *From British Peasants to Colonial American Farmers* (Chapel Hill, North Carolina, 2000).

Lovejoy, David S. *The Glorious Revolution in America* (New York, 1972).

The Creation of the British Atlantic World edited by Elizabeth Mancke and Carole Shammas (Baltimore, Maryland, 2005).

The Oxford History of the British Empire volume two: The Eighteenth Century edited by Peter Marshall (Oxford, 1998).

Olson, Alison G. *Anglo–American Politics 1660–1775: The relationship between parties in England and Colonial America* (Oxford, 1973).

Olson, Alison G. *Making the Empire Work: London and American Interest Groups 1690–1790* (Cambridge, Massachusetts, 1992).

Pestana, Carla Gardina *The English Atlantic in an Age of Revolution 1640–1661* (Cambridge, Massachusetts, 2004).

Pole, J. R. *Political Representation in England and the Origins of the American Revolution* (1966).

Sosin, Jack M. *English America and the Restoration Monarchy of Charles II: Transatlantic Politics, Commerce and Kinship* (Lincoln, Nebraska, 1980).

Speck, W. A. *British America 1607–1763* (1985).

Steele, Ian K. *Politics of Colonial Policy: The Board of Trade in Colonial Administration 1696–1720* (Oxford, 1968).

Steele, Ian K. *The English Atlantic 1675–1740: An exploration of communication and community* (Oxford, 1986).

Webb, Stephen Saunders *The Governors-General: the English army and the definition of the Empire 1519–1681* (Chapel Hill, North Carolina, 1979).

Webb, Stephen Saunders *1676: The End of American Independence* (New York, 1984).

Webb, Stephen Saunders *Lord Churchill's Coup: The Anglo-American Empire and the Glorious Revolution Reconsidered* (New York, 1995).

MIGRATION

Andrews, K. R. *Trade, Plunder and Settlement: Maritime Enterprise and the Genesis of the British Empire 1480–1630* (Cambridge, 1984).

The Westward Enterprise: English Activities in Ireland, the Atlantic and America 1480–1650 edited by K. R. Andrews and Nicholas Canny (Detroit, 1979).

Bailyn, Bernard *The Peopling of British North America* (New York, 1986).

Breen, T. H. and Foster, Stephen 'Moving to the New World: the character of early Massachusetts immigration', *William and Mary Quarterly* 1973, xxx, 189–222.

Campbell, Mildred 'Social origins of some early Americans', *Seventeenth-Century America* edited by James M. Smith (Chapel Hill, North Carolina, 1959), pp. 63–89.

Europeans on the Move: studies on European Migration 1500–1800 edited by Nicholas Canny (Oxford, 1994).

Cressy, David *Coming Over: Migration and communication between England and New England in the seventeenth century* (Cambridge, 1987).

Dickson, R. J. *Ulster Emigration to Colonial America 1718–1775* (1966).

Dobson, D. *Scottish Emigration to Colonial America 1607–1785* (Athens, Georgia, 1966).

Ekirch, A. Roger *Bound for America: the transportation of British convicts to the colonies 1718–1775* (Oxford, 1987).

Galenson, David W. '"Middling People" or "common sort"? The social origins of some early Americans re-examined', *William and Mary Quarterly* 1978, xxxv, 499–524.

Games, Alison *Migration and the origins of the English Atlantic World* (Cambridge, Massachusetts, 1999).

Lockhart, A. *Some Aspects of Emigration from Ireland to the North American Colonies between 1660 and 1775* (New York, 1976).

Quinn, D. B. *England and the Discovery of America 1481–1621* (New York, 1974).

Quinn, D. B. *Set Fair for Roanoke: Voyages and Colonies 1584–1606* (Chapel Hill, North Carolina Press, 1985).

Thompson, Roger *Mobility and Migration: East Anglian Founders of New England 1629–1640* (Amherst, Massachusetts, 1994).

INDIANS

Axtell, James *The European and the Indian: Essays in the Ethnohistory of Colonial North America* (Oxford, 1981).

Axtell, James *The Invasion within: The contest of cultures in colonial North America* (Oxford, 1985).

Axtell, James *After Columbus: Essays in the Ethnohistory of Colonial North America* (Oxford, 1988).

Axtell, James *After 1492: Encounters in Colonial North America* (Oxford, 1992).

Braund, Kathryn E. Holland, *Deerskins and Dufffels: The Creek Indian Trade with Anglo–America 1685–1815* (Lincoln Nebraska, 1993).

Calloway, Colin G. *New Worlds for all: Indians, Europeans and the remaking of early America* (Baltimore Maryland, 1997).

Calloway, Colin G. *After King Philip's War: Presence and Persistence in Indian New England* (Hanover, New Hampshire, 1997).

Reinterpreting New England Indians and the Colonial Experience edited by Colin G. Calloway and Neal Salisbury (Boston, Massachusetts, 2003).

Cronon, W. *Changes in the Land: Indians, Colonists and the Ecology of New England* (New York, 1983).

Gleach, Frederick W. *Powhatan's World and Colonial Virginia: A conflict of cultures* (Lincoln Nebraska, 1997).

Hinderaker, Eric and Mancall, Peter C. *At the Edge of Empire: The Back country in British North America* (Baltimore Maryland, 2003).

Jennings, Francis *The Invasion of America: Indians, Colonialism and the cant of conquest* (Chapel Hill, North Carolina Press, 1975).

Jennings, Francis *The Ambiguous Iroquois Empire: The Covenant Chain Confederation of Indian Tribes with English Colonies from its beginnings to the Lancaster Treaty of 1744* (New York, 1984).

Mancall, Peter C. *Deadly Medicine: Indians and Alcohol in early America* (Ithaca, New York, 1995).

Merrell, James H. *Into the American Woods: Negotiators on the Pennsylvania Frontier* (New York, 1999).

Merrit Jane T. *At the crossroads: Indians and Empires on a mid-Atlantic Frontier 1700–1763* (Chapel Hill, North Carolina, 2003).

O'Brien, Jean M. *Dispossession by Degrees: Indian Land and Identity in Natick Massachusetts, 1650–1790* (Cambridge, 1997).

Richter, Daniel *The Ordeal of the Longhouse: The peoples of the Iroquois League in the era of European Colonisation* (Chapel Hill, North Carolina, 1992).

Richter, Daniel *Facing East from Indian Country: A native history of early America* (Cambridge, Massachusetts, 2003).

Beyond the Covenant Chain: The Iroquois and their neighbors in Indian North America 1600–1800 edited by Daniel Richter and James H. Merrell (Syracuse, New York, 1987).

Shannon, Timothy J. *Indians and Colonists at the Crossroads of Empire: The Albany Congress of 1754* (Ithaca, New York, 2002).

Shoemaker, Nancy *A Strange Likeness: Becoming Red and White in Eighteenth-Century America* (Oxford, 2004).

Vaughan, Alden T. *New England Frontier: Puritans and Indians 1620–1675* (3rd edition, Norman Oklahoma, 1995).

White, Richard *The Middle Ground: Indians, Empires and Republics in the Great Lakes Region 1650–1815* (Cambridge, 1991).

ROANOKE ISLAND

Kupperman, Karen *Roanoke, the abandoned colony* (Totawa, New Jersey, 1984).
Miller, Lee *Roanoke: solving the mystery of the lost colony* (2000).
Stick, David *Roanoke Island: The beginnings of English America* (Chapel Hill, North Carolina, 1983).

CANADA

Eccles, W. J. *The French in North America* (1998).
Faragher, J. M. *A great and noble scheme: the tragic story of the expulsion of the French Acadians from their American homeland* (2005).
Greer, A. *The People of New France* (1997).
Griffiths, N. E. S. *From Migrant to Acadian: a North American People 1604–1755* (2005).

THE CHESAPEAKE

Breen, T. H. *Tobacco Culture: the mentality of the great tidewater planters on the eve of the Revolution* (Princeton, 1985).
Billings, W. M. *Sir William Berkeley and the forging of Colonial Virginia* (Baton Rouge, Louisiana, 2004).
Brown, Robert E. and B. Katherine, *Virginia 1705–1786: Democracy or Aristocracy?* (East Lansing, Michigan, 1964).
Earle, Carville *The Evolution of a Tidewater Settlement System: All Hallow's Parish, Maryland 1650–1783* (Chicago, 1975).
Colonial Chesapeake Society edited by Lois Green Carr, Philip D. Morgan and Jean B. Russo (Chapel Hill, North Carolina, 1988).
Carr, Lois Green, Walsh, Lorena S. and Menard, Russell R. *Robert Cole's World: Agriculture and Society in early Maryland* (Chapel Hill, North Carolina, 1991).
Gleach, Frederic W. *Powhatan's World and Colonial Virginia: a Conflict of Cultures* (1997).
Greene, Jack P. *The Quest for power: The Lower Houses of Assembly in the southern Royal Colonies* (Chapel Hill, North Carolina, 1963).
Hatfield, April Lee *Atlantic Virginia: Intercolonial Relations in the seventeenth century* (Philadelphia, 2004).
Horn, J. *Adapting to a New World: English Society in the Seventeenth-Century Chesapeake* (Chapel Hill, North Carolina, 1994).
Izaac, Rhys *The Transformation of Virginia 1740–1790* (Chapel Hill, North Carolina, 1982).
Kolp, John G. *Gentlemen Freeholders: Electoral Politics in Colonial Virginia* (Baltimore, Maryland, 1998).
Main, Gloria *Tobacco Colony: Life in early Maryland* (Princeton, 1982).
Morgan, E. S. *American Slavery, American Freedom: The Ordeal of Colonial Virginia* (New York, 1975).
Perry, J. *The formation of a society on Virginia's eastern shore 1615–1655* (Chapel Hill, North Carolina, 1990).
Rutman, D. B. and A. H. *A Place in Time: Middlesex County Virginia 1650–1750* (New York, 1984).
Colonial Chesapeake in the seventeenth century: Essays in Anglo-American Society and Politics edited by Thad W. Tate and David L. Ammerman (Chapel Hill, North Carolina, 1979).

NEW ENGLAND

Allen, D. G. *In English Ways: The movement of Societies and the transferal of English local law and custom to Massachusetts Bay in the seventeenth century* (Chapel Hill, North Carolina, 1982).

Anderson, V. D. *New England's Generation: The Great Migration and he Formation of Society and Culture in the Seventeenth Century* (Cambridge, 1991).

Boyer, Paul S. and Nissenbaum, S. *Salem Possessed: The Social Origins of Witchcraft* (Cambridge MA, 1974).

Breen, T. H. *The Character of the Good Ruler: a study of Puritan Political Ideas in New England 1630–1730* (New Haven, Connecticut, 1970).

Bremer, Francis *John Winthrop: America's Forgotten Founding Father* (Oxford, 2003).

Bushman, Richard L. *From Puritan to Yankee: Character and Social Order in Connecticut 1690–1765* (Cambridge, Massachusetts, 1967).

Demos, John *A Little Commonwealth: Family Life in Plymouth Colony* (Oxford, 1970).

Demos, John *Entertaining Satan: Witchcraft and the culture of early New England* (Oxford, 1982).

Donahue, Brian *The Great Meadow: Farmers and the Land in Colonial Concord* (New Haven, Connecticut, 2004).

Godbeer, R. *The Devil's Dominion: Magic and Religion in Early New England* (Cambridge, 1992).

Greven, Philip *Four Generations: Population, Land and Family in Colonial Andover, Massachusetts* (Ithaca, New York, 1970).

Haffenden, Philip *New England in the English Nation 1689–1713* (Oxford, 1974).

Heyrman, C. L. *Commerce and Culture: The maritime communities of colonial Massachusetts* (New York, 1984).

Innes, Stephen *Labor in a New Land: Economy and Society in Seventeenth-Century Springfield* (Princeton, 1983).

Johnson, Richard *Adjustment to Empire: The New England Colonies 1675–1715* (New Brunswick, New Jersey, 1981).

Karlsen, Karen *The Devil in the shape of a woman: Witchcraft in colonial New England* (New York, 1987).

Lockridge, Kenneth 'Land, Population and the Evolution of New England Society, 1630–1790', *Past and Present* 1968, xxxix, 153–91.

Lockridge, Kenneth *A New England town: the first hundred years; Dedham, Massachusetts 1636–1736* (New York, 1970).

Lucas, Paul R. *Valley of Discord: Church and Society along the Connecticut River, 1636–1725* (Hanover, New Hampshire, 1976).

Martin, J. F. *Profits in the Wilderness: Entrepreneurship and the Founding of New England Towns* (Chapel Hill, North Carolina, 1991).

Norton, Mary Beth *In the Devil's Snare: The Salem witchcraft crisis of 1692* (New York, 2003).

Reis, E. *Damned Women: Sinners and Witches in Puritan New England* (Ithaca, New York, 1997).

Van Deventer, David E. *The Emergence of Provincial New Hampshire* (Baltimore, Maryland, 1976).

Vickers, D. *Farmers and Fishermen: Two centuries of work in Essex county, Massachusetts, 1630–1830* (Chapel Hill, North Carolina, 1994).

Weisman, R. *Witchcraft, Magic and Religion in seventeenth-century Massachusetts* (Amherst, Massachusetts, 1984).

Zuckerman, Michael *Peaceable Kingdoms: New England Towns in the Eighteenth Century* (New York, 1970).

THE MIDDLE COLONIES

Archdeacon, Thomas *New York City, 1664–1710: Conquest and Change* (Ithaca, New York, 1976).

Balmer, R. H. *A Perfect Babel of Confusion: Dutch Religion and English Culture in the Middle Colonies* (Oxford, 1989).

Bodle, Wayne 'The myth of the Middle Colonies Reconsidered: The process of regionalization in early America', *Pennsylvania Magazine of History and Biography* 1989, cxiii, 527–48.

Bonomi, Patricia *A Factious People: Politics and Society in Colonial New York* (New York, 1971).

Bonomi, Patricia *The Lord Cornbury Scandal: The politics of reputation in British America* (1988).

The World of William Penn edited by Richard S. and Mary Maples Dunn (Philadelphia, 1986).

Geiter, Mary K. *William Penn* (2000).

Gough, R. J. 'The Myth of the Middle Colonies': an analysis of regionalization in early America', *Pennsylvania Magazine of History and Biography* 1983, cviii, 93–149.

The Demographic History of the Philadelphia Region 1600–1800 edited by S. E. Klepp (Philadelphia, 1989).

Landsman, Ned *Scotland and its first American colony 1683–1765* (Princeton, 1985).

Lemon, J. T. *The Best Poor Man's Country: A geographical study of south eastern Pennsylvania* (Baltimore, Maryland, 1972).

Levy, B. *Quakers and the American Family: British Settlement in the Delaware Valley* (Oxford, 1988).

Nash, Gary B. *Quakers and Politics: Pennsylvania 1691–1726* (Princeton, 1968).

Newcomb, Benjamin H. *Political Partisanship in the American Middle Colonies 1700–1776* (Baton Rouge, Louisiana, 1995).

Authority and Resistance in Early New York edited by William Pencak and Conrad Edick Wright (New York, 1988).

Rink, O. A. *Holland on the Hudson: An Economic and Social History of Dutch New York* (Ithaca, New York, 1986).

Ritchie, Robert C. *The Duke's Province: A study of New York Politics and Society 1664–1691* (Chapel Hill, North Carolina, 1977).

Salinger, S. V. *'To serve well and faithfully': Labor and Indentured Servants in Pennsylvania 1682–1800* (Cambridge, 1987).

Tully, Alan *Forming American Politics: Ideals, Interests and Institutions in Colonial New York and Pennsylvania* (Baltimore, Maryland, 1994).

Tully, Alan *William Penn's Legacy: Politics and social structure in provincial Pennsylvania 1726–1755* (Baltimore Maryland, 1977).

THE LOWER SOUTH

Chaplin, Joyce *An Anxious Pursuit: Agricultural Innovation and Modernity in the Lower South 1730–1815* (Chapel Hill, North Carolina, 1993).

Ekirch, A. Roger *'Poor Carolina': Politics and Society in Colonial North Carolina 1729–1776* (Chapel Hill, North Carolina, 1981).

Morgan, P. D. *Slave counterpoint: black culture in the eighteenth-century Chesapeake and Low country* (Chapel Hill, North Carolina, 1998).

Olwell, Robert *Masters, Slaves and Subjects: The culture of power in the South Carolina Low country 1740–1790* (Ithaca, New York, 1998).

Roper, L. H. *Conceiving Carolina: Proprietors, Planters and Plots 1662–1729* (2004).

Sirmans, Eugene *Colonial South Carolina, a political history 1663–1763* (Chapel Hill, North Carolina, 1966).

THE WEST INDIES

Curtin, P. D. *The Rise and Fall of the Plantation Complex: Essays in Atlantic History* (1998).

Dunn, R. S. *Sugar and Slaves: The Rise of the Planter Class in the English West Indies 1624–1713* (1973).

West Indies Accounts: Essays in the history of the British Caribbean and the Atlantic Economy in honour of Richard Sheridan edited by Roderick A. MacDonald (1993).

Sheridan, R. B. *Sugar and Slavery: An Economic History of the British West Indies 1623–1775* (1974).

RELIGION

Bonomi, Patricia *Under the Cope of Heaven: Religion, Society and Politics in Colonial America* (Oxford, 1986).

Butler, Jon *The Huguenots in America: A refugee people in New World Society* (Cambridge, Massachusetts, 1983).

Butler, Jon *Awash in a sea of faith: Christianising the American People* (Cambridge MA, 1990).

Crawford, M. J. *Seasons of Grace: Colonial New England's Revival Tradition in its British Context* (Oxford, 1991).

Erikson, Kai T. *Wayward Puritans: a study in the sociology of deviance* (New York, 1966).

Foster, Stephen *The Long Argument: English Puritanism and the shaping of New England Culture 1570–1700* (Chapel Hill, North Carolina, 1991).

Gura, P. F. *A Glimpse of Sion's Glory: Puritan Radicalism in New England 1620–1660* (Middletown, Connecticut, 1984).

Hall, David D. *Worlds of Wonder, Days of Judgment: Popular Religious Belief in Early New England* (Cambridge, Massachusetts, 1990).

Hall, T. D. *Contested Boundaries: Itinerancy and the Reshaping of the Colonial Religious World* (Durham, North Carolina, 1994).

Hambrick Stowe, C. E. *The Practice of Piety: Puritan Devotional Disciplines in Seventeenth-Century New England* (Chapel Hill, North Carolina, 1982).

Knight, J. *Orthodoxies in Massachusetts: Rereading American Puritanism* (Cambridge, Massachusetts, 1994).

Lambert, Frank *Inventing 'the Great Awakening'* (Princeton, 2001).

Morgan, E. S. *Visible Saints: The History of a Puritan Idea* (Ithaca, New York, 1965).

Nash, G. B. *The Urban Crucible: Social change, political consciousness, and the origins of the American Revolution* (Cambridge, Massachusetts, 1979).

Pestana, Carla Gardina *Baptists and Quakers in Colonial Massachusetts* (Cambridge, 1991).

Pettit, N. *The Heart Prepared: Grace and Conversion in Puritan Spiritual Life* (New Haven, Connecticut, 1966).

Pointer, R. W. *Protestant Pluralism and the New York Experience: a study in eighteenth-century religious diversity* (Bloomington, Indiana, 1988).

Pope, R. *The Half-Way Covenant: Church Membership in Puritan New England* (Princeton, 1969).

Porterfield, A. *Female Piety in Puritan New England: The emergence of religious humanism* (Oxford, 1992).

Schwartz, Sally *'A mixed multitude': The struggle for toleration in Colonial Pennsylvania* (New York, 1988).

Stout, H. S. *The New England Soul: Preaching and Religious Culture in Colonial New England* (Oxford, 1986).

Tracy, P. *Jonathan Edwards, Pastor: Religion and Society in Eighteenth-Century Northampton* (New York, 1980).

Westerkamp, M. J. *Triumph of the Laity: Scots-Irish Piety and the Great Awakening 1625–1760* (Oxford, 1988).

SLAVERY

Berlin, Ira *Many Thousands Gone: The first two centuries of slavery in North America* (Cambridge, Massachusetts, 1998).
Bontemps, Alex *The Punished Self: Surviving Slavery in the Colonial South* (Ithaca, New York, 2001).
Frey, Sylvia and Wood, Betty *'Come shouting to Zion': African American Protestantism in the American South and British Caribbean to 1830* (Chapel Hill, North Carolina, 1998).
Gallay, Alan *The Indian Slave Trade: The rise of the English Empire in the American South* (New Haven, Connecticut, 2003).
Jordan, Winthrop *White over Black: American Attitudes towards the Negro 1550–1812* (Chapel Hill, North Carolina, 1968).
Kay, Marvin L. Michael and Cary, Lorin Lee *Slavery in North Carolina 1748–1775* (Chapel Hill, North Carolina, 1995).
Kulikoff, Alan *Tobacco and Slaves: the development of southern cultures in the Chesapeake 1680–1800* (Chapel Hill, North Carolina, 1986).
Mullin, Gerald W. *Flight and Rebellion: Slave resistance in eighteenth-century Virginia* (Oxford, 1972).
Nash, Gary *Forging Freedom: The Formation of Philadelphia's Black Community 1720–1840* (Cambridge, Massachusetts, 1987).
Sobel, Mechal *The World they made together: Black and White Values in eighteenth-century Virginia* (Princeton, 1987).
Slavery and the Rise of the Atlantic System edited by Barbara Solow (Cambridge, 1991).
Walvin, James *Slaves and Slavery: The British Colonial Experience* (Manchester, 1992).
Wood, Betty *Slavery in Colonial Georgia 1730–1775* (Athens, Georgia, 1984).
Wood, Betty *Women's work, men's work: The informal slave economies of Lowcountry Georgia* (Athens, Georgia, 1995).
Wood, Betty *The Origins of American Slavery: Freedom and Bondage in the English Colonies* (New York, 1997).
Wood, Peter H. *Black Majority: Negroes in Colonial South Carolina from 1670 through the Stono Rebellion* (New York, 1974).

WOMEN

Berkin, Carol *First Generations: Women in Colonial America* (New York, 1997).
Brown, Kathleen M. *Good Wives, Nasty Wenches and Anxious Patriarchs: Gender, Race and Power in Colonial Virginia* (Chapel Hill, North Carolina, 1996).
Carr, Lois Green and Walsh, Lorena S. 'The Planter's Wife: The Experience of White Women in seventeenth-century Maryland', *William and Mary Quarterly* 1977, xxxiv, 542–71.
Dayton, Cornelia Hughes *Women before the bar: Gender, Law and Society in Connecticut 1639–1789* (Chapel Hill, North Carolina, 1995).
Fisher, Kirsten *Suspect Relations: Sex, Race and Resistance in Colonial North Carolina* (Ithaca, New York, 2001).
Kamensky, Jane *Governing the Tongue: The politics of speech in early New England* (Oxford, 1997).
Sturtz, Linda L. *Within her power: Propertied Women in Colonial Virginia* (2002).
Ulrich, Laurel Thatcher *Good Wives: Image and Reality in the Lives of Women in Northern New England 1650–1750* (New York, 1982).
Westerkamp, Marilyn J. *Women and Religion in early America 1600–1850: The Puritan and Evangelical Traditions* (New York, 1999).
Wulf, Karin *Not all Wives: Women of Colonial Philadelphia* (Ithaca, New York, 2000).

THE REVOLUTIONARY ERA

Alexander, J. K. *Samuel Adams: America's Revolutionary Politician* (2002).

Appleby, Joyce *Thomas Jefferson* (2003).

Black, Jeremy *George III: America's Last King* (2006).

Breen, T. H. *The Marketplace of Revolution: How Consumer Politics shaped American Independence* (Oxford, 2004).

Brodsky, A. *Benjamin Rush, Patriot and Physician* (2004).

Chernow, R. *Alexander Hamilton* (2004).

Christie, I. R. and Labaree, B. W. *Empire or Independence, 1760–1776* (1976).

Clark, J. C. D. *The Language of Liberty, 1660–1832* (Cambridge, 1994).

Conway, Stephen *The British Isles and the American Revolution* (2000).

Countryman, Edward *The American Revolution* (1985).

Dowd, Gregory Evans *War under Heaven: Pontiac, the Indian Nations and the British Empire* (2002).

Draper, Theodore *A struggle for power: The American Revolution* (1996).

Ellis, J. H. *His Excellency George Washington* (2004).

Foner, Eric *Tom Paine and Revolutionary America* (Oxford, 2005).

Empire and Nation: The American Revolution in the Atlantic World edited by Eliga, H. Gould and Peter, S. Onuf (2005).

McCullough, David *John Adams* (2001).

McDermott, S. *Charles Carroll of Carrollton, Faithful Revolutionary* (2002).

Macksey, Piers *The War for America 1775–1783* (1993).

Maier, Pauline *From Resistance to Revolution: Colonial Radicals and the development of American opposition to Britain 1765–1776* (1971).

Middlekauf, R. *The Glorious Cause: The American Revolution, 1763–1789* (1982).

Morgan, E. S. *Benjamin Franklin* (New Haven, Connecticut, 2003).

Morrison, J. H. *John Witherspoon and the founding of the American Republic* (2005).

O'Shaughnessy, A. J. *An Empire Divided: The American Revolution and the British Caribbean* (2000).

Thomas, P. D. G. *Revolution in America: Britain and the Colonies 1763–1776* (1992).

Unger, H. G. *John Hancock, Merchant King and American Patriot* (2005).

Wood, Gordon S. The American Revolution: A History (2002).

Subject Glossary

Acts and Laws

Affirmation Act 1696; Book of General Laws and Liberties; Coercive Acts; Declaratory Act; Duke's Laws; Hat Act; Iron Act; Molasses Act; Naval Stores Act; Navigation Act; Parson's Case; Plantation Duties Act; Poynings Law; Proclamation of 1763; Quartering Act; Quebec Act; Quo Warranto; Stamp Act; Stamp Act Congress; Staple Act; Sugar Act; Townshend Duties; Two Penny Act Controversy; Vice Admiralty Courts

Board of Trade

Blathwayt, William; Board of Trade; Randolph, Edward

British Army

Abercromby, James; Amherst, Jeffrey; Andros, Sir Edmund; Bellamont, Richard Coote, earl of; Braddock, Edward; Bradstreet, John; Burgoyne, John; Cornbury, Edward Hyde, Viscount; Cornwallis, Charles Marquess; Gage, Thomas; Howe, William; Loudon, John Campbell, Fourth Earl; Nicolls, Richard; Washington, George

Canada

Acadia; Canada; Carleton, Sir Guy; New France; Nova Scotia

Charter Colonies

Virginia; Massachusetts; Rhode Island; Connecticut

Chesapeake Bay

Bacon, Nathaniel; Bacon's Rebellion; Berkeley, Sir William; Blair, James; Brent, Margaret; Byrd, William; Calvert, George, first Baron Baltimore; Calvert, Cecil, Second Baron Baltimore; Calvert, Charles, Third Baron Baltimore; Carroll, Charles; Carter, Robert; Charles Town; Chesapeake Bay; Claiborne, William; Coode, John; Culpeper, Thomas, Second Baron Culpeper; Dale, Sir Thomas; Gates, Sir Thomas; Headright; Henry, Patrick; Hunter, Robert; Jefferson, Thomas; Madison, James; Maryland; Mason, George; Smith, John; Spotswood, Alexander; Virginia; Virginia Company; West, Thomas, Baron De La Warr; Yeardley, Sir George

Colonial Governors

Andros, Sir Edmund; Argall, Sir Samuel; Bellamont, Richard Coote, earl of; Berkeley, Sir William; Bernard, Sir Francis; Blackwell, John; Burnet, William; Carver, John; Clinton, George; Clinton, Sir Henry; Codrington, Christopher; Colden, Cadwllader; Coode, John; Cornbury, Edward Hyde, Viscount; Dale, Sir Thomas; Dongan, Thomas; Dudley, Joseph; Endecott, John; Fletcher, Benjamin; Gates, Sir Thomas; Gorges, Sir Ferdinando; Hamilton, Andrew; Hancock, John; Haynes, John; Henry, Patrick; Hunter, Robert; Jefferson, Thomas; Mason, John; Morris, Lewis; Nicolls, Richard; Spotswood, Alexander; Stoughton, William; Vane, Henry Sir; Williams, Roger; Winthrop, John; Wolcott, Roger; Wyatt, Sir Francis; Wyatt; Sir Francis; Yeardley, Sir George

Crown Colonies

Carolinas; Crown Colonies; New Jersey; New York; Virginia;

Declaration of Independence

Adams, John, Declaration of Independence; Jefferson, Thomas,

Education

College of William and Mary; Harvard College; King's College; Princeton University; William and Mary College; Yale College

French and Indian War
Abercromby, James; Peace of Paris 1763;
  Pepperell, Sir William; Wilkes, John

Friends of America
Burke, Edmund; Pitt, William; Rockingham,
  Marquess of; Charles Watson-Wentworth,
  Second Marquess of; Wilkes, John

Glorious Revolution
Coode, John; Glorious Revolution; James II;
  Leisler, Jacob; William III

Indians
Albany Congress; Albany Plan of Union;
  Bradstreet, John; Chain of Friendship;
  Colden, Cadwallader; Covenant Chain;
  Deerfield; Eliot, John; Indians; Johnson,
  Sir William; King Philip's War; Mason,
  George; Metacom; Pequot War;
  Pocahontas; Pontiac's War; Powhatan
  Confederacy; Rogers, Robert; Rolfe, John;
  Smith, John; Walking Purchase; Weiser,
  Conrad; Williams, Roger

Lower South
Carolinas; Culpeper, John; Florida; Georgia;
  North Carolina; Oglethorpe, James
  Edward; Regulators; Roanoke Island;
  South Carolina; Stono Rebellion

Middle Colonies
Bradford, Andrew; Charter of Privileges;
  Clinton, George; Clinton, Sir Henry;
  Colden, Cadwallader; Cornbury, Edward
  Hyde,Viscount; Delaware; Dickinson,
  John; Dongan, Thomas; Dulany, Daniel I;
  Dulany, Daniel II; Dutch; Elizabethtown
  Grant; Fletcher, Benjamin; Free Society of
  Traders; Frelinghuysen, Theodore;
  Galloway, Joseph; Germantown; Hamilton,
  Andrew; Keith, George; Leisler, Joacob;
  Livingston, Robert; Lloyd, David; Logan,
  James; Middle Colonies; Morris, Lewis;
  Morris, Robert; New Jersey; New York;
  New York Charter of Liberties and
  Privileges; New York City; Nicolls,
  Richard; Penn, Thomas; Penn, William;
  Pennsylvania; Rush, Benjamin;
  Susquehanna Company; Tennent, Gilbert;
  Tennent, William

Monarchs
Anne; Charles I; Charles II; George I;
  George II; George III; James I; James II;
  Mary; William III

New England
Book of General Laws and Liberties; Boston;
  Boston Massacre; Boston Tea Party;
  Bradford, William; Bradstreet, Anne;
  Bradstreet, John; Bradstreet, Simon;
  Brewster, William; Carver, John; Child,
  Robert; Clarke, John; Coddington, William;
  Connecticut; Cotton, John; Council for New
  England; Davenport, John; Deerfield;
  Dominion of New England; Dudley, Joseph;
  Dummer, Jeremiah; Dyer, Mary; Eaton,
  Theophilus; Edwards, Jonathan; Endecott,
  John; Gaspee Incident; Gorges, Sir
  Ferdinando; Gorton, Samuel; Hancock,
  John; Haynes, John; Hooker, Thomas;
  Hutchinson, Anne; Hutchinson, Thomas;
  Massachusetts; Mather, Cotton; Mather,
  Increase; Mather, Richard; Mayflower
  Compact; Morton, Thomas; New England;
  New Hampshire; New Haven; Otis, James;
  Phips, Sir William; Plymouth Colony;
  Puritans; Rhode Island; Shirley, William;
  Stoughton, William; Williams, John;
  Williams, Roger; Winthrop, John

Press
Bradford, Andrew; Bradford, William;
  Campbell, John; Daye, Stephen; Franklin,
  Benjamin; Zenger, John Peter

Proprietorships
Berkeley, John; Calvert, George, First Baron
  Baltimore; Calvert, Cecil, Second Baron
  Baltimore; Calvert, Charles, Third Baron
  Baltimore; Penn, Thomas; Penn, William;
  Proprietary Colonies; Carteret, George;
  New Jersey; New York; Pennsylvania;
  Carolinas; Delaware

Religion
Anglican Church; Antinomian Controversy;
  Backus, Isaac; Baptists; Blair James;
  Bradford, William; Cambridge Platform;
  Clarke, John; Coddington, William;
  Congregationalists; Cotton, John;
  Davenport, John; Dyer, Mary; Edwards,
  Jonathan; Eliot, John; Endecott, John;

Frelinghuysen, Theodore; Great
Awakening; Half-Way Covenant; Hooker,
Thomas; Huguenots; Hutchinson, Anne;
Johnson, Samuel; Keith, George; Mather,
Cotton; Mather, Increase, Mather,
Richard; Methodists; Moravians;
Presbyterians; Price, Richard; Priestley,
Joseph; Puritans; Quakers; Roman
Catholics; Rush, Benjamin; Salem Witch
Trials; Society for the Promotion of
Christian Knowledge; Society for the
Promotion of the Gospel in Foreign parts;
Tennent, Gilbert; Tennent, William;
Whitefield, George; Williams, Roger;
Winthrop, John

Navy
Antigua; Carteret, George; Clinton, George;
Codrington, Christopher; Howe, Richard;
Jones, John Paul; Nova Scotia; Phips,
Sir William

Sciences
Bartam, John; Franklin, Benjamin; Priestly,
Joseph; Rush, Benjamin

Slavery
Barbados; Carter, Robert; Economy;
Georgia; Indentured Servants; Jamaica;
Jefferson, Thomas; Pain, Thomas;
Population; Slavery; Slave Trade; Virginia;
West Indies; Wheatley, Phillis; Whitefield,
George

Societies
American Philosophical Society, Society for
the Promotion of Christian Knowledge;
Society for the Propagation of the Gospel
in Foreign Parts

Trade
Free Society of Traders; Fur Trade; Hancock,
John; Jefferson, Thomas; Mercantilism;
Navigation Act; New Mediterranean Sea
Company; New Pennsylvania Company;
Ohio Company; Plantation Duties Act;
Slave Trade; Susquehanna Company;
Virginia Company

Treaties
Peace of Paris 1763; Peace of Paris 1783;
Treaty of Utrecht; Treaty of Westminster

Wars
King George's War; King Philip's War; King
William's War; Queen Anne's War; War of
Jenkins' Ear; War of the Austrian
Succession; War of the league of Augsburg;
War of the Spanish Succession

War of American Independence
Adams, John; Adams, Samuel; Boston
Massacre; Boston Tea Party; Continental
Congress; Cornwallis, Charles Marquess;
Dartmouth, William Legge, Second Earl;
Deane, Silas; Dickinson, John; Dulany,
Daniel II; Fox, Charles James; Franklin,
Benjamin; Gage, Thomas; Gaspee
Incident; Galloway, Joseph; Sackville,
Germain, George Sackville; Grafton,
Henry Fitzroy, Third Duke; Grenville,
George; Hamilton, Alexander; Hancock,
John; Henry, Patrick; Hillsborough, Wills
Hill, First Earl; Howe, Richard; Howe,
William; Hutchinson, Thomas; Jay, John;
Jefferson, Thomas; Jones, John Paul; Lee,
Richard Henry; Loyalists; Madison,
James; Mason, George; Morris, Robert;
North, Frederick, Lord; Otis, James;
Paine, Thomas; Pitt, William;
Rockingham, Charles Watson-Wentworth,
Second Marquess of; Rogers, Robert;
Shelburne, William Petty, Second Earl;
Stamp Act Congress; Tarleton, Banastre;
Townshend, Charles; Virginia Resolves;
War of American Independence;
Washington, George; Witherspoon,
Jonathan

West Indies
Antigua; Bahamas; Barbados; Bermuda;
Codrington, Christopher; Jamaica;
Providence Island; West Indies; Western
Design

Witches
Mather, Cotton; Mather, Increase; Salem
Witch Trials

Women
Adams, Abigail; Bradstreet, Anne; Brent,
Margaret; Coverture; Hutchinson, Anne;
Murry, Judith Sargent; Wheatley, Phillis;
Women